S0-CBA-828

PARIS

GUIDE

BE A TRAVELER - NOT A TOURIST!

OPEN ROAD TRAVEL GUIDES SHOW YOU
HOW TO BE A TRAVELER – NOT A TOURIST!

*Whether you're going abroad or planning a trip in the United States, take Open Road along on your journey. Our books have been praised by **Travel & Leisure, The Los Angeles Times, Newsday, Booklist, US News & World Report, Endless Vacation, American Bookseller, Coast to Coast**, and many other magazines and newspapers!*

Don't just see the world – experience it with Open Road!

ABOUT THE AUTHORS

Robert F. Howe is a veteran journalist, screenwriter, and freelance author who has reported for the *Baltimore Sun* and *Washington Post*. Diane Huntley previously worked for former US Senator Alan Cranston of California. After living in Paris for a number of years , they now reside in New York, where Rob is a senior editor at *People* magazine and Diane is a vice president of the Magazine Publishers of America.

BE A TRAVELER, NOT A TOURIST - WITH OPEN ROAD TRAVEL GUIDES!

Open Road Publishing has guide books to exciting, fun destinations on four continents. As veteran travelers, our goal is to bring you the best travel guides available anywhere!

No small task, but here's what we offer:

• All Open Road travel guides are written by authors with a distinct, opinionated point of view – not some sterile committee or team of writers. Our authors are experts in the areas covered and are polished writers.

• Our guides are geared to people who want to make their own travel choices. We'll show you how to discover the real destination – not just see some place from a tour bus window.

• We're strong on the basics, but we also provide terrific choices for those looking to get off the beaten path and experience the country or city – not just see it or pass through it.

• We give you the best, but we also tell you about the worst and what to avoid. Nobody should waste their time and money on their hard-earned vacation because of bad or inadequate travel advice.

• Our guides assume nothing. We tell you everything you need to know to have the trip of a lifetime – presented in a fun, literate, no-nonsense style.

• And, above all, we welcome your input, ideas, and suggestions to help us put out the best travel guides possible.

PARIS

GUIDE

BE A TRAVELER - NOT A TOURIST!

Robert F. Howe & Diane Huntley

OPEN ROAD PUBLISHING

OPEN ROAD PUBLISHING

We offer travel guides to American and foreign locales. Our books tell it like it is, often with an opinionated edge, and our experienced authors always give you all the information you need to have the trip of a lifetime. Write for your free catalog of all our titles, including our golf and restaurant guides.

Catalog Department, Open Road Publishing
P.O. Box 284, Cold Spring Harbor, NY 11724

E-mail:
Jopenroad@aol.com

3rd Edition

Text Copyright ©2001 by Robert F. Howe & Diane Huntley
Maps Copyright ©2001 by Open Road Publishing
- All Rights Reserved -

Library of Congress Control No. 00-134123
ISBN 1-892975-40-8

Front cover photo©FPG International. Back cover photos courtesy of French Government Tourist Office, New York.

The authors have made every effort to be as accurate as possible, but neither they nor the publisher assume responsibility for the services provided by any business listed in this guide; for any errors or omissions; or any loss, damage, or disruptions in your travels for any reason.

TABLE OF CONTENTS

MAPS

SIDEBARS

ACKNOWLEDGMENTS

We would like most of all to thank our parents, whose guidance over the years instilled us with the confidence and daring to realize our dream of living in Paris.

Special thanks also go to our publisher, Jon Stein, who phoned up out of the blue one day and said, "Hey, how would you guys like to write a guidebook to France?"

Our fondness for the Good Life is what drives and shapes this book — at least, that's the way we see it. And no one helped us hone our appreciation for the good things in life more than John Anderson and Molly Moore, with whom we shared some of the best of our French adventures.

Ralph Earle, an unrepentant oenophile who claims to know it all, deserves our appreciation for providing invaluable guidance with the wine section here. (Though we're sure that his wife, Jane, who is the real brains of the family, must have done the heavy lifting.)

Thanks, too, to John Baxter, Christopher Mesnooh, Richard Paxson, Mister Nathaniel F. Queen Jr., Roger Ray, Skye Tallmadge, and Jeri and Andy Turpin for helping us explore and review some of Paris's finest culinary hideaways.

And lastly, thanks to all our friends in Paris (especially Angela Walker, who cared for the cats when we were out of town, Simone Gallo at the American Library in Paris, who helped us with research, Frederique and Patrick Lallement, who fueled us with an endless supply of magnificent pastries, and Kelly Roughton, who provided invaluable updates so that we could bring you the best and latest information) for putting up with our constant babbling about the book.

See, it was all worthwhile.

1. INTRODUCTION

Paris has mesmerized Americans since Benjamin Franklin snapped up the assignment as America's first ambassador to France. His portrait still stands in the freshly redecorated Ambassador's residence on rue du Faubourg Saint-Honoré and, judging by the picture, he was pretty pleased to be here.

Who can blame him? Paris is the international symbol of the Good Life — of leisurely strolls along the grand avenues, of hours spent gossiping over *Pastis* at an outdoor café, of inventive meals accompanied by bold vintage wines, of *haute couture* that's actually worn, of enduring works of art, of inspiring monuments celebrating turning points in world history, and of beautiful men and women who magically keep their figures despite the buttery pastries they devour daily.

Sitting over a glass of *vin ordinaire* in a local bistro, you're likely to hear a half dozen languages — and those exotic voices don't just belong to tourists. The city and its residents represent a cultural buffet, with diverse customs and international restaurants, music, and movies at every turn. You can buy fruits from a Moroccan vendor in the local marché, admire 17th-century Swedish arts at the quintessentially French Grand Palais, sip an afternoon *cervesa* at a local Mexican joint, dine on a 26-dish Lebanese feast, take in a Brazilian cabaret, and have a nightcap in a Left Bank *bôite* featuring hard-core Rap-sters from the Bronx. We try to capture that tremendous diversity in our guide.

We've steered you toward the best that Paris has to offer. We describe the various central neighborhoods so you can choose a hotel that you'll find most interesting and comfortable. We highlight our favorite sights, urging you to skip some of the most obvious (and therefore crowded) stops because there are so many museums, monuments, and parks with more character and charm.

And we've steered you to some absolutely fabulous restaurants. There's no moment quite so poignant during a Parisian holiday as toasting the last drops of a fine wine at the end of a memorable meal. And to help you through these incredible feasts, we've put together two extensive chapters explaining French food and wine, including a Food Dictionary to make sure you get what you order!

Here's looking at you, kid.

2. OVERVIEW

A BRIEF GUIDE TO THIS GUIDE

Paris, said to be the third most densely populated city in the world, doesn't feel like it at all.

Yes, in spots there are narrow streets made virtually impassable by legions of residents and tourists on foot, and there are traffic jams to rival any ever seen on the L.A. freeways. But, despite its size and congestion, Paris feels more like a gathering of modestly-sized neighborhoods, each with its own distinct charm and character.

That's why we've organized the heart of this guidebook — the hotels, restaurants and sights — by neighborhoods. If you picture this magnificent city as a collection of communities with diverse personalities, rather than as a massive stockyard for monuments and museums, we think you're more likely to come away with a more affectionate appreciation of Paris, Parisian culture and, dare we predict, the notorious Parisians themselves. More to the point, we think you'll have more fun.

The division into neighborhoods is a practical one as well. Most of your visit is likely to be on foot (if you're doing this trip properly, your feet should ache at the close of every day), so you'll probably want to tour the city in manageable sections.

This guide will help you choose which sections of Paris to visit. And, at the end of the day, if you just don't have the energy to travel across town for dinner, this guide will also identify a good restaurant near your hotel.

ARRONDISSEMENTS

The divisions and neighborhoods we've created for the purposes of this guide roughly parallel the Parisian *arrondissements*.

What's an *arrondissement*? Glad you asked, because it's an essential bit of knowledge whether you're following our guide, reading a local map, or trying to locate a shop you saw advertised in the newspaper.

The Paris *arrondissements* are essentially political wards whose current boundaries were established in the 1800s. There are 20 *arrondissements*, beginning at the western half of the Île de la Cité and spiraling outward

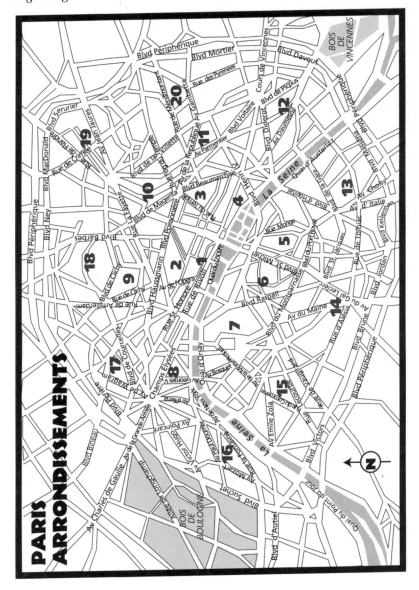

and clockwise, crossing the Seine several times and resembling, as they say, the chambers of a snail's shell.

Each *arrondissement* has its own city hall and independently elected mayor — though, in truth, the executives of most of the 20 *arrondissements* are products of Jacques Chirac's political machine. Chirac, a conservative Gaullist elected president in 1995, was the mayor of all of Paris from 1977 until he won the presidency.

But the *arrondissements* are more than expedient political devices. The borders were drawn largely where distinct neighborhoods already existed — communities defined over time by their proximity to a religious enclave, or their role as a center of government, education or commerce. Some are largely residential developments that sprang out of the fields as the city expanded.

After awhile, you'll get the hang of it, realizing instantly, for instance, that the 5th *arrondissement* is the Latin Quarter or that the Champs-Élysées bisects the 8th.

Our locator maps should help you, but you should also buy a pocket-sized book available just about anywhere titled *Paris par Arrondissement*. Even Parisians don't leave home without them.

LEFT BANK VERSUS RIGHT BANK

In Chapter 9, *Where to Stay,* we describe the central Paris districts in greater detail to help you choose where you want to search for a hotel, but we also wanted to get in a quick word of advice here.

The Left and Right banks are so-named because — and this is incredibly obvious when you think about it — the **Left Bank** is on the left side of the **Seine** as it flows westward toward the Atlantic Ocean, and the **Right Bank** is on the right side. Voilà!

Of course, long ago, the names also took on political overtones. The Left Bank, being home to the universities and intellectuals, was left-leaning politically, while the Right Bank, which is where big business has been conducted for centuries, was considerably more conservative and further right politically.

In general, we prefer the Left Bank. It's less stuffy, less crowded, and more livable, with more small shops and more parks and open areas. It's humming with activity, but it's not as frenzied as the central part of the

USAGE IN THIS BOOK

*Each of our listings of hotels, restaurants, and sights, includes the address and, in parentheses, the number of the **arrondissement** and the name of the nearest **Métro stop** – example: (1st, M:Louvre). Whenever you ask for directions or grab a cab, it will help matters enormously if you can identify the arrondissement of your destination.*

*We also use **FF** to denote a French franc, which will remain in use until the new unified European currency, the **Euro**, is put into general circulation (current plans call for the Euro to be introduced in 2002, though you will already see signs in shops calculating the cost of various goods in Euros). Currently, one franc equals roughly 15 cents; or conversely, $1 equals 6.7 FF. The exchange rate has improved enormously in the last year or so because the FF is already tied directly to the Euro, and the Euro has fallen more than 15 percent and is currently valued almost 1 to 1 with the dollar in currency markets. Our advice: Go, while the going is good. (Visitors in the early 1980s had it especially good when, because of a deep recession in Europe, the exchange rate reached 10 to 1.) If you want up-to-the-minute quotes, most major banks and newspapers (or the Wall Street Journal) carry daily conversion charts.*

Right Bank, which is doubly congested because it is a business district and home to some of the bigger tourist attractions — most notably, the **Louvre** and the **Georges Pompidou Arts Center**.

We find the cafés and bistros on the Left Bank a bit more neighborly as well. The Right Bank has fewer bistros and many cater to business folks on lunch breaks.

On the other hand, if you're looking for luxury, stay on the Right Bank, where six of the seven Michelin three-star restaurants are located, and where all eleven of the palace-style hotels can be found. *Haute couture* and pricey shops also abound on the Right Bank, especially along the **rue du Faubourg Saint-Honoré** and **rue François 1er**, both of which are in the 8th arrondissement.

An important exception to these generalizations is the area around the **Bastille** on the Right Bank. After the **Bastille Opera House** opened in 1989, that area blossomed with hip clubs and restaurants, becoming the

Soho of Paris. It has a much more Left Bank feel to it than other Right Bank neighborhoods.

GETTING THE MOST OUT OF YOUR VISIT

There is so much to do in Paris it's sometimes tough to decide where to start. There are the museums, the monuments, the cafés, the shops, the parks, the open markets, the cabarets, the jazz clubs, the boats on the Seine, the gardens blazing with blossoms, and on and on and on.

One thing you should accept before you drive yourself crazy is that you can't see it all in one visit. Too many people try and end up racing from one museum to another to the point that all the paintings and sculptures begin to look alike. Then they climb aboard the plane home and realize that they never really saw the city at all.

Our advice: Tour the city on foot and don't try to wedge in more than three or four major sights a day. Also, take time to window-shop and people-watch. You learn a lot about the culture that way – plus the live theater of daily life here is as entertaining as in any city in the world.

And from time to time, just set the maps aside and wander. You'll be amazed what fascinating little streets, shops, and bistros you'll discover purely by accident.

And for listings of events going on in town pick up a copy of *Pariscope*. It costs only 3FF and is remarkably comprehensive, whether you're interested in symphony orchestras, movies, theater, sports, clubs or even puppet shows for the kids.

SPECIAL RECOMMENDATIONS

Two things you really should do even if you're the kind of person who hates doing the obvious touristy things: take a boat tour along the Seine and see a cabaret. They may sound hokey, but you won't regret either one.

WHEN TO VISIT

Spring and fall.

The winters are cold, dreary, and damp. And some restaurants and shops close up for the holidays.

During the summer, it can get uncomfortably hot and there are ten zillion tourists milling around (that's no exaggeration). Also, some hotels and restaurants hike up the prices during the summer months.

And you could be especially frustrated by August because that is when the French take their annual vacation – seemingly all of them. That means shops and bistros by the dozens close down for two to four weeks. Believe it or not, we have seen hotels hang a sign on the door announcing that the staff has gone south for August, the peak of the tourist season. Go figure.

FOOD & WINE

French cuisine is deservedly renowned, and we talk about it at greater length in chapters 7 and 8. But we bring it up here as well because we just can't resist talking about food and wine.

For the French, food isn't merely fuel consumed so you can get back to work. It's meant to be fussed over in the kitchen and appraised leisurely at a restaurant table that is yours for the whole evening. Ingredients are usually farm-fresh, even when purchased in the heart of the city.

You should make an effort to try traditional dishes, such as *coq au vin*, rabbit in mustard sauce, duck breast (*magret de canard*), snails, onion soup (*grantinée* or *soupe à l'oignon*), goat cheeses (*chèvres*), the bread and pastries, and anything else you can fit under your belt.

And set aside at least one meal for *haute cuisine* at one of the many truly fine restaurants, where the blend of ingredients is inventive and the presentation on the plate a work of art.

Not surprisingly, there are wines to fit any kind of meal. Bordeaux and Burgundies are the best known, but try the Alsatian white wines and the striking red and white Côtes du Rhone wines.

But a word of warning. As is true in any major city, there is a lot of bad food in Paris. Many cafés serve the original French version of fast food, such as grilled cheese sandwiches with ham (*croques monsieurs*), omelets which are often overdone, and crêpes made long in advance and re-heated. And their wine can sometimes taste something like battery acid.

We would advise against anything but the most fundamental snack or lunch at almost any café or bistro you find along the Champs-Élysées, the rue de Rivoli, the boulevard Saint-Germain, the boulevard Saint-Michel, or just about any other major thoroughfare. These are fabulous places to sip an espresso and watch the world pass by, but most of the good food (inexpensive as well as gourmet) is further off the beaten track.

Do a little research before you pick a restaurant for dinner (of course, we highly recommend our picks), make a reservation, and be prepared on occasion to take a cab across town. The research will pay off.

THE FRENCH

"The French are rude, and they hate Americans."

That hasn't been our experience at all, and we strongly doubt you'll have any problem. Still, it's a common notion – one that's rooted in historic precedent and subtle cultural differences.

Historically, some of the blame goes to Charles de Gaulle, if only because he was the ultimate French role model for the latter half of the 20th century. He disliked and distrusted Americans and, no doubt, some of that rubbed off on the general population.

During the early stages of World War II, France essentially rolled over when the war swept its way. And sadly, collaboration with the Germans was not uncommon – both through overt support and through the acquiescence of a silent and terrified majority.

When the war ended, de Gaulle, angry with his countrymen, angry with his dependence on American and British might to liberate France, and angry with America's sudden cultural and economic dominance of the free world, distanced himself from the United States. He didn't want to be seen, or to see himself, as just a different kind of collaborator – as the man who allowed the Americans to shape the future of France.

Bursting with pride, he sought psychological, social, and economic independence for France. He pulled his country's military support out of the NATO alliance and met freely with the Soviet leadership during the height of the Cold War – in part as a way to thumb his nose at America and Great Britain. He was saying France did not need help and would forge its own place in the new world order. And, to his credit, he did succeed in pulling his people out of a mire of despair and destruction.

His success at resurrecting a proud economic and military world power is all the more remarkable when one remembers that, aside from certain flashes of cultural and artistic brilliance, things had gone badly for France for the better part of a century. The French had been soundly thrashed in the Franco-Prussian war of 1870, the First World War, the

Second World War, Vietnam in the 1950s, and Algeria in the 1950s and 1960s.

SETTING THE RECORD STRAIGHT

So let's try to set the record straight. Though proud to a fault and wary because America's cultural influence continues to grow thanks to the might of its industry, banking, institutions, and globally influential media, the French do not hate Americans.

In fact, you will find that most people are friendly and many are even eager to help. No doubt, you'll have an easier time as a visitor if you speak some French, just as any foreigner fares better in the States if he speaks some English, or at least tries.

Remember also that this is an enormous, busy city, and you will inevitably run into someone who missed the Métro, or just lost their job, or broke up with their girlfriend, and they're going to be cranky. New York, Washington, Los Angeles, San Francisco – we've lived in them all and they're just the same.

The root of so many street-level misunderstandings between American tourists and the locals is that French society is more formal than American. We Americans will talk with any stranger who comes along, throwing our arms around their shoulders, and inviting them home to meet the family.

The French don't do that. Strangers are strangers and family is sacred, and never the twain shall meet. You can witness the formality of the French in their language.

Vous, the formal (both singular and plural) word for "you," is the preferred choice over *tu*, the familiar form. You would only begin a relationship with *tu* when addressing a child. You would only *tutoyer* an adult (use the familiar form *tu*) after you had known them for months and become pretty good friends. Often even then a French person might feel uncomfortable using the familiar term.

This is less and less the case with today's French youth, which profited from the social changes brought about in the late 1960s and which is mesmerized by what they see on television as the ease and perks of American society.

With adults, the formality appears in some pretty interesting ways – ways that can affect your visit.

For instance, when you enter a small shop, it is expected that you would say, "*Bonjour, Madame*" or "*Bonjour, Monsieur*" to the shopkeeper. The thinking is that just because they want to sell their products doesn't diminish the fact that this is their space and that "guests" should show proper courtesy.

It is also expected that, when you leave, you say, "*Au revoir, Madame, merci*," whether or not you have purchased anything.

When entering a doctor's office or a small restaurant where there is just a handful of patrons, it is not at all unusual for a French adult to say, "*Bonjour Messieurs*" or "*Bonjour Mesdames*," to the other patients or diners.

Because so many Americans rush in and out of shops, manhandling the merchandise without even glancing at the owner, they are sometimes considered rude and are greeted in kind. French people have told us that they sometimes feel as if American tourists view them and their shops or cafés as nothing more than commodities to be bought and sold.

THE LANGUAGE BARRIER

The most obvious barrier between the two cultures is the language.

Even though hotel and restaurant employees often speak some English, the French working class speaks less English than is generally assumed. And often, those who do speak passing English feel too ashamed of the poor quality of their English to use it. Having said that, though, you are likely to run across an occasional waiter who will answer you in English after you have ordered in French – in our view, an annoying habit.

On the other hand, the French are generally encouraging if you blurt out even the most abysmal phrase of French. It seems sometimes as if they will insist that you speak French well even when you yourself weren't quite sure what you said.

But try anyway. And don't be afraid of accidentally saying something incredibly stupid. That happens to everyone. A real-life example: A friend of ours who paid a visit insisted on ordering his own breakfast at a local café. Very proudly, he said, "*Une tartine avec des préservatifs, Madame.*" Well, the Madame was quite taken aback. What he had thought he'd said was, "A sliced baguette with butter and preserves." Little did he know that though *préservatifs* may sound like preserves, it actually means condoms.

So, yes, it may cause some embarrassment at times, but the bottom line is that you will have a more successful and fun trip if you attempt a bit of French and fail, than if you had not tried to speak the language at all.

THE MONEY BARRIER

Money represents another difference between the cultures that occasionally grates.

An average middle-class French person is not driven by profit in the same way that many Americans are. After leaving school, a French person often hunts down a respectable job and willingly (almost unconsciously) settles in for the very long haul.

They might move up the ladder over the years, but the French rarely quit and change jobs without a very compelling reason. They also do not move around the country as often as Americans do, so they are not used to the idea of enormous change.

The net result is that they are relatively secure (or at least not restless) when it comes to money. Their salaries are surprisingly low, but they generally live within their means without fretting about it.

Oh, they regularly bitch and moan about salaries, staging countless work slow-downs and demonstrations. But mostly their beefs against the government are good-natured. (Cafés do very well when peaceful demonstrations visit their neighborhoods, but they lose lots of glass on those rare occasions when things turn ugly.)

In essence, the French adore the government because of the financial perks built into the system (sort of the adoration of a child toward a parent). The state takes care of virtually all their medical expenses, and employers are obliged by law to pay all or part of their transportation costs. And the law requires that employees receive at least five weeks vacation a year and that they be paid for thirteen months work in every twelve.

They are not generally comfortable discussing money matters and, in their view, just because a wealthy tourist wants to buy their product or services, that does not mean that they should humble themselves in a cloak of gracious servitude. Quite the contrary. The attitude can be reversed so that the tourist should feel privileged to have access to the shop owner's wares.

POLITICAL HURDLES

It's true that the United States and France are often embroiled in some kind of official political squabble. That was true back when de Gaulle pulled French military support out of NATO, as it was recently when the French moaned about the allegedly mercenary dominance of the American film industry during the GATT world trade negotiations in 1994.

What you see is a love-hate relationship. The French are obsessed with Americans and American goods. A big rage in the 1990s was for boys to wear caps emblazoned with the names of American sports teams. When asked about the caps, they sometimes admit they don't even know what sport the team plays. For that matter, we've seen caps for teams we've never heard of either.

But there is a fear of American culture, largely because American cultural influences are growing increasingly powerful. This goes back to the argument over the American film industry during GATT.

The French, especially the politicians, feel that their culture is under attack by the American media. And, truth be told, the French culture and others are under fire – not by a malicious conspiracy masterminded by American CEOs huddled in smoky backrooms, but by naturally evolving market forces and consumer tastes.

As we write this, fourteen of the twenty most popular films (judged by ticket sales) over the past twelve month-period in Paris are American-made—topped by *Star Wars: Episode One*, *Tarzan* and *Matrix*. The highest ranking French film was *Astérix et Obélix contra César*, based on the long-lived Astérix cartoon character. Not exactly high-brow stuff. But then, films like these were also at the top of the American charts, demonstrating again that we are not as far apart as some would say.

The proportions are about the same for the top 20 popular music videos. And the four primary French television stations (TF1, France 2, France 3 and M6) are crowded with reruns of such American standards as Suddenly Susan, Dr. Quinn Medicine Woman, Dallas and Magnum PI.

Why are there so many American films in French theaters and American television series on French airwaves? Because Americans crank out a huge volume of product, and the European rights are cheap. The French film and television industries simply cannot afford to produce enough original programming to fill the increasing demand of its viewers.

But there is another factor: The French, especially young viewers, are growing accustomed to American sitcoms. They like them. Even French adults, while genuflecting in front of such native film giants as François Truffaut, have developed a hankering for the big-budget, action-oriented American pictures.

So what to do? During GATT, the French politicians tried to limit the import of American films and raise tariffs on the films, saying they would use the money to subsidize French productions. The French won the skirmish, but shortly afterward American filmmakers displayed an increasing interest in cooperative ventures with French producers.

This backdoor approach will likely result in increasing French media dependencies on American money and know-how.

LANGUAGE AS THE NATIONAL SOUL

In a more extreme effort to slow what is largely seen as an inevitable cultural takeover by American media giants, French politicians in 1994 passed a law that would have made it illegal to use English words in any advertising campaign or notice if a French word existed to express the same thought.

As an example, car ads touting "air bags" would have had to be rewritten to boast about *"coussins gonflables de sécurité,"* meaning "inflatable security cushions." It doesn't exactly sing, does it? What with economic globalization, such terms as *"le start-up"* had filtered into common usage. That term was banned in 2000; in its place, officials said, please use *jeune pousse* (meaning a young plant shoot).

Essentially, the law was struck down because it violated free speech tenets of the French constitution. The ruling declared that the government could restrict only the use of English in official contexts. In the most extreme example, this might have required that the government change all the "Stop" signs (which do, in fact, read "Stop") to read *"Arretez."*

Not surprisingly, since lawmakers were really only targeting American businesses and French "collaborators" with American businesses, the proposed law was shelved.

An interesting related debate raged in early 2000, when pilots for Air France were enraged because the government actually told them they would have to start speaking English with French air control towers. At most major airports all around the world, most conversations between pilots and air traffic controllers are conducted in English for safety's sake. That way, the reasoning goes, everyone can listen in and know where all the planes are and where they are headed. The French had resisted this while flying in France, continuing to communicate in their native tongue with French air traffic controllers. The British especially complained bitterly, saying their pilots sometimes grew confused, not understanding the exchanges between Air France pilots and the tower at De Gaulle, so not knowing if they were headed for some kind of disaster. But even after the government issued the edict, Air France pilots were urged by their unions to ignore the directive and to continue to speak French. (By the way, regardless of whether they are speaking French or English, the French flight crews are among the safest in the skies, so you need not worry.)

We may be somewhat amused by this strutting and fretting, but we should remember how touchy many American communities have been when proposals have been made to institute bilingual English-Spanish ballots or school texts.

Think how you'd feel if two-thirds or more of the movies and television you watched in your own home were in French, with subtitles in English or with annoying dubbed voices. And what if your kids were obsessed with Roberto Donadoni of the AC Milan soccer team, but couldn't name a single player on the San Francisco Giants.

Maurice Druon, head of the Académie Française, the institutional and intellectual keeper of the French language and heritage, once noted that he wanted to find a way to recapture the French pride in their own language. "France remains a great power," he said (in French). "We possess a universal language, we are one of the few nuclear powers, we are the fourth largest exporter in the world, we have the world's third largest economic maritime sovereignty. But here at home, national pride is taken as bad taste. We welcome all the exotic nationalities, but to embrace our own is to be accused of arrogant nationalism."

He ends up with this plea: "It's necessary to constantly remind ourselves that language gives voice to our souls."

3. SUGGESTED ITINERARIES

Here are three suggested itineraries, for three, four, and seven days. You'll find each hotel, restaurant, and activity described in the pages that follow. Simply check out the relevant chapters or look them up in the index and go to town – literally!

For each, we recommend the same four choices for your hotel: for special occasions, the Hôtel Le Relais Saint-Germain or Duc de Saint-Simon. For the budget conscious traveler who still wants something special, we suggest the Hôtel des Grands Écoles or the Hôtel des Grands Hommes.

We suggest you quickly stop by several of the monuments, admiring them from the outside. For others, we suggest you take time for the full tour. You should check our listings to see which days museums and other sights might be closed, but keep in mind that times may change.

You'll probably want to catch a cab to most of the dinner restaurants; you will be very glad you did. And remember, as with any itinerary, no matter how perfect, set it aside from time to time and follow your own instincts and appetites.

THREE DAYS IN PARIS

Day 1

Check into hotel.

Tour Notre-Dame de Paris.

Stroll through the Square de l'Île de France behind Notre-Dame overlooking the Île Saint-Louis.

Lunch – The Brasserie Balzar.

Stroll through Luxembourg Gardens.

Stop by Saint-Sulpice.

Window-shop at the galleries and boutiques along all the tiny side streets
between the boulevard Saint-Germaine and the river.

Rejuvenating coffee or cocktail – Aux Deux Magots.

Back to your hotel to freshen up.

Dinner – Le Petit Marguery.

Day 2

Tour the Musée d'Orsay.

Lunch – The Musée d'Orsay Café.

Tour the Musée National Auguste Rodin.

Take the elevator to the top of the Tour Eiffel.

Take a one-hour cruise on the river.

Rejuvenating coffee or cocktail – Choose an outdoor café along the
avenue de la Bourdonnais.

Back to your hotel to freshen up.

Dinner – Les Bookinistes.

Day 3

Stop by the Arc de Triomphe.

Stroll down the avenue des Champs-Élysées.

Peek into the Virgin Megastore.

Stop by the Place de la Concorde.

Tour the Madeleine.

Lunch — l'Écluse.

Tour the Opéra Garnier.

Stop by the Musée National du Louvre.

Stop by the Flower Market on Île de la Cité.

Stop by the booksellers who line the banks of the Seine.

Rejuvenating coffee or cocktail – Choose an outdoor café by the Seine
near the boulevard Saint-Michel.

Back to your hotel to freshen up.

Dinner – Le Bistro d'à Côté in the 17th arrondissment.

FOUR DAYS IN PARIS

The same three days outlined above, plus:

Day 4

Stop by the Georges Pompidou Center.

Tour the Musée Picasso.

Lunch — Jo Goldenberg.

Stop by the place des Vosges.

Stop by the place de la Bastille.

Stroll down the main street of the Île Saint-Louis.

Rejuvenating coffee or cocktail – Choose an outdoor café on the Quai
d'Orléans on the Île Saint-Louis.

Back to your hotel to freshen up.

Dinner – Chardenoux.

SEVEN DAYS IN PARIS

Day 1

Check into your hotel.

Tour Notre-Dame de Paris.

Stroll through the Square de l'Île de France behind Notre-Dame overlooking the Île Saint-Louis.

Lunch – The Brasserie Balzar.

Stop by the Panthéon.

Stroll through the Jardin des Plantes.

Rejuvenating coffee or cocktail – The rooftop café of Institut du Monde
Arabe.

Back to your hotel to freshen up.

Early dinner – Polidor.

Day 2

Tour La Musée de Cluny.

Stroll through Luxembourg Gardens.

Lunch – La Coupole.

Stop by Saint-Sulpice.

Window-shop at the galleries and boutiques along all the tiny side streets
between the boulevard Saint-Germain and the river.

Rejuvenating coffee or cocktail – Aux Deux Magots.

Back to your hotel to freshen up.
Dinner – Le Petit Marguery.

Day 3
Tour the Musée d'Orsay.
Lunch — The Musée d'Orsay café.
Tour the Musée National Auguste Rodin.
Tour the Hôtel des Invalides.
Rejuvenating coffee or cocktail — The outdoor section of the café Vauban almost directly across the street from the entrance to Napoleon's tomb.
Back to your hotel to freshen up.
Dinner – Les Bookinistes.

Day 4
Take the elevator to the top of the Tour Eiffel.
Take a one-hour cruise on the river.
Early lunch – Au Bon Accueil.
Stop by the Trocadéro.
Stop by the Arc de Triomphe.
Stroll down the avenue des Champs-Élysées.
Peek into the Virgin Megastore.
Stop by the Place de la Concorde.
Rejuvenating coffee or cocktail – Angelina.
Stroll through the Jardin des Tuileries.
Back to your hotel to freshen up.
Dinner – Le Bistro d'à Côté in the 17th arrondissment.

Day 5
Stop by the Château de Vincennes.
Tour the Parc Floral.
Lunch – The crèperie in the park.
Tour the Musée National du Louvre.
Rejuvenating coffee or cocktail – Café Marly at the Louvre.
Stop by the Flower Market on Île de la Cité.
Stop by the booksellers who line the banks of the Seine.

Back to your hotel to freshen up.

Dinner – Tan Dihn.

Day 6

Tour the Opéra Garnier.

Tour the Madeleine.

Lunch – l'Écluse.

Tour the Montmartre neighborhood.

Rejuvenating coffee or cocktail – Choose an outdoor café at the Place de Tertre near Sacré-Coeur.

Back to the hotel to freshen up.

Early dinner – Perraudin.

Go to a cabaret – The Lido or Crazy Horse.

Day 7

Stop by the Georges Pompidou Center.

Tour the Musée Picasso.

Lunch – Jo Goldenberg.

Stop by the place des Vosges.

Stop by the place de la Bastille.

Stroll down the main street of the Île Saint-Louis.

Rejuvenating coffee or cocktail at one of the outdoor cafés on the Quai d' Orléans on the Île Saint-Louis.

Back to your hotel to freshen up.

Dinner – Chardenoux.

4. A SHORT HISTORY

BEGINNINGS

(4,000 BC-986 AD)

Many people like to think of the French as being nothing more than ... well ... French, as if the people and their culture sprang out of the ground like the chesnut trees that dot Paris.

But, in truth, the French civilization grew out of a lively stew of Western peoples – the Britons, Greeks, Romans, Vikings, Franks, a variety of Germanic tribes, and a host of barbarians, just to name a few. Their story goes something like this:

Agricultural villages cropped up in the vast and fertile Paris Basin more than 4,000 years BC. Even prehistoric farmers recognized a good thing when they saw it.

But what we think of as Paris did not begin to take root until about 300 BC, when a band of once marauding Celts known as the **Parisii** decided it was time to settle down.

Their name, said to be derived from a Celtic word meaning "boat," was tribute to their skill as traders. And being traders, they sought out a home on a major river — in this case the Seine, where there also happened to be a well-traveled north-south highway. Savvy, too, about the ways of war, the Parisii were drawn to the natural protection offered by an island in the middle of the Seine. That island became known as the **Île de la Cité**, and is still today at the very heart of Paris.

Thus, Paris truly sprang from the serpentine river that now divides the city roughly in half as it flows from the east toward the west.

The Romans arrived in 52 BC, bringing order to the chaos in their typically militaristic, but admirably efficient fashion. They soundly defeated the local tribes in a battle on the Left Bank not far from where the **École Militaire** (7th *arrondissement*) now stands, and, by the first century AD, they had rebuilt the settlement on the Île de la Cité and renamed it Lutetia.

The Romans were the first to significantly expand the town off of the island and onto the Left Bank. In the neighborhood later called the Latin Quarter, they built temples, a forum, baths, and an amphitheater known as **Arènes**, the remains of which can be found off of the rue Monge (5th *arrondissement*).

The Roman years through to the 5th century were noted by an expanding wine trade (what a surprise), devastating, though temporary, barbarian occupation, and the heroics of two Christian saints. Romans objected when **Saint Denis**, Paris's first Christian bishop, attempted to convert Parisians en masse. For his troubles, he was beheaded on a Right Bank hilltop later named **Mons Martyrium**, or **Montmartre** (18th *arrondissement*). Legend has it that Saint Denis retrieved his severed head and marched to where the cathedral by his name now stands six miles north of Paris's Porte de la Chapelle.

Sainte Geneviève won the hearts of Parisians in 451. The settlement had been abandoned at the time by Roman troops who feared Attila the Hun, who was marching through France. But **Geneviève**, a 15-year-old of intense religious fervor, convinced Parisians not to flee, insisting that Attila would not come. Fortunately, for largely unknown reasons, he steered clear and Geneviève was canonized. In her honor, the hill on which the Sorbonne and the Panthéon now stand became known as **Mount Sainte-Geneviève** (5th *arrondissement*).

The next several centuries were rough ones, marked by war, floods, epidemics and even neglect. No wonder it was called the Dark Ages. **Clovis I**, king of much of what became France, provided a bright note in the late 400s, making Lutetia his capital and formally changing the name to Paris.

Unfortunately, Clovis's heirs fought viciously over the empire, essentially ripping it apart. In the late 700s, when **Charlemagne** consolidated power, he largely abandoned Paris, which consequently fell into decline. Matters worsened the following century when Vikings and Normans repeatedly pounded the city.

CIVILIZATION TAKES HOLD
(987-1335)

After a quick succession of nominal kings with such unflattering tag lines as "the Bald," "the Stammerer," "the Fat" and "the Simple," **Hugh Capet** took the throne in 987, declaring Paris his base and setting in motion a period of magnificent growth.

Civilization began to take hold in the 11th century. Guilds for river traders, butchers and other trades were established. They grew increasingly influential over time and laid the groundwork for citizen participation in government. A mercantile class began to develop the Right Bank, where **Louis VI** had established a huge marketplace just west of rue Saint-Denis (1st *arrondissement*). That market, **Les Halles**, remained in various incarnations until the 1960s, when it was finally removed because it had become an eyesore and caused increasingly horrendous traffic jams.

It was also during this time that **Philippe II** built a wall around Paris and constructed a relatively simple fortress named the **Louvre** (1st *arrondissement*). It was not until the late 1300s that the Louvre was expanded and transformed into a grand palace.

Notre-Dame (4th *arrondissement*), which would become the gem of Gothic architecture in the city, was begun on the Île de la Cité in 1163, followed not long afterward by the elegant **Sainte-Chapelle** cathedral a stone's throw away. In the 1200s, the **University of Paris** and the still famous **Sorbonne** college were established on the Left Bank in the Latin Quarter (5th *arrondissement*).

The city center had begun to take a now recognizable shape, with government based on the Île de la Cité, intellectual pursuits on the Left Bank, and business concerns on the Right.

WAR & RENAISSANCE
(1336-1593)

The 14th and 15th centuries were a bit rockier. There was natural havoc in the form of the Black Death in the mid-1300s. And there was political upheaval stemming from high taxes, peasants' rights (or lack thereof), and a seemingly interminable war with England.

In 1336, **Edward**, king of England and duke of Gascony (southwestern France), renounced his allegiance to **Philip VI**, king of France, and so began the Hundred Years debacle that would sap France's resources for well over a century. The French throne was seized by the English in 1418 and not recaptured until 1437. Even **Joan of Arc**, in 1429, failed to recover Paris for the French – though she certainly changed the tide.

The French Renaissance of the 16th century was somewhat kinder to Paris. Reflecting Italian architectural inspiration, a magnificent **Hôtel de Ville** (4th *arrondissement*), or city hall, was built on the Right Bank across from Notre-Dame. The Louvre was expanded and finally became the official seat of the throne. In 1564, **Catherine de Medicis** ordered the **Palace of the Tuileries** and a magnificent garden be constructed just west of the Louvre.

At the close of the century, the classical **Pont Neuf** was constructed, connecting the western tip of the Île de la Cité with both banks, as it does today. It was the first bridge without houses on its sides and is the oldest of the more than thirty bridges in the city.

The city was expanding westward and, thanks to the money of the bourgeois class and the intellect of the Parisian universities, had gained a reputation as a European center of the arts and highbrow debate. Unfortunately, one debate, fueled in the later 1500s by the printing presses that hummed overtime in Paris, pitched the Catholic power structure against an increasingly aggressive tide of Protestantism.

The result: more bloodshed, probably the worst of which occurred in Paris in August 1572 when, on Saint-Bartholomew's day, thousands of Protestants known as **Huguenots** were slaughtered in accordance with a devious plan arranged by **Charles IX**, Catherine de Medicis, and others. Bodies littered the Seine. The story is partially told in the 1995 French film, *Queen Margot*.

THE CITY TAKES SHAPE
(1594-1788)

A civil war catalyzed by events in Paris and fed by religious and class differences flamed on for years before **Henri IV** converted to Catholicism, was welcomed back to Paris in 1594 by the local powers, and enacted the **Edict of Nantes** meant to stabilize Catholic and Protestant relations.

And, for awhile, things were better. Growth continued rapidly on the Right Bank in the early to mid-1600s. The elegant **Place des Vosges** (4th *arrondissement*) was built in the Marais (meaning "marsh") district, the

Louvre and Tuileries palaces were linked, and the **Palais Cardinale** (later **Palais Royal**) was constructed for **Cardinal de Richelieu**.

On the river, the **Pont Royal** spanning the Seine west of the Île de la Cité was built and the **Île Saint-Louis** (4th *arrondissement*) was fashioned from two tiny islands just east of the Île de la Cité. On the Left Bank, the luxurious **Jardin des Plantes** (5th *arrondissement*) was established, as was the marvelous **Luxembourg Palace** (now home to the French Senate, 6th *arrondissement*) with gardens that draw even locals by the thousands.

Louis XIV (1643-1715), the **Sun King**, continued the orgy of growth with the invaluable aid of **Jean-Baptiste Colbert**, his superintendent of buildings and finance minister. Broad avenues replaced ramparts, the early version of the **Champs-Élysées** (8th *arrondissement*) was laid out just west of the expanding city, the **Place des Victoires** was built, then the **Place Vendôme**. The **Hôtel des Invalides** (7th *arrondissement*), far west on the Left Bank, was erected for destitute military veterans, and even further west, eight miles from the current Porte d'Auteuil, **Versailles** went up.

Versailles, the palace of palaces, with such luxuries as 1,400 fountains, required the efforts of 36,000 builders and artisans. Of course, when Louis moved into Versailles, Paris proper lost a bit of its luster. Those left behind were displeased (which Louis intended) and the seeds of revolt were planted.

The decades after Louis XIV's death saw some of the city's most brilliant minds flower. **Voltaire**, **Rousseau**, **Diderot** and others were the cream of the crop. Arts and literature flourished, as did the bourgeois class that seemed always to profit no matter how many wars the country continued to wage with Holland, England and others.

The poor, crammed into cramped and stinking neighborhoods, couldn't help but notice others' stunning prosperity and were not amused. Food shortages spurred riots from 1775 through 1788, the year that the Paris council rejected the crown's proposal for new taxes that would dig into their own bourgeois pockets.

REVOLUTION & THE EMPIRES
(1789-1870)

Revolution came knocking on the doors of the 400-year-old **Bastille** prison on July 14, 1789. In truth, there were only a handful of prisoners at the Bastille (12th *arrondissement*), but the raid and its subsequent destruction symbolized what the populace thought would be a new order. The Revolution also galvanized Paris as the indisputable centerpoint of French existence, whether considered in political, economic or artistic terms.

Violence became a way of life for several decades. The Revolution claimed 1,200 lives in the September massacres of 1792, the first year of the formally declared **First French Republic** (France is now on its Fifth). Many of the dead were loyalists to the crown, and many happened simply to have been in the wrong place at the wrong time. The following January, Louis XVI was taken to the guillotine in the Place de la Concorde (8th *arrondissement*) and executed, followed the next autumn by **Marie Antoinette**, his queen.

The thirst for blood worsened during the **Reign of Terror** in 1793 and 1794, when the National Assembly passed the Law of Suspects by which anyone suspected of treason was automatically judged guilty. Another 20,000 people in Paris alone were guillotined.

The national bloodletting was finally quelled by one of the most violent men of all, **Napoleon Bonaparte**, a military genius who, at least, used his knowledge constructively in establishing a strong city police force. During his dictatorship, which lasted until 1814, he brought peace to the streets of Paris, even while he led hundreds of thousands of French youths to death in ultimately futile foreign campaigns.

After Napoleon's final exile to the island of Sainte-Héléna, the task of governing Paris and the nation bordered on the impossible. Paris was reeling from economic strain. A cholera epidemic wiped out 19,000 residents in 1832, and two more revolutions, one in 1830 and a second in 1848, transformed the streets of Paris into a battleground between the classes.

Once again the people looked for a savior and once again they turned to a Bonaparte. Profiting from the General Assembly's decision in 1848 to hold the country's very first national presidential election, Napoleon's ambitious nephew won by a landslide. Three years later, under the pretext that the General Assembly was attempting to strip the people of the right to vote, Napoleon shut down the Assembly and, exactly one year later, declared himself **Napoleon III, Emperor**. (Clever man.)

Apparently, it was a good thing he did. Ultimately, wisdom triumphed over his hunger for pure power. He enlarged the powers of the Assembly and the Senate, allowed for a freer press, increased the country's industrialization, and put **Baron George-Eugene Haussmann**, prefect of Paris, in charge of a total facelift for the city.

Haussmann is largely responsible for the lasting grandeur of Paris, having ruthlessly cleared slums, opened up the grand avenues, vastly improved the water and sewage systems, constructed new docks, and developed park land. Under his watch, Paris blossomed into a cultural world capital, hosting two world's fairs.

THE THIRD REPUBLIC
(1870-1944)

Then Napoleon III made a mistake, going to war against Prussia in 1870 with an ill-equipped army. Less than a year later, the Prussians marched down Haussmann's beautiful avenues. The Second Empire was over.

The last of the 1800s and the years leading up to World War I were politically chaotic in Paris, with the government of the Third Republic changing leaders as if it were trying on hats. Happily, at the same time, the architectural and cultural forces inside the city thrived.

In 1889, the **Tour Eiffel** (7th *arrondissement*) was erected in preview of yet another world's exposition. The first Métro stop opened in 1900 and the **Sacré-Coeur Basilica** (18th *arrondissement*), the monument to the soldiers who fell in the disastrous war with Prussia, was completed on the peak of Montmartre in 1910.

Literature, music and the art world flourished like never before, led by giants such as **Gustave Flaubert**, **Emile Zola**, **Charles Baudelaire**, **Maurice Ravel**, **Claude Debussy**, **Edouard Manet**, **Henri Matisse**, **Pierre-Auguste Renoir** and **Vincent Van Gogh**. The list goes on and on.

Ugly reality and international crisis returned in 1914, when the German army slogged its way through Belgium to within a few miles of Paris. The French government fled to Bordeaux and the French army threw everything they had at the Kaiser's crew, even using taxis to rush troops to the front.

The Germans were held in the battle of the Marne, but the French lost hundreds of thousands of men in the first few months of what would become history's most gruesome exercise in military futility.

The Germans were effectively defeated four years later at Verdun, by **General Philippe Pétain** (who would later run the traitorous Vichy government during World War II). But the cost of trench warfare was huge. The French lost more than 1.3 million men, and suffered another 3 million wounded. Almost half of the young men were gone, industries were crippled, farms were laid waste, inflation boomed, and the national debt grew to ominous proportions.

It wouldn't be until the late 1920s that the French economy began once again to pick up speed. But this momentum too was quickly lost in the Great Depression that began in 1929 with the crash of the New York Stock Exchange.

The hideous economy brought out the most fanatical right wingers in both France and Germany, where the Nazi party grew quickly and Hitler began to undo the binders placed on his country by the Treaty of Versailles that had ended World War I.

France essentially stood by as Hitler marched on Czechoslovakia, then Austria, then Denmark, Holland and Belgium. War was at hand and the French, having hidden their heads in the sand, were ill prepared mentally, politically, and militarily to defend themselves against the storm of German tanks and bombers that swept across French borders.

On June 14, 1940, Hitler's rejuvenated German troops occupied Paris. A turncoat French government was established in the central spa town of **Vichy** with Pétain as its head. It was a disgraceful government, rooting out Jews, executing resisters, and providing laborers to the German armies.

(Recent research suggests that the late **François Mitterand**, the Socialist president of France from 1981 to 1995, had more intimate ties to the Vichy government than was originally believed and maintained relations with some former Vichy leaders up through the 1980s. He responded that his relationship was necessary during the war years to aid resistance fighters.)

Finally, American, British, Canadian, and a token band of French troops landed on the beaches at Normandy on June 6, 1944. At great cost of lives, both military and civilian, the war was turned. In the following weeks, Allied armies devastated several French cities – an unfortunate necessity in flushing the German army out of France.

Members of the French resistance, sensing that the end of war was near, increased their harassment of the German occupation forces and, a little more than two months later, Paris was freed.

The liberation of Paris was both the city's most exhilirating and terrifying moment. True, the Allied troops seemed sure to drive out the Germans, but Hitler ordered that bombs be placed under most of the significant Paris monuments. Level the city, Hitler demanded.

But German **General von Choltitz**, based in Paris, could not bring himself to carry out the orders. Thus, when American troops and a French garrison led by **General Jacques Leclerc** drove into Paris on August 19, they found the city intact.

General Charles de Gaulle, having marshaled the free French forces from exile in England, returned to his capital in a triumphant march down the Champs-Élysées August 26, 1944.

The Vichy government was instantly dissolved, Paris resumed its rightful place as the seat of power, an estimated 9,000 collaborators were executed, and, in a disturbingly brutish attempt to purge the nation of its demons, women who had shown favors to German troops were stripped naked and paraded with shaved heads up and down the streets.

POSTWAR GUILT

Despite reveling in a giddy atmosphere of regained freedom, France was also emotionally and politically troubled immediately after the war.

Plainly put, the French felt a stinging sense of guilt. They were intimately aware that collaboration with the Nazis had been painfully commonplace and that the famed Resistance forces, though active throughout the war, had not received the unwavering popular support they might have.

Even today, in discussions with French families, you are likely to hear tirades against the rampant corruption and empty denial of those who did nothing to thwart the German occupation forces. At the same time, without fail, these families proclaim that their own fathers or grandfathers numbered among the few unerringly loyal Resistance members.

(This phenomenon of reconstructive memory is not a peculiarly French phenomenon. A huge majority of Americans remember voting for John F. Kennedy in 1960, even though Kennedy could not possibly have won all those votes in his squeaker against Richard Nixon. The collective, self-healing memory shifted after Kennedy was shot, when the nation suffered an overpowering and unifying sense of grief and guilt.)

Jean-Paul Sartre, **Simone de Beauvoir**, **Albert Camus**, and other writers were at the heart of Parisian postwar intellectual debate, and it is easy to sense their discomfort in virtually all their writings from that era.

Sartre's *Troubled Sleep*, written in the late 1940s and de Beauvoir's *The Mandarins*, published in 1954, are especially unforgiving in their dissection of the wartime struggle with collaboration and the postwar turmoil during which the past actions of even the dearest friends were held to the scrutiny of hindsight.

These themes were also debated at length in articles pubished in *Les Temps Modernes*, a periodical founded by Sartre in 1945.

THE ECONOMIC BOOM

Economically, France was in very sad shape after the war. It had lost thousands of factories, hundreds of miles of roads and train tracks, and a staggering number of farms and homes. If there was a silver lining, it was that the nation's needs meant there would be jobs and, with jobs, relative prosperity.

Like the United States, France enjoyed an economic boom, especially in the 1950s and 1960s and especially in Paris, as younger generations abandoned small farming towns for the promise of education and better-paying jobs in the big city.

The coal and electric industries were nationalized, as were the country's largest banks and transportation companies. The government fashioned a remarkable net of social services and made them available to everyone. And schools sprang up everywhere to cope with the soaring population.

High tech industry took off. The French, having once lagged far behind other European states in industrialization, gradually assumed a leadership role in the latter half of the century.

They developed supersonic passenger planes (the SSTs, produced jointly with Britain), the 200 mph **TGV** (*"train grande vitesse,"* meaning "very rapid train"), an enviable network of toll highways criss-crossing the nation, and a phone system that offers users a free home computer called a **Minitel**. With a Minitel (if you can get your fingers to fit those tiny keys), you can look up phone numbers, reserve theater or plane tickets, consult psychics, join a singles club, etc., etc., etc.

Despite occasional slow-downs, such as during the 1973 worldwide oil crisis caused by steep increases in the price of Arab crude, the French economy continued to grow, finally surpassing the British. Today in Europe, its economy is second only to Germany's.

France also played a key role in the creation of the **Common Market**, an increasingly powerful political tool that would bind European neighbors in an economic alliance that would theoretically prevent future wars. The alliance began in 1957, with the signing of the **Treaty of Rome** by France, Western Germany, Italy, Belgium, Holland, and Luxembourg.

Initially hesitant nations, impressed with the lower tariffs of unification and pressured by the increasing globalization of modern industry, later joined. Today, the European Community numbers fifteen countries—most of the affluent European nations. Trade barriers have been eliminated and residents of any one country can live or work in any other member country. Plus, there are ambitious plans to expand the membership in the next several years by as many as thirteen new countries, reaching into Eastern Europe all the way to the borders of Russia.

POSTWAR PARIS

Paris itself grew like crazy after the war.

In the period from 1945 to 1959 alone, more than 60,000 housing units were built in the city. Paris expanded so quickly, in fact, that by the early 1960s, the government decided it was once again time to clear some slums and modernize.

To attract tourists and improve the national image as a world power, classic monuments and buildings, black with soot after years of neglect, were also encased in scaffolds and blasted clean.

In the 1970s and 1980s, the government improved the local transportation system with a freeway (the **Périphérique**) that circled the city and with a network of commuter trains (the **RER**) that branched out into suburbs in all directions.

New monuments also rose, though they sometimes introduced unwelcome modern elements to revered neighborhoods. In the 1970s, for example, the food markets that had occupied **Les Halles** for centuries were replaced by a largely unpleasant multi-level mall sinking several stories into the ground.

Under **President Georges Pompidou's** watch, a hugely unpopular **Montparnasse** office tower (15th *arrondissment*, visible from anywhere in the city) was erected in the name of "Progress" in the neighborhood near the **Select Café** and other Left Bank landmarks.

For some, the last straw of modernism was the **Pompidou Arts Centre** (4th *arrondissement*), completed just north of the **Hôtel de Ville**. A tribute to Pompidou (who followed de Gaulle as president in the early 1970s), the center and its fine museum of contemporary art was designed with the ductwork, escalators, and other unsightly organs on the exterior of the structure.

Still, the Pompidou (or *Beaubourg* as many locals call it in reference to its immediate neighborhood) has defied its critics and become the most visited building in Paris.

POLITICS: DE GAULLE & COMPANY

Politically, postwar France had a somewhat dicey start. De Gaulle, having formed the provisional government, put a formal end to the Third Republic and gave women the vote for the first time ever.

Still, he did not like the look of the various parties squabbling for power and, pouting mightily because they did not accept him as the obvious national father-figure, entered a political semi-retirement in 1947.

What immediately followed was not a pretty sight. Domestically, barely-contained chaos reigned. Prime ministers were supplanted on average every six months.

Internationally, the Vietnamese (led by Paris-educated **Ho Chi Minh**) stomped the French at **Dien Bien Phu** in 1954, then drove them out of the country (thus setting the stage for American "intervention").

In Africa, France granted independence to Tunisia and Morocco in 1956, but failed to move quickly enough in **Algeria**. The subsequent Algerian fight for independence was so fierce that France committed as many as 350,000 troops at a given time to quell the rebellion, and still they failed. Algeria became the French counterpart to America's Vietnam.

Algerian-backed terrorist acts became commonplace in Paris. Worse, in the late 1950s, a handful of French military leaders actually switched sides, invading Corsica in 1958 and threatening a military coup over their own nation.

As the French looked to Louis Napoleon for peace and stability in the mid-1800s, they now pleaded for de Gaulle's return. He was allowed to draft a new constitution giving the president enormous powers and, in short order, to assume the presidency himself.

Still, it would be 1962 before de Gaulle granted Algeria independence. (Even today there are Algerian hostilities toward the French, this time led by Muslim extremists who object to Algeria's subservient economic relationship with the "infidels" of mother France. A series of bombings shook Paris in 1995 and a bomb on a Métro train killed several commuters in 1996.)

The beginning of the end of de Gaulle's 10-year "reign" came in **May 1968**. Students, enraged over their antiquated university system, the war in Vietnam, and an assortment of often vague anti-establishment issues, staged violent riots in Paris that quickly spread throughout the country.

The date is hailed as a political turning point by the political left, which insists that the student demonstrations and subsequent sympathy strikes by millions of labor union members brought France into the modern era in terms of social awareness and political equality.

There was change in substance as well, especially in what had been a hugely overcrowded and impersonal university system. The massive universities were decentralized, students were granted a role in school management, and the student-professor ratio was eased. Labor unions also won concessions on unemployment, low wages, and job safety.

De Gaulle's initial response to the demonstrations was to dismiss the boisterous students as a minor and insignificant nuisance. Only after several days passed and after unions joined students in the streets did de Gaulle address the nation over the radio, rallying support from the right with platitudes about national pride.

In an obvious backlash to the violence of the riots, de Gaulle supporters staged their own demonstrations and, within weeks, reelected Gaulist members to the National Assembly by a huge majority. It looked initially as if de Gaulle had maintained his political hold.

In reality, however, the war hero's allure had dimmed. For many, he was suddenly viewed as someone to be placed, with eternal thanks, on a pedestal in a museum. He was a symbol of the past at a time when the French were increasingly hungry for a progressive and prosperous future.

In 1969, de Gaulle floated a referendum in front of the voters, proposing various government reforms that included greater regional autonomy and reforms in the French Senate. He was a great believer in the political utility of referendums, having bypassed political opponents in the past by taking his cause to the people, who had shown him unquestioning support. This time, however, things were different. The referendum was soundly defeated.

Once again pouting mightily, de Gaulle skulked off the job. He never formally resigned. He said he was going off to write his memoirs and he died a year later.

AFTER DE GAULLE

De Gaulle was followed by other conservatives, first Pompidou, who had once served as de Gaulle's prime minister and who died in office of cancer, and then, in 1974, **Valéry Giscard d'Estaing**. A dashing younger man, Giscard shocked the staid older generations and won favor with younger supporters by lowering the voting age to 18 and making abortion and contraceptives more easily available.

But the significant national political shift that some had predicted right after the May 1968 strikes did not come until 1981, when a coalition of French intellectuals, liberals, and Communists backed socialist François Mitterand for president and he won.

The election was fascinating in that de Gaulle and Mitterand had sparred for decades. Mitterand had actually worked for the Vichy government during the war, while de Gaulle had fled to exile. Mitterand was ever the intellectual, while de Gaulle had capitalized on a military career base.

In the years after the war, Mitterand had staked out the moderate left, while de Gaulle symbolized the conservative right. In 1965, the only year de Gaulle was elected president by popular vote, Mitterand was his challenger, winning 45 percent of the vote.

Thus, the election in 1981 of Mitterand seemed to signal the final rejection of de Gaulle and his stodgy political principles. But for all their placard-waving activism, the French are wary of sudden change.

POSTWAR FRENCH PRESIDENTS

Fourth Republic

Vincent Auriol (socialist) 1947-1954

Rene' Coty (conservative) 1954-1958

Fifth Republic

Charles de Gaulle (Gaullist) 1959-1969

Georges Pompidou (Gaullist) 1969-1974

Valéry Giscard d'Estaing (conservative) 1974-1981

François Mitterand (socialist) 1981-1995

Jacques Chirac (Gaullist) 1995-

As a result, Mitterand's leftist visions were quickly dulled by compromise and practicality. Voters insured he would toe a moderate line in 1986 and again in 1991 when they elected a conservative majority in the General Assembly, forcing him to recommend equally cautious prime ministers.

The return to the conservative party line was completed in May 1995, when **Jacques Chirac**, the Gaullist mayor of Paris since 1977 who had also twice served as prime minister (under Giscard and Mitterand), was elected to succeed Mitterand (who died of prostate cancer just a few months after the election).

Chirac had been a hugely popular mayor, holding highrises at bay, opening new squares, refurbishing the Champs-Élysées, and hiring a green-clad army of workers to scour the streets of Paris daily. He even instituted a motorcycle-bound dog-doo patrol (though they seem to be losing the battle).

But his followers quickly turned on him when he and his prime minister Alain Juppé began to try to tame the nation's unemployment and lower its annual debt so that France would qualify for the European Community's goal of converting to a common currency by 1999. The mere suggestion of trimming the national debt by slightly reducing the treasured social perks drew angry crowds to the streets in 1995 and 1996. By the spring of 1997, little had been accomplished and the deadline for union was drawing closer.

Once adored, Chirac saw his approval ratings fall below 40 percent. Juppé, well, he became reviled by about two-thirds of the people. Though much of the debate does center on economics and the nation's entrenched social welfare system, there is a greater truth that lies beneath the debate. The French simply aren't very keen on a melting pot approach to Europe. To give up the Franc is as distasteful to many as the replacement of the corner café with yet another McDonald's. It's another war and many resurrected the age-old battle cry: *Vive La France!*

An extraordinary event in French politics occurred in 1997. Wanting to extend the life of his power base, Chirac resorted to one of De Gaulle's old tricks and attempted to bolster his support by dissolving the parliament and holding a special election. His thinking was that his majority government had only three of its five years left; he wanted to extend that by creating a new government that would have its full five-year term ahead of it. Chirac thought victory was a foregone conclusion; after all, he had a seemingly insurmountable hold on the government, with a 484 to 93 seat advantage.

Stunningly, he seemed to forget that he and Juppé had grown terribly unpopular. The result: Led by Socialist Lionel Jospin, who had lost to Chirac in the presidential campaign of 1995, the left retook a majority of the parliament, winning 320 seats. Reluctantly, Chirac appointed Jospin Prime Minister, thus beginning another era in French politics of what they call cohabitation—meaning the President and Prime Minister are from different parties and have to find some way to get along.

Jospin had little experience in such lofty ranks of government, having served once as Education Minister and only having been chosen to oppose Chirac in 1995 because there was no one else willing to step up to the plate against the then-popular mayor of Paris. But his arrival, whether it was of his doing or not, marked a sea change. The economy took a turn for the better. Aside from squabbling with the British, who refused to enter the newly formed European Community, economic unification with its neighbors seemed to go smoothly and without the horrible cultural compromises critics had predicted. Unemployment drifted from almost 13 percent, down to just above 10. Rather than fight privatization, Jospin effectively opened the door to lifting government control of some major corporations and allowing them to go public. Almost more remarkable, especially to Americans, some French corporations began to give American industrial giants a run for their money. The French-led Airbus consortium, for instance, began selling more new planes than Boeing

Jospin did live up to his promise of cutting the work week from 39 hours down to 35, the thinking being that if employees worked fewer hours, then employers would have to make up the difference by hiring more people–thus, easing unemployment. So far, all the move seems to have done is spawn more protests. Though, with some help from government incentives, some of the larger corporations are going through an aggressive hiring phase. It remains to be seen what the impact will really be, when the new law goes into full effect in 2002.

With the improving economy and currently soaring Bourse (the French Wall Street), public opinion has shifted. In polls, the people concede that they are relatively happy–an enormous concession from such a serious and formal populace. Jospin's numbers were so good they even resuscitated Chirac's popularity. Facing reelection in 2002, he is said once again to have a chance–unless Jospin challenges him for the top spot. Then he'll have a battle on his hands. This is true especially since the younger voters look at Gaullism as a relic now best left to history classes. Chirac will have to show he is a man of the times.

But, of course, little lifted the public malaise so thoroughly as the 1998 World Cup soccer games. Though hosted by France, the locals were given little hope against such titans as the Brazilians. But, having scrapped past the Croatian team in the semis, France whipped the Brazilian team. The Champs-Élysées was instantly awash with Parisians touting their epic triumph. The French *joie de vive* was back and more intoxicating than ever.

FRENCH GOVERNMENT
President

Beginning with a law passed in 1962, the President is elected by popular vote every seven years. If no individual wins an absolute majority of the vote on a first ballot, a second ballot is held 15 days later between the two leading candidates. According to the 1958 constitution, the President names the Prime Minister, presides over the Council of Ministers and the military, negotiates foreign military and trade treaties, and signs or vetoes proposed laws. In emergencies, the President can dissolve the National Assembly, call for new elections, or usurp the Prime Minister's powers.

The president is headquartered in the **Palais de l'Élysée**, *55 rue du Faubourg-Saint-Honoré (8th, M:Champs-Élysées)*.

Prime Minister

Named by the President, the Prime Minister is responsible for running the national government, executing the national laws, managing the national defense, and naming civil servants. The Prime Minister serves for an undetermined amount of time. Because of firings and resignations, there have been thirty-eight since the end of World War II, as opposed to six Presidents.

The Prime Minister is based in the **Hôtel Matignon**, *47 rue de Varenne (7th, M:Varenne)*.

Ministers

Ministers of the various national departments are nominated by the President, though they must be accepted by the Prime Minister. There are a total of anywhere from twenty-five to fifty ministers and sub-ministers at any given time. They exist on three levels of power, with the most powerful being the four Ministers of State: Social Affairs, Interior, Justice, and Defense. Though ministers help the Prime Minister govern and to set and propose policy and law, they must also answer to the National Assembly, which can periodically call a minister to their chamber and grill him or her about policy decisions.

National Assembly

Deputies of the National Assembly (the equivalent of the U.S. House of Representatives) are elected by popular vote to five-year terms, though the President can, under grave circumstances, dissolve the sitting body and order new elections. There are 577 deputies, with each of the country's 96 *départements* (the equivalent of states) represented according to population. The deputies propose law, adopt the national budget, and vote on military and trade treaties.

The **National Assembly** building is located on the *Quai d'Orsay across the Seine River from the Place de la Concorde (7th, M:Invalides)*.

Senate

Senators are elected to nine-year terms by electoral colleges in each of France's 96 *départements*. A third of the Senate is up for reelection every three years. There are 283 Senators. Representation of the *départements* is awarded on the basis of a complicated population chart that grants a certain number of Senators for a certain range of populations. The Senate powers parallel to those of the National Assembly.

The Senate is located in the **Luxembourg Palace** *(6th, M:Odéon)*.

Conseil Constitutionnel

A nine-member body appointed to nonrenewable nine-year terms. The President, National Assembly, and Senate each appoint three members. This council manages all elections and reviews the constitutionality of proposed laws.

5. PLANNING YOUR TRIP

Though Paris is one of the world's largest and most densely populated metropolises, it is surprisingly easy to navigate. The central core of Paris, where you will no doubt spend the bulk of your time, is relatively compact. You can, and should, cover a huge amount of ground by foot. And when your feet begin to ache, the Métro system, which is both extensive and safe, will save the day.

Shops, newsstands, change bureaus, and cafés are always within easy reach, and, despite what you've heard, most Parisians are helpful and friendly — especially if you attempt even a tiny bit of poorly phrased French.

ORIENTATION

Paris, the capital of France, occupies a series of gently rolling hills in the north-central part of the country and is divided into **Left Bank** and **Right Bank** halves by the **Seine river**, which spills into the Atlantic Ocean 200 kilometers northwest at the port of Le Havre. The city is within easy reach of London to the northwest, Brussels to the north, Munich to the east, and Milan to the southeast.

Paris proper has a population of roughly 2.1 million people, with a Métropolitan total hovering around 10 million. The climate is not exactly sensational, but it rarely grows cold enough to snow and or hot enough to melt the pavement under your feet.

Set your watch **six hours ahead of the East Coast** of the United States — though, for a few days each spring and fall, the difference is seven hours (spring) or five hours (fall) because the French do not follow the same timetable for switching back and forth from daylight savings time.

CLIMATE & WEATHER

You're not coming to Paris for the climate. Oh, there are nice days during the spring and fall, when you might need a light jacket or sweater in the evenings. But the winters hover in the 30s and the summers can feel somehow even hotter than the 75 degree norms. And then there's the rain. Lots of it. It's not uncommon for three or four showers to blow through during the course of a day, or for clouds to sit on the city for days on end.

Fortunately, Paris is even beautiful when it's gray.

WHAT TO PACK

You'll probably want to bring at least one semi-formal or business-like outfit (ties, dresses, that sort of thing) for the better restaurants. It's not that formal attire is required, but you will feel more at ease if you don't look out of place. Plus, a special meal out will feel that much more special.

A lot of hotels have hair dryers, but they don't work very well, so you should toss one into your bag. And don't forget a converter and an adapter for the 220 volt power here. Converters and adapters can easily be found at Radio Shacks and travel shops.

If you're traveling extensively outside Paris, you will also want to find a store where you can buy a Michelin Atlas and the current Michelin Red Guide, which lists thousands of hotels and restaurants. The Red Guide's city maps complement the Atlas and can help guide you directly to the center of town and to your hotels.

A bit of trivia: The Michelin Man – you know, the tubby guy composed of a pile of tires – is known in his home country of France as Bibendum. More trivia: Bibendum is also the name of one of London's hippest restaurants and is set in ye olde tyre shop in the Knightsbridge section of town.

PASSPORTS & VISAS

You will, of course, be obliged to show a **current passport**. No special visas are currently required of American visitors who intend to stay less than three months. If you are staying longer, you need to contact the French Embassy in Washington to ask how to apply for a **long-stay visa**, which is a somewhat tortured process brought to you by the nation who coined the word "bureaucracy." Contact the **French Embassy** at: *4101 Reservoir Rd. NW, Washington, D.C., 20007; Tel. 202/944-6000.*

No vaccines are required. Even though France has nationalized medicine, little if any assistance would be available to you as a tourist, so be sure that you have proper health insurance.

CUSTOMS
Arriving

Customs won't really be a factor for you until you return to the States. However, when you arrive in France you will be funneled through a French Customs area, where signs will lead you to one line if you have something to declare, and another line if you don't. Usually, you sail right through. On occasion, French authorities will stop someone and check their bags. Mainly, they do it to keep up appearances.

Returning

During your flight home, you will be given a small Customs form to complete. You are supposed to declare the total value of all the items you acquired that were gifts or purchases (even from duty-free shops) and that are in your possession. Only one form is required per family.

As a United States resident, you are allowed, duty-free, no more than one liter of booze (no matter what type), and no more than 200 cigarettes or 100 cigars (no Cuban cigars at all, for the obvious reason). You are also allowed a total exemption of $400 worth of items. Though bakery goods and cured cheeses are allowed, other fresh food is forbidden. All plants (even cuttings and seeds) must be declared. If you are carrying more than $10,000 in currency of any kind, that too must be declared.

If you exceed your $400 exemption, you will be asked to pay a flat 10 percent duty on the next $1,000 worth of goods. After you pass the $1,400 plateau, each item you bring in is assessed a duty that applies to that particular type of item (there are countless formulas).

Duty can be paid by cash, check and, in some locations, credit cards. Traveler's checks can be used if the checks do not total more than $50 more than your assessed duty.

For more information: Tel. 202/512-1800 in the Washington D.C. area, or Tel. 01.43.12.12.12 in Paris.

ARRIVALS & DEPARTURES
By Air

Paris has two main airports: **Orly**, a few miles south of the city, and **Roissy-Charles-de-Gaulle**, a few miles to the north. Both have all the conveniences and frustrations of a large urban airport.

There are plenty of duty free shops where you can find everything from silk scarves to CDs a little cheaper than they are in Paris stores (though not necessarily cheaper than in retail stores in North America). Often, there are long lines at the ticket counters, so when your airline suggests you show up for a departure two or three hours before boarding time, they are not kidding.

Stepping off the plane, you will be guided en masse down various hallways and corridors until you reach small glass booths where you present your passport for what will probably be a cursory glance and stamp of arrival. From there, you move on to the luggage area and, afterwards, through customs (see above).

For information about Charles de Gaulle: Tel. 01.48.62.12.12. For information about Orly: Tel. 01.49.75.15.15.

Airlines

Some airlines have non-stop service from American cities to Paris. It's usually a bit more expensive, but it's worth the money in our view. If you have had to wait around to switch planes in the States, you will be dog-tired when you arrive here and your first day will be lost in a fog of exhaustion.

Travel agents can help find charter services. The **Alliance Français**, which is a Paris-based language school with tiny campuses in many major American cities, is one of many cultural organizations that offer package deals.

If you want to do a bit of comparison pricing, which we suggest, here are some numbers you can try:

- **Air France**, *US Tel. 800/237-2747, Paris Tel. 08.02.80.28.02*
- **American**, *US Tel. 800/433-7300, Paris Tel. 08.01.87.28.72*
- **Continental**, *US Tel. 800/525-0280, Paris Tel. 01.42.99.09.09*
- **Delta**, *US Tel. 800/221-1212, Paris Tel. 01.47.68.92.92*
- **Northwest**, *US Tel. 800/225-2525, Tel. Paris 01.42.66.90.00*
- **TWA**, *US Tel. 800/221-2000, Paris Tel. 08.01.89.28.92*

- **United**, *US Tel. 800/241-6522, Paris Tel. 08.01.72.72.72*
- **USAir**, *US Tel. 800/428-4322, Paris Tel. 01.49.10.29.00*

For air travel inside France:
- **Air Inter**, *Paris Tel. 01.45.46.90.00*

FROM THE AIRPORT TO THE CITY
By Taxi

If you have a lot of luggage, splurge and take a cab. It will cost 150FF to 300FF, but it will get your vacation off to a smoother, happier start. Remember that you will probably have flown through the night, gotten very little sleep, and will be tired and probably cranky.

Note also that your fare will be a bit higher than what the meter says because you will be charged extra for bags that go in the trunk.

By Bus

You can save money by taking the **Air France bus** into town (regular buses are also available but are slower and are not really equipped to handle tourists with lots of luggage). Air France buses leave Charles de Gaulle for Porte Maillot, then the Arc de Triomphe about every 15 minutes, from 6 a.m. to 11 p.m. The ride can take a half hour to an hour, depending on traffic, and costs 60FF-70FF. From Porte Maillot or the Arc de Triomphe, both of which are on the Right Bank, you will have to continue to your hotel by cab or Métro.

Air France buses from Orly, at a charge of 45FF, will drop you off at either the Gare Montparnasse or the Invalides Air Terminal, both of which are near the center of the Left Bank. Both Air France bus lines also work in reverse and can be taken to the airports at the end of your stay.

Air France bus information: Tel. 01.41.56.89.00.

Another bus, the **Roissybus**, is a bit cheaper and will take you to the Opéra Garnier area in the heart of the Right Bank. *Roissybus information: Tel. 01.48.04.18.24.*

By Train

RER trains can also bring you into town from the airports. From Charles de Gaulle catch a short connector bus from the airport to the

Roissy RER station, where you will take the B3 RER line into the very heart of Paris (fare is about $9). There are several stops, running north to south through the city. From Orly, catch the C2 RER line, which will stop at several stations along the Seine on the Left Bank.

Trains run frequently from before 6 am to just after midnight.

By Car

Each airport has the usual array of **car rental agencies** eager to accommodate, especially if you drive a stick. But as far as cars go, just say no. Parking in Paris is expensive and often non-existent.

The rules of the road are different than in the United States and accidents are stunningly common and complicated to resolve.

By Van

There are more and more companies providing door to door transport to and from the airport by van. Some have a minimum requirement of two people, sometimes even four. But prices are reasonable, reservations can be made in advance, and most have English-speaking staff. Rates range from about 60 to 90FF per person, depending on how many are in your party and whether you are going to De Gaulle or Orly. For the companies that will give a single a van, you'll pay a premium of about 150FF—which is still not horrible.

- **Airport Connection**, *Tel. 01.44.18.36.02, Fax 01.45.55.85.19*
- **Paris Airports Service**, *Tel. 01.49.62.78.78, Fax 01.49.62.78.79*
- **Parishuttle**, *Tel. 01.43.90.91.91, Fax 01.43.90.91.10*
- **Airport Shuttle**, *Tel. 01.45.38.55.72, Fax 01.43.21.35.67, www.airportshuttle.fr*

ARRIVING FROM DESTINATIONS OTHER THAN THE AIRPORTS
By Train

A friend recently asked us to meet her daughter at the train station. Well, that was fine, except for the fact that Paris has **six SNCF train stations** — **Montparnasse** and **Austerlitz** on the Left Bank and **Saint-Lazare**, **Gare du Nord**, **Gare de l'Est** and **Lyon** on the Right Bank. The Paris station where you arrive is determined by your place of geographic origin.

For instance, if you are coming into Paris from Brittany, along France's west coast, you will arrive at the Gare Montparnasse. If you are arriving from Burgundy country to the southeast of Paris, you will be deposited at Gare de Lyon.

Information about SNCF destinations and fares: Tel. 01.53.90.20.20 for the Paris suburbs and 08.36.35.35.35 for France and Europe. Travel agencies in the U.S. and Paris can also help with train schedules and ticket purchases.

All six SNCF stations are on Métro lines, so it is fairly simple to continue to your hotel by Métro. Taxi stands are also located at train stations.

- **Gare d'Austerlitz**, *55 quai d'Austerlitz (5th, M:Gare d'Austerlitz)*, serving southern France, southwestern France, Spain and Portugal.
- **Gare de l'Est**, *place du 11 Novembre, 1918 (10th, M:Gare de l'Est)*, serving eastern France, southern Germany, Luxembourg, northern Switzerland and Austria.
- **Gare de Lyon**, *20 boulevard Diderot (12th, M:Gare de Lyon)*, serving southern France, southeastern France, central France, Italy, Switzerland, and the Alps.
- **Gare Montparnasse**, *17 boulevard Vaugirard (15th, M:Montparnasse)*, serving western France.
- **Gare du Nord**, *18 rue de Dunkerque (10th, M:Gare du Nord)*, serving northern France, northern Germany, Belgium, Great Britain, and Holland.
- **Gare Saint-Lazare**, *13 rue d'Amsterdam (8th, M:Saint-Lazare)*, serving Normandy and Great Britain.

By Car

A very successful and intelligent attorney friend of ours drove his family into Paris not long ago and became so thoroughly confused so quickly that he hailed a cab and paid the driver to lead him caravan-style to his hotel. Paris does not have a logical street grid, there are many tricky traffic circles, even relatively straight streets change names every three or four blocks, and French drivers are statistically dangerous.

In short, there is little we can offer in terms of advice or solace if you arrive in Paris by car — except to find your destination as quickly and safely as possible, then park your car for the duration. Your hotel will tell you the nearest garage, though there are not many.

If you park on the street, you will see that most spaces are marked *Payant*. This means the space is metered and that somewhere nearby on the sidewalk you will see a four-foot electronic meter with a '**P**' on top that asks you how much time you would like. After you pay, the meter spits out a small receipt with the expiration time printed prominently. This slip goes on your dashboard. Parking tickets are very expensive.

GETTING AROUND TOWN
Maps, A Must

Again, because this city follows no grid and a single street can change names several times, a good map is essential. Printemps, Galeries Lafayette, and other local department stores circulate very useful free maps in hotels, some restaurants, and travel bureaus. Their maps also contain lots of helpful information.

If you stay more than a few days, however, you need to pick up a copy of *Paris par Arrondissement* for about 60FF. This tiny book is the bible of Paris maps, even for Parisians. It includes every tiny street in Paris proper as well as many of the close-in suburbs, it has Métro and bus maps, and notes various landmarks, open markets and government offices. Virtually any bookstore, many newsstands, and most hotel shops carry this book.

By Foot

Bring comfortable shoes because Paris, with its grand avenues, countless shops and bistros, and beautiful parks, is made for walking. You will walk and walk and walk, then stop for a leisurely coffee or Pernod, and then walk some more.

One strategy is to choose a neighborhood that you want to explore thoroughly, take the Métro to the heart of that neighborhood, and then walk the day away. We have divided the key sections of this guide into manageable and logical neighborhoods, or quarters.

Oh, and watch out for dog droppings!

By Métro

The Métro system is remarkable — so remarkable that you will note that every time we give you an address for a hotel, a museum or whatever, we include the arrondissement and the Métro stop.

Rarely will you wait more than five minutes for a train. The Métro's 14 lines criss-cross the city, making every neighborhood accessible. All lines run from 5:30 in the morning to just past midnight.

And it's cheap. You can buy single tickets, but it makes much more sense to ask for a *carnet*, which is a packet of 10 tickets for only 55FF. You can travel anywhere in the city, changing as many times as you like, on a single ticket. When you buy the carnet ask for *un plan* also, which is a free map of the Métro system.

Métro stations are clearly marked at the street level so they are easy to find. Sometimes you will spot a big yellow 'M' in a circle. Other times, you will see the wonderful green metal Art Deco stations.

The drawbacks: the system can get crowded, especially along central lines like the number 1 that runs beneath the Champs-Élysées; the system shuts down at 12:30 am; and you sometimes have to walk what seems like a long block underground to transfer lines. *Métro information: Tel. 01. 43.46.14.14.*

By Rail

The **RER**, or *Reseau Express Régional*, is a system of four light rail train lines that are used primarily to ferry commuters into Paris during the day and back to their suburban neighborhoods at night. However, there are inner city stops, so the RER supplements the Métro. And there are several suburban sights to see within reach of the RER system, including Versailles.

Prices vary according to the distance you cover, but are reasonable. If you use the RER only to cover a few stops inside the city, simply use one of your Métro tickets.

By Bus

The Paris bus system, with more than 40 lines, is even more comprehensive than the Métro system. The advantage, of course, is that you are above ground and can watch the scenery go by. Disadvantages are that traffic can slow you down and buses are often quite crowded. The Parisian sense of space is different from the American, so don't be surprised if you are pressed in tightly on all sides.

The bus system uses the same tickets as the Métro. If you travel out of the city proper, you may be asked to give up a second ticket. When you step on the bus there will be a small machine behind the driver. Simply push your Métro ticket into the slot and it will be properly punched.

Bus service begins at 6:30 am and ends around 9 pm, with some lines working until just after midnight.

Bus Tours

There are a bunch of them. Some specialize, offering everything from art-related tours to late-night tours of live sex shows. Prices run a little more than 100FF a day for an adult, and half price for children. Special tours can run as high as 1,000 FF.

- **Les Cars Rouges**, *3 rue Talma (16th, M:La Muette), Tel. 01.53.95.39.53*
- **Cityrama**, *4 place des Pyramides (1st, M:Tuileries), Tel. 01.44.55.60.00 and 01.42.60.30.14.* One of the most popular.
- **Excursions Parisiennes**, *51 rue de Maubeuge (9th, M:Notre-Dame de Lorette), Tel. 01.42.80.42.54*
- **Paris-Vision**, *214 rue de Rivoli (1st, M:Tuileries), Tel. 01.42.60.30.01; also at 1 rue Auber (9th, M:Opéra), Tel. 01.49.27.00.06 and 01.47.42.85.84.* One of the best and most popular. Variety, including cabarets and even the Loire Valley. Mini-vans available.
- **ParisBus**, *place du Trocadéro(16th, M:Trocadéro), Tel. 01.42.30.55.50*
- **Paris Bus Service** (minibus from hotel by special arrangement), *20 avenue Franklin Roosevelt, 94300 Vincennes, Tel. 01.43.65.55.55.* Based in the suburbs.
- **Tax Voyages** (minibus from hotel by special arrangement), *7 rue Jules Verne, 93400 Saint-Ouen, Tel. 01.40.12.88.08.* Based in the suburbs.

By Boat

Yes, you can actually get around town by boat — well, sort of. There is a service called **BatOBus**, which has five stops along the Seine, stretching from the Tour Eiffel to the Île de la Cité. *Single trips are 20FF, or you can hop on and off all day with passes for 65FF; Tel. 01.44.11.33.44.*

There are also several boat tours that swing up and down the Seine day and night for hour-long narrated tours. Boats depart about every half hour beginning in mid-morning and ending at about 10 pm. Prices run 40 to 50FF per person and half price for children. Most of the boats are huge, but the short trips are still somehow romantic.

There are dinner tours as well, though they are said to have disadvantages — dinner distracts you from the sights and the sights distract you from a pretty expensive dinner.

- **Bâteaux Mouches**, *Pont de L'Alma (7th, M:Alma-Marceau or Pont de l'Alma), Tel. 01.42.25.96.10*
- **Bâteaux Parisiens**, *Tour Eiffel/Pont d'Iena (7th, M:Alma-Marceau or Pont de l'Alma), Tel. 01.44.11.33.44; also at Notre-Dame/Quai Montebello (5th, M:Saint-Michel), Tel. 01.43.26.92.55*
- **Vedettes de Paris**, *Port de Suffren (8th, M:Bir-Hakeim or Pont de l'Alma), Tel. 01.47.05.71.29 and 01.45.50.23.79*
- **Vedettes du Pont Neuf**, *Square du Vert-Galant (1st, M:Pont Neuf), Tel. 01.46.33.98.38*
- **Yachts de Paris**, *Port de Javel-Haut (15th, M:Javel). Tel. 01.44.37.10.20. A dinner cruise on a yacht that lasts from about 8 p.m. to 11 p.m. Fare per person: 890FF*

For tours of the **Paris canals** that cross the northeast section of the city, try:
- **Canauxrama**, *13 quai de la Loire (19th, M:Jaures), Tel. 01.42.39.15.00. Fare 80FF*
- **Paris Canal**, *19 quai de la Loire (19th, M:Jaures), Tel. 01.42.40.96.97. Fare 100FF*

By Taxi

Taxi stands are scattered throughout the central part of the city, primarily at major intersections, circles, or monuments. You can also hail a cab from the sidewalk, though they are not supposed to stop if there is a taxi stand close by. You can also order a cab by phone, though there is an extra charge to come to your door.

Rates should be posted on the left side window. If you have baggage there is an additional fee, and rates are a bit higher after 10 pm. Tip is included in the fare, though it is common, even expected, that you offer 5 to 20FF depending on the length of the trip (and whether the driver imperiled your life).

You know the cab is available if its bright roof light is on. If the small light beneath that sign is on, the cab is occupied or on call.

Complaints should be addressed to **Service Taxi-Préfecture de Police**, *36 rue des Morillons, 75015 Paris, Tel. 45.31.14.80.*

Some taxi services that will get you to the airport or around town:

- **Aero Taxi**, *Tel. 01.47.31.30.30*
- **Alpha Taxis**, *Tel. 01.45.85.85.85*
- **Artaxi**, *Tel. 01.42.41.50.50*
- **G7**, *Tel. 01.41.27.69.99*
- **Taxis Bleus**, *Tel. 01.49.36.10.10*
- **Taxis Radio Etoile**, *Tel. 01.42.70.41.41*

By Car

Car rental agencies abound, but, as we've said several times now, driving is not fun, parking is a hassle and expensive, and statistically the French have truly horrible road records. Once a week there was an accident on our relatively open and safe street.

However, you may want to rent a car for a leisurely drive down to the **châteaux country** in the Loire Valley or somewhere else. Your American driver's license will suffice and, though some credit card companies provide some insurance when you pay for the rental with their card, it is still a very good idea to buy all the basic insurance coverage when you rent the car. (Often you can get them to include the insurance, or *assurance*.)

Rules you must remember: one, the car coming from the right always has the right of way; two, stop signs are routinely ignored by other drivers; and three, seatbelts are absolutely required by law, even in the backseat.

Car rental agencies, most of which have several neighborhood offices, can be found in the *Location* section of the Yellow Pages. Avoid the central number and call the office nearest your hotel.

Cars can also be rented by your tourist agent back home, or through toll free numbers in the United States *(Tel. 800/555-1212 for information of toll-free numbers in the US).*

Car rental agencies in Paris include:

- **Avis**, *Tel. 01.46.09.92.12, Fax 01.40.71.81.81*
- **Car Rental**, *Tel. 01.48.08.31.31*
- **Eurodollar**, *Tel. 01.49.38.77.77, Fax 01.49.38.77.72*
- **Europcar**, *Tel. 01.30.44.90.00 or 01.30.43.82.82*
- **Eurorent**, *Tel. 01.45.67.82.17, Fax 01.40.65.91.94*

• **Hertz**, *Tel. 01.47.88.51.51*
• **Prestige Limousines**, with chauffeur, *Tel. 01.42.50.81.81*

By Bicycle

Limited use of bicycles could be fun, but stay away from crowded streets and keep your eyes wide open at all times. Rental agencies, some of which have bicycle tours, include:

• **Autothèque**, *80 rue Montmartre (2nd, M:Montmartre), Tel. 01.42.36.87.90*
• **La Maison du Vélo**, *11 rue Fenelon (10th, M:Gare du Nord), Tel. 01.42.81.24.72*
• **Mountain Bike Trip**, *6 place Etienne-Pernet (15th, M:Felix-Faure), Tel. 01.48.42.57.87*
• **Paris-Vélo**, *2 rue du Fer-à-Moulin (5th, M:Censier-Daubenton), Tel. 01.43.37.59.22*
• **Ride-a-Bike Tours** *(call for location but English is spoken). Tel. 01.47.81.38.18*

GUIDED WALKING TOURS

There are a few guided walking tours:
• *Anne Hervé, Tel. 01.47.90.52.16*
• *Association for Safeguard of Historical Paris, 44 rue Francois Miron (4th M:St. Paul), Tel. 01.48.87.74.31*
• *Paris Contact, 46 rue Lepic (18th, M:Abbesses), Tel. 01.42.51.08.40.*

By Helicopter

Helicopter rides viewing Paris are offered by **Paris Helicopters** in the suburb of Bourget, *Tel. 01.48.35.90.44.*

FOR MORE INFORMATION

Write the **French Tourist Office** nearest you:

• *444 Madison Avenue, Suite 222, New York, New York 10020. Tel. 212/757-1125*
• *645 North Michigan Ave., Suite 630, Chicago, Illinois 60611. Tel. 312/337-6301*
• *2305 Cedar Spring Road, Suite 205, Dallas, Texas 75201. Tel. 214/720-4010*
• *9454 Wilshire Boulevard, Suite 303, Beverly Hills, California, 90212. Tel. 310/272-2661*

6. BASIC INFORMATION

ELECTRICITY

The current in France runs at a menacing 220 volts and the plugs are shaped differently. If you have an electric razor or a hair dryer or whatever, you will need an electric current converter and a plug adapter. Even so, say folks with more experience than we have, machines with motors may eventually burn out. Message: bring cheap hairdryers.

HEALTH SERVICES

Health care in France is first-rate and completely modern, which is not to say French doctors do everything exactly the way American doctors do. There is nationalized health care and, on occasion, this will cover an emergency suffered by a foreign visitor. But you are still much better off having your own medical and dental coverage. Forms for your American insurance carrier will be completed in French and you will be billed in francs. Your Stateside carrier will convert the francs to dollars when they reimburse you.

Paris has an **American Hospital**, *84 boulevard de la Saussaye, Neuilly-sur-Seine, Tel. 01.46.01.41.25.25.* Neuilly-sur-Seine is a close-in suburb to the west, not far from the Pont de Neuilly Métro stop and at the end of the no. 82 bus line. The hospital has a bilingual staff.

A comprehensive listing of English speaking doctors can be obtained from a women's organization known as **WICE,** *20 boulevard du Montparnasse, 75015 Paris (15th, M:Montparnasse), Tel. 01.45.66.75.70.* Another listing is included in *Bloom Where You're Planted*, a helpful book for local Americans published by **The American Church in Paris**, *65 quai d'Orsay, 75007 Paris (7th, M:Invalides), Tel. 01.47.05.07.99.*

Various emergency medical phone numbers are listed later in this chapter under "Essential Phone Numbers." Help of all kinds is available around the clock.

Pharmacies around town are clearly marked with green neon crosses. Medicines, including common aspirin, can only be purchased at a pharmacy.

Some pharmacies in Paris where you are likely to find someone who speaks English:
- **British & American Pharmacie**, *1 rue Auber (9th, M:Opéra), Tel. 01.47.01.42.01.49.40*
- **Pharmacie Dhery** (open 24 hours), *84 avenue des Champs-Élysées (8th, M:George V), Tel. 01.45.62.02.41*
- **Pharmacie Opéra**, *6 boulevard des Capucines (9th, M:Opéra), Tel. 01.42.65.88.29*
- **Pharmacie Swann**, *6 rue Castiglione (1st, M:Concorde), Tel. 01.42.60.72.96*

IN PRINT IN ENGLISH
Library
- **The American Library**, *10 rue du Général Camou, 75007 Paris (7th, M:École Militaire), Tel. 01.53.59.12.60*

Newspapers
- *The International Herald Tribune*, which is largely a blend of pieces from the paper's owners: The Washington Post and The New York Times. 10FF, daily except Sunday.
- *USA Today*
- *The European edition of The Wall Street Journal*
- *The Financial Times, of London*
- *The European*

Magazines
A variety of the usual is available in the big cities, including *Time, Newsweek, Vanity Fair, Glamour, Rolling Stone*. There are also several local products in Paris, where more than 20,000 Americans are said to live:
- *France USA Contacts* (FUSAC), a bi-weekly advertiser which is quickly becoming the Bible of classified ads for Americans in Paris. On the web at *www.fusac.fr*. Free.

- *Paris Voice*, a monthly tabloid. Free.
- *Pariscope*, an essential weekly listing every cultural and nightlife event in town. Has an English-language section. 3FF.
  - *TimeOut, Paris Guide*. Free.

LANGUAGE CLASSES

As we've said many times, you'll have more fun if you know the language. You won't feel so 'foreign' and the locals will treat you with a bit more respect—even if you're not very good. If you have the time, attending a school can help you with your language skills and you can also meet some new friends. Costs vary wildly, but it's quite easy to find some program that fits your schedule and budget.

- **La Sorbonne**, *47 rue des Écoles (5th, M:Maubert-Mutualité)*, *Tel. 01.40.46.22.11*
- **Alliance Française**, *101 boulevard Raspail (6th, M:Rennes)*, *Tel. 01.45.44.38.28*
- **Berlitz**, *35 avenue Franklin Roosevelt (8th, M:Roosevelt), Tel. 01.40.74.00.17*
- **Accord**, *14 boulevard Poissoniere (9th, M:Bonne Nouvelle)*, *Tel. 01.55.33.52.33, Fax. 01.55.33.52.34*
- **École France Langue**, *2 rue de Sfax (16th, M:Victor Hugo)*, *Tel. 01.45.00.40.15*

LOST & FOUND

If you are fortunate enough to have had a sympathetic soul find your things, you can retrieve them at the **Lost and Found Bureau**, *36 rue des Morillons (15th, M:Convention)*, *Tel. 01.55.76.20.20*. The office is open Monday through Friday from 8:30 a.m. to 5 p.m.

PLACES OF WORSHIP

The *International Herald Tribune* publishes a weekly list of services. Or, for information about services, *phone 01.46.33.01.01 Monday through Friday*. A few churches and temples where services are conducted in English:

- **Adath Shalom**, *22bis rue des Belles-Feuilles (16th, M:Porte Dauphine)*. *Tel. 01.45.53.84.09*
- **American Cathedral** (Episcopal-Anglican), *23 avenue George V (8th, M:George V)*. *Tel. 01.47.20.17.92*

- **American Church**, (Protestant), *65 quai d'Orsay (7th, M:Invalides). Tel. 01.47.05.07.99*
- **Church of Christ**, *4 rue Deodat-Severac (17th, M:Malesherbes). Tel. 01.42.27.50.86*
- **Internatinal Baptist Fellowship**, *123 avenue du Maine (14th M:Mouton-Duvernet). Tel. 01.47.01.49.15.29*
- **Saint-George's Anglican Church**, *7 rue Auguste-Vacquerie (16th, M:Kléber). Tel. 01.47.20.22.51*
- **Saint-Joseph's Catholic Church**, *50 avenue Hoche (8th, M:Charles-de-Gaulle);. Tel. 01.42.27.28.56*
- **Saint-Michael's Church** (Anglican), *5 rue d'Aguesseau (8th M:Madeleine). Tel. 01.47.01.42.70.88*

PEEING IN PARIS

The three most important things in the life of a tourist are: one, appropriate attire for the weather; two, comfortable footwear; and three, a place to answer nature's call. Layering and the willingness to sacrifice some style in favor of comfort will probably get you through the first two. But what about number three? In a strange city? In a foreign country, where they don't have the same standards about these things that many of us do?

It takes a little knowledge, that's all. And, on occasion, strong thigh muscles.

Every café and restaurant has a bathroom. Usually they're in the basement (*sous sol*) and usually there's one sink in a common area that also often has a telephone.

If you're a woman and haven't traveled much you may one day open the door with the silhouette of a woman on it, look at the hole in the floor inside, and think there's been some mistake or that someone stole the toilet. But no. It's called a Turkish toilet and it requires balance and good quads.

As a general rule, French bathrooms (*toilettes*) are not as clean as those you might be used to back home. Paper towels are rare (we'd love to have the hot air dryer concession). And it's not uncommon for women to have to walk past an occupied urinal to get to the ladies room.

Where to go (so to speak):

- Those hulking green cabins you sometimes see half-blocking the sidewalk represent the current incarnation of the streetside *pissoir* and they are better than you might imagine. The cost of a couple of francs is minimal compared to extreme discomfort. They are heated and surprisingly clean for what they are. (They clean themselves seconds after you've stepped out.)
- All first class hotels have immaculate rest rooms. Keep your eyes peeled for the sign, look like you're registered, and see how the other half lives.
- Department stores almost always put the bathrooms on an upper floor, the theory being that you'll be tempted by all their fine wares to and from.

POST OFFICES

Whether you're visiting France's largest cities or tiniest hamlets, there is a post office near you. Paris is loaded with them. Look for the yellow *Poste* signs. There are often markers on city street corners, pointing the way to the nearest *Bureau de Poste*.

Offices are open from 8 a.m. to 7 p.m. Monday through Friday, and 9 a.m. to noon on Saturdays. The **main post office** in Paris, *52 rue du Louvre (1st, M:Louvre)*, is open 24 hours a day for telegrams, phone calls, and general delivery *(poste restant)*.

Air mail letters with one or two pages are 4,40FF to the United States.

Tabacs (bars which also carry tobacco) also sell stamps. In fact, the lines in a tabac are often shorter and quicker than they are in the post office, where the French do everything from pay their utility bills to conduct their banking.

Helpful phrase: *"Je voudrais des timbres pour les États-Unis, s'il vous plaît."* Just hold up your fingers for how many you want.

MONEY & BANKING

Like Sally Bowles says in *Cabaret*, money makes the world go around. For France, and especially Paris, bring lots. You will spend more than you expect, and probably more than you want. But what's the point of coming all this way if you have to remember it as a time when you deprived yourself of the available pleasures just because things cost a bit much?

French **francs** come in coins for 1, 2, 5, 10 and 20FF, and in bills for 20, 50, 100, 200 and 500FF. **Centimes**, the French equivalent of cents, come in coins for 5, 10, 20 and 50 centimes.

Changing Money

The franc has consistently traded at somewhere between 5:1 and 7:1 on the dollar. The financial section of your local newspaper or your local banker should be able to tell you where it stands on any given day.

So, you ask, where do you pick up a few hundred francs? Some, but not all, American banks will have a modest amount of foreign currency in the vault. Likewise, some, but not all, French banks will exchange francs for dollars. Those that do will have a sign reading *Change* outside the door. Some of the upper crust hotels will help you out, but only if you are a guest and only at a crummy rate.

Whether you have cash or travelers checks, the most common way to change money is at a *Change* bureau – usually a tiny storefront with signs outside showing the going rates of about twenty currencies.

Change bureaus often brag that they don't charge you for the change. Nonsense. They give you less than the full market value of your currency (compare their posted exchange rate with currency tables in that morning's *International Herald Tribune*), so there is a charge built into the exchange. You can sometimes find better exchange rates if you shop around a bit. And, on rare occasions, you might even talk the broker into a better rate.

If you wander on a day trip into the countryside, remember that in the smaller towns and villages, it can sometimes be difficult to change money. So plan ahead, making sure you have enough cash to get you through.

DOLLAR-FRANC & DOLLAR-EURO EXCHANGE RATES

*Current plans call for use of the French franc until 2002, when the Euro will be officially introduced. You will note that already most prices in stores are posted in francs and in Euros. Your credit card charges are already calculated in Euros. At the time of this writing, **one dollar is worth roughly 6.7 FF**. The Euro and the dollar are almost one to one.*

Credit & ATM Cards

Most banks will give you a cash advance on a credit card.

Or – and this is the easiest method of all – if your ATM card is hooked into one of the major electronic banking systems, just do what you do at home: Find an ATM (they look just like they do in the States), punch in your secret four-digit personal identification code, and count the cash when it comes out the slot.

Banks will charge you a flat fee for these transactions (as they do in the States), or charge you a percentage by giving you a lower-than-market-value exchange rate, or both, depending on how greedy your bank is. (If you charge an advance at a French bank, it too will factor in a small cut.)

Important: You can save the cost of conversion fees by using your credit cards for meals and purchases because your bank will give you the full market value when it exchanges your charge in francs for its payment in dollars.

American Express

I was ticked off when I learned that even preferred customers are charged a conversion fee at American Express. What's the point of being preferred if you have to pay all the fees anyway?

However, American Express still does a bigtime business in converting dollars to francs and issuing travelers checks to American tourists. The main offices in Paris are: *11 rue Scribe (9th, M:Opéra), Tel. 01.47.77.70.07; and 12 Rond Pont Champs-Élysées (8th, M:Franklin-Roosevelt), Tel. 01.42.25.15.16. For information in the US: Tel. 800/221-7282.*

The offices are closed Sundays.

A Special Tip

Another way to save conversion fees is to join the **American Automobile Association** in the United States and to buy travelers checks in French francs instead of dollars.

AAA gives you virtually the full market value on your exchange, has no service charge, and supplies you with French franc travelers checks that will be honored at the full face value by virtually any bank or change bureau, as well as by most French stores, hotels and restaurants.

Sure, you still have to pay the membership fees for AAA, but that will come in handy next time you get a flat tire in the middle of the night.

SAFETY & TAKING PRECAUTIONS

France, even downtown Paris, experiences nothing approaching the violent crime that plagues American cities. This does not mean you should not exercise caution. Wallets and purses do get stolen, vandals do break into cars, and people are occasionally mugged.

Avoid empty dark streets late at night, watch out for pickpockets on crowded buses and subway cars, and keep your cool if those around you are losing theirs. Of the primary tourist neighborhoods in Paris, Pigalles and Les Halles are the only two where we sometimes feel a bit uncomfortable. Though this happens less frequently than some would lead you to believe, you should also be very careful when suddenly swarmed by a gaggle of small usually colorfully dressed children. The gypsy children may seem friendly, but they also can lift your wallet in a heartbeat.

Police are often nearby. The **emergency police phone number is 17**. To visit or call the central police station: *208 rue Faubourg Saint-Honoré (8th, M:Ternes), Tel. 01.42.89.55.78.*

SOCIAL ORGANIZATIONS

- **Alcoholics Anonymous**, *Tel. 01.46.34.59.65*
- **American Catholic Women's Organization**, *50 avenue Hoche (8th, M:Charles De Gaule), Tel. 01.42.27.28.56*
- **American Chamber of Commerce**, *212 avenue George V (8th, M:George V), Tel. 01.47.23.70.28*
- **American Club**, *34 avenue de New York (16th, M:Alma-Marceau), Tel. 01.47.23.64.36.*
- **American Women's Group in Paris**, *22bis rue Pétrarque, 75016 Paris (16th, M:Trocadéro). Tel. 01.47.55.87.50 or 01.47.55.87.51; 49 rue Pierre-Charron, 75008 Paris (8th, M:Franklin-Roosevelt). Tel. 01.43.59.17.61*
- **Association of American Residents Overseas**. *Tel. 01.42.04.09.38*
- **Canadian Women's Group**, *5 rue de Constantine (7th, M:Invalides), Tel. 01.45.51.35.73*
- **Council on International Educational Exchange**, *1 place de l'Odéon (6th, M:Odéon), Tel. 01.46.34.16.10*
- **Democrats Abroad**, *5 rue Bargue (15th, M:Vaugirard), Tel. 01.45.66.49.05.*
- **Republicans Abroad**, *26 boulevard Suchet (16th, M:Ranelagh), Tel. 01.45.24.44.99*

- **University Club of Paris**, *34 avenue de New York (16th, M:Iéna), Tel. 01.47.23.64.36*
- **WICE**, a women's organization, *20 boulevard du Montparnasse, 75015 Paris (15th, M:Montparnasse). Tel. 01.45.66.75.70*

TELEVISION

Most of the better hotels will have cable, which will include a CNN channel, as well as Sky news from Great Britain and a handful of German and Italian channels. You might have about 30 options, which is more than many of the Parisians have themselves. Though cable and miniature satellite dishes have been available for some time, they are quite expensive and many simply settle for the standard six channels. **TF1** and the government-owned **France 2** and **France 3** are like the ABC, CBS and NBC of France, offering news, adventure shows, some sitcoms, more circuses than you ever imagined possible, endless soccer matches, occasional movies and lots and lots of talk shows. **M6** is similar with more foreign programming dubbed into French. **Arte** tends to feature more avant-guard movies. **Canal+** is a pay channel.

It is not unusual to find an American film in English, especially later in the evening. As you flip from channel to channel you will also spot dubbed reruns of such standard U.S. fare as *Cagney and Lacey, Dallas* and *Melrose Place*. Why? Basically, it is a great deal cheaper for them to pay fees to air old programs than to produce new ones of their own.

If you're curious about what's on, you can pick up a copy of *Télé-Z* for just 2FF.

TELEPHONES

France, which not long ago had an absolute disgrace of a telephone system, has now advanced beyond most countries.

If you are in the US and want to phone a number in Paris directly, dial 011 for the international line, 33 (for the country code representing France), 01 (for the French area code representing Paris), then the eight-digit number of the party.

Virtually any country in the world can be dialed direct from France, though you must tap into an international line by dialing 19, then the country code. To phone someone in the United States, you would dial 19, then 1, then the area code, then the phone number you want.

Not so long ago, you could dial anywhere in the city using just the eight-digit number. Because of the increase of wireless phones, pagers, etc., **you now must also dial the 01 Paris code before dialing the number itself.**

Codes for other countries can be found in the front of a French phone book (yellow or white pages). Or, if your French is good, dial 12 for directory assistance.

If you want to make a long distance call through AT&T, dial *08.00.99.00.11*; this will allow you to make direct calls or request operator assistance. For an MCI operator, dial *08.00.99.00.19*. For a Sprint operator, dial *08.00.99.00.87*.

If you are in Paris and want to phone a hotel or restaurant somewhere else in France, you will need to look up the area code for that region. Again, the Yellow Pages will provide that information, or you can phone Information at 12. If you are in France and want to phone someone in Paris, dial 01, then the eight-digit number.

By the way, France does not have a compatible touch tone system, so you won't be able to dial your bank's computer back home to check your balance. And, you'll be sad to know, you cannot dial 800 lines from France. You can only reach 800 lines by calling the operator and charging the call on a credit card as if it were a regular phone number.

Public Telephones

Though there are still coin-operated public phones in some bars, France was one of the first countries to eliminate coin-operated public phones on the streets. Hoping to discourage vandals who kept breaking into public phones in search of a few francs, the French devised phones that use cards that resemble credit cards.

These cards can be purchased most easily in **Tabacs** (bars that also sell tobacco, stamps, and other odds and ends – look for the Tabac sign outside), Métro stations, and post offices. They are available for 40FF and last seemingly forever. These can even be used to phone the United States from a pay phone.

In a rare burst of marketing genius, makers of the cards have circulated a myriad of designs and they are now collected in France the same way baseball cards are collected in the States. To buy a phone card, say: *"Je voudrais une télécarte, s'il vous plaît."*

ESSENTIAL PHONE NUMBERS

Information: 12
Medical Emergency: 15
Police: 17
Fire and Any Emergency: 18
Poison Center: 01.40.37.04.04
American Hospital: 01.46.01.41.25.25
Ambulance: 01.48.42.22.00
SOS Medecins (medical emergency): 01.47.07.77.77
SAMU (medical emergency): Left Bank 01.45.67.50.50
Right Bank 01.42.01.45.50.50
24-Hour House Calls: 01.45.01.45.31.03
24-Hour Pharmacy: 01.42.42.42.50
Dental Emergency: 43.37.51.00
SOS Help (crisis line): 01.47.23.80.80
SOS Avocats (legal help): 01.43.29.33.00
American Embassy: 01.43.12.22.22
American Consulate: 01.42.96.12.02
American Church: 01.40.62.05.00
American Express (for stolen card): 01.47.77.72.00
American Express (for stolen checks): 05.90.86.00
Visa (for stolen card): 01.42.77.11.90
Information in US: (19) 1+Area Code+555-1212

TIPPING

In hotels, if someone carries your bags to your room, it is common to give a small tip of 10 or 20FF, depending on the amount of luggage, the character of the hotel, and whether the porter accidentally drops your luggage down two flights of stairs. It is also common to leave small loose change in an ashtray in the room in the morning as a tip for the maid who cleans your room – though this is often done only at the end of your stay.

In restaurants, the tip is included in the price of the meal (*servis compris*). If you have enjoyed a fine meal, it is common to leave an additional tip of 5 to 50FF, depending on the meal and the restaurant.

In the now rare case where the tip is not included, that fact will be prominently noted on the menu (*servis n'est pas compris*). If that is the case, a 10 to 15 percent tip is normal.

Five to 10FF should cover the cloak room attendant. Bathroom attendants expect 2 to 5FF.

For taxis, tip is included, though you might offer another 5 to 20FF, depending on the distance and your mood.

TOURIST OFFICE

The **central tourist office**, *127 avenue des Champs-Élysées (8th, M:George V), Tel. 01.49.52.53.54. Fax 01.49.52.53.00*, is open during the week from 9 a.m. to 8 p.m. Smaller offices are also found at the Tour Eiffel and all the train stations except Gare Saint-Lazarre.

City Hall, *29 rue de Rivoli (4th, M:Hôtel de Ville), Tel. 01.42.76.43.43*, has an information office open Monday through Saturday from 9 a.m. to 6 p.m.

For an English version phone recording of **current entertainment and events**, *call 01.49.52.53.56*.

There are other guide books as well. Of course, they are not nearly as good as ours, but if you insist on a second opinion, you could try the Michelin Paris Guide.

WATER

Yes, you can drink the water. In fact, virtually every bistro or restaurant will want to know if you would like bottled water with or without bubbles (*gazeux* or *sans gaz*) with your meal. However, you can save a few francs simply by requesting a small pitcher of tap water (*un pichet d'eau*).

If you want to be extra cautious, as many people recommend, order bottled water and avoid any brush with local waterborne germs.

FRENCH FACTOIDS

• A person can buy a handgun only after first receiving a permit from the police. A person can obtain the permit only if he can prove he is an active member of a shooting club or if he can prove his life is in danger.

- Handwritten applications for jobs are sometimes required because the applicant's handwriting is analyzed to see if he or she possesses personality traits appropriate to the job.
- If you own a television, the government assesses you for an annual tax, the proceeds of which go to subsidize the state run channels of France 2 and France 3.
- State subsidies for pregnant women and new mothers can extend as long as to the child's third birthday. The amount is increased if the mother breast-feeds her baby, though a social worker must witness the breast-feeding at least once for the mother to qualify.
- Employment classifieds can indicate what age and sex the company seeks in its applicants. The company can also note that it is interested only in physically attractive candidates.
- The great majority of employees are paid once a month and are paid by direct deposit into their bank accounts.
- You cannot cash a check written to you even if you take it to the bank on which the check was drawn. You can only deposit the amount into your own account.
- French women were given the right to vote in 1945.
- Jacques Chirac, who became the mayor of Paris in 1977, was the first person ever elected to the post by popular vote. All past mayors had been appointed by the national government.
- The president of France has been elected by popular vote only since 1965. (The law was changed in 1962, but 1965 was the first election, pitting de Gaulle, who won 54.5 percent of the vote, against his longtime political foe, François Mitterrand.)
- There are approximately 25,000 Americans living in France.
- When you include the membership subscription and the various taxes, Parisians pay a tax of just under 60 percent on their electric bill.
- The legal age for drinking, driving, and voting in France is 18.
- The oldest continuous family line belongs to the Capétians, who can be traced back to 852.
- The French pay anywhere from 5 to 56 percent of their income in taxes.
- The use of contraceptives was legalized in 1967. Abortion became lawful in 1975.
- Women were guaranteed equal rights under the constitution in 1946.

- On average, French women outlive French men, 81.3 years versus 73.1 years.
- The French spend an average of less than two hours a day watching television.
- The highest recorded temperature was 111.2 degrees in Toulouse in southwestern France on August 8, 1923. The lowest recorded temperature was minus 41.8 degrees on January 17, 1985, in the town of Mouthe near the Swiss border east of Dijon.
- There are about 80 daily newspapers in France.
- About 75 percent of the power used in France is generated by nuclear plants, the largest such percentage in the world.
- There are four murders per 100,000 people in France a year.
- France has the fourth largest economy in the world.
- France has the highest literacy rate in the world.
- Despite their reputation for eating well, the French rank 30th in terms of how many calories they consume daily.
- The average waiter makes 11,000FF per month. The average manager of a business earns 50,000FF monthly.
- The French consume more medicine per capita than any other nationality in the world.
- The French franc was devalued by 100-fold in 1958, so that overnight, 100 francs became a single franc.
- In France, where Michelin is one of the largest independent corporations, the Michelin man is known as Bibendum.

7. THE CUISINE OF FRANCE

It was hearty country cooking that first made a name for French cuisine – dishes like a *cassoulet* made with sausage, preserved duck, and white beans, or a *petit salé* of tender roast pork in a pool of lentils, or *coq au vin*, a free range chicken stewed in red wine laden with onions, carrots, and herbs.

The ingredients were fresh off the farm and the results enough to warm the coldest toes on the most bitter winter night.

Haute cuisine came along ages ago and jazzed things up with marvelously rich sauces. When many people think of French cuisine, they still envision plates drenched in heavy cream sauces. Not so anymore – not for some time.

About two decades ago, culinary superstars lightened the cholesterol load, combined ingredients that had never before shared a plate, invented clever new sauces based on wines and natural meat juices, and refined the presentation on the plate to an art form that was dubbed *nouvelle cuisine*.

Today, the best chefs say that nouvelle cuisine, with its characteristically puny portions, is dead. Well, yes and no.

The current end-all, be-all is a kind of haute cuisine that often combines the best of traditional dishes with the inventiveness of nouvelle ingredients. Sort of the best of both worlds.

You should make it a point to try both traditional and haute cuisine. Bistros and brasseries are usually home to the traditional, while full blown restaurants are more likely to offer creative menus with unexpected, sometimes bizarre, combinations of ingredients.

In both cases, you will note that, as on the farm, no food product is tossed carelessly into the waste bin. Browse through one of the city's many amazing market streets and you'll see what we mean. Vendors hawk everything from celery root and fresh beets, to trays of brains, intestines, feet, and ears. During game season in the fall, butchers showcase entire pheasants, small deer, hares, and even whole wild boars.

What you see in the marketplace is exactly what might end up on your plate that night. So, for instance, if you're squeamish about organ meat, read the menu very carefully. *Ris de veau* is not a tender veal medallion. It is veal sweetbreads, which are very popular, but may not be to your taste.

And *andouilette*, a staple at good restaurants and bad, is a sausage stuffed not with ground pork, but with heavily-herbed chewy strips of a pig's small intestines – not one of our favorites.

Even with game, which we absolutely love, take some care. Most is truly game, which is to say wild – we've had fine pheasant in quality restaurants where we've picked shotgun pellets out of the meat. The meat was magnificent; the pellets were not.

EATING OUT

No matter how many times you've eaten in French restaurants in the United States, you are likely to find yourself at a loss from time to time in Paris. Bring along our guide with its *Food Dictionary* (see below) and be prepared to ask questions.

There are dishes – not just organ meat, but certain types of fish – that rarely if ever appear on American menus. And the names given the dishes

TIPS FOR EATING OUT

• *The word* **Entrées** *on the menu indicates the appetizers.* **Plats** *are the main courses.*

• **Garçon** *for waiter is no longer appropriate or amusing.* **Monsieur** *is more polite.*

• *Water is not automatically served at the table. You can avoid the cost of bottled water, which is what the waiter will suggest, by ordering* **un carafe d'eau**, *which is a small pitcher of tap water. The water's just fine, though purists insist that bottled water is the safest for travelers going anywhere outside their own country.*

• *When ordering meats, the French word for rare is* **saignant**, *and very rare is* **bleu**. *Medium rare is* **à point**, *and medium well is* **bien cuit**.

• *Traditional French cooking calls for green salads (***salades vertes***) to be served between the main course and dessert, but it is no longer unthinkable to request a salad as an appetizer. Salads are rarely included with a meal.*

• *Cheese can be ordered between the main and dessert courses, and you should take advantage of the fabulous choices here. French cheese, especially the amazing variety of goat cheeses (***chèvre***), has not been processed the same way as cheese is in the States and, consequently, is generally fresher and richer.*

• *Coffee (***un café***) is espresso and is served in a demitasse. A* **café creme** *is espresso with steamed milk. Some places serve American coffee (***café filtre***). Your coffee will not be served until you have finished eating. You can ask, but nine times out of ten, your request will be ignored.*

• *When asking for the check, say,* **L'addition, s'il vous plaît.**

• *The tip and tax are included in the price, though with a good meal it is customary to leave the waiter another five to fifty francs depending on the service and the bill.*

often reflect the style of preparation or even the name of the chef or the friend who taught the chef how to make the dish – all of which is something even the best dictionary may fail to explain. You may recognize a word or two, but still have no idea what you're ordering unless you ask.

Though chicken and beef are available in several forms, you should sample other staples of French cuisine, such as rabbit, duck, lamb, and veal. Rabbit roasted in a mustard sauce can be miraculous. *Magret de canard*, the breast of a duck, is served medium rare like a good steak. *Gigot*, or leg of lamb, and *blanquette de veau*, a veal stew in white sauce, are both standard fare worth your attention. Well-known appetizers include *escargots* (snails steeped in butter and garlic), a salad with rounds of warm goat cheese (*chèvre*), *patés* of all kinds, and herring with warm potatoes.

Of course, the French are also famous for their sweet tooth. Dessert menus offer a dizzying variety of pastries, fruit tarts, and sorbets.

Reservations are highly recommended and few restaurants (especially decent ones) will seat you before 7:30.

We've listed many of our favorite bistros and restaurants in Chapter 10, *Where to Eat*. Window shop as you stroll the streets during the day and you're likely to find a gem or two that we have not included in this guide. Menus, even for the best restaurants, are posted outside so you know what you're getting into.

Often you will see a *formule* or *prix fixe* selection noted on a menu. Those selections offer fewer options, but are usually ten to thirty percent cheaper than if you were to order the same dishes *à la carte*. Some *prix fixe* menus even offer a half bottle of wine per person.

And don't forget that the French adoration for food extends beyond their native cuisine. Paris is liberally seeded with restaurants featuring dishes from all over the world – Italian, Chinese, Vietnamese, Lebanese, Spanish, and just about any other kind of food you can imagine. Fusion has also finally crossed the Atlantic from the States. Several new restaurants blend Asian elements with traditional French dishes.

You wouldn't go to Chicago just to gnaw on ribs. Likewise you should branch out in France.

TYPES OF RESTAURANTS
Auberge

A term that has taken on an alluring cachet in recent years. Once referring strictly to a country inn with a few rooms and hearty home-cooking (usually prepared by the owner and served by his wife or children), the term is now used by city restaurants that want to lure customers keen on a blend of gourmet and country cuisine.

Bistro

A small, usually informal neighborhood restaurant which is often family-owned and where the food is traditional country cooking.

Brasserie

A term that once referred to a beer pub, where the action was mostly at the bar. Now many brasseries have been transformed into bistro-like restaurants, though brasseries are often larger and less intimate.

Café

A small informal establishment offering coffees, teas, alcoholic beverages, and simple meals, such as omelets or salads. Often with outdoor seating, this is where you can sit for as long as you like, reading a good book, contemplating the future, or watching the people.

FOOD STORES

When you want to put together a meal on your own, you can go to various small supermarkets or, better yet, do it like the natives do: one specialty shop after another. The names of these stores in French are:

alimentation - *small food store*
boucherie - *butcher's shop*
boucherie chevaline - *horsemeat butcher*
boulangerie - *bakery*
cave - *wine shop*
charcuterie - *like a deli*
confiserie - *candy shop*
crèmerie - *dairy products*
emporter - *carry-out*
épicerie - *general store*
fleuriste - *florist*
fromagerie - *cheese shop*
marchand de légumes - *vegetable store*
poissonerie - *fish shop*
traiteur - *prepared foods*
triperie - *tripe shop*
volailler - *poultry shop*

Restaurant

This name is supposed to signal a more serious and formal dedication to food, complete with linen tablecloths. You cannot wander in for a quick coffee.

Tabac

A French-style bar, serving coffee and booze of all kinds, and with a counter near the door where you can buy cigarettes, payment cards for public phones, lottery tickets, and Métro tickets.

THE THREE MEALS

Petit Déjeuner (Breakfast)

Breakfast is served at hotels and cafés from about 7:30 to 10:00 a.m. It is usually a light meal with coffee or tea (for types of coffee, see *café* below under Beverages) and a small basket of bread and pastries with butter and jam. Orange juice (*jus d'orange*) is common, but is usually extra. Cereals can be found at some hotels, and, on rare occasions, so can eggs and a kind of Canadian-style bacon. Eggs are normally considered a lunch food.

Common breakfast pastries include *chansons aux pommes* (flaky pastries with apple filling), *croissants* (crescent-shaped rolls), *pains au chocolat* (flaky pastry with a small amount of chocolate in the middle), and *tartines* (small half baguettes with butter and, if you ask jam).

A brief aside: If you want jam or preserves, ask for *confiture*. We've had friends request *préservatifs*, which is a good way to cause a sudden silence in the room. *Préservatifs* are condoms.

Déjeuner (Lunch)

Lunches generally stretch from about 11:30 a.m. to 2:30 p.m., after which many places refuse to serve any food at all until dinner.

For ages, lunch was the major meal of the day, but that custom has grown more and more outdated as the French work day grows busier. Fewer people are ordering steaks and more are choosing the *salades composées*, such as the *salade Niçoise* with tuna or a *salade paysanne* with egg and small bits of bacon called *lardons*.

Omelets and fries are still very popular, as are *croques monsieur* and *croques madame*, which are similar to grilled cheese sandwiches, but with ham, chicken or an egg. You won't find many hamburgers, and even if you do, you'll probably be disappointed by them.

If you're on a march through the city and don't want to sit for lunch, **crêpe stands** offer an alternative. A crépe with strips of ham, shredded Guyère, and an egg will fuel your fires for a couple of hours at least.

Traiteurs (delis) are scattered around and offer pastas, prepared meats, and salads to go for reasonable prices. Bakeries also prepare cheap baguette sandwiches or tiny quiches and pizzas that you can wolf down while sitting on a park bench. They're not haute cuisine, but they'll keep you on your feet and they're cheap.

TAKE A COOKING CLASS

If you are a shameless foodie–as we are–then you might want to consider taking a class or two. Some of the finest cooking schools are here, which is no surprise. But some offer classes as short as a single day, which is a surprise. Each offers a variety of subjects and plans, but whatever you choose, you will no doubt have some fun, make new acquaintances and surely fill up on the fruits of your labor.

RITZ ESCOFFIER EDOCLE DE GASTRONOMIE FRANCAISE, 15 place Vendome (1st, M:Opéra), Tel. 01.43.16.30.50. Fees range from about 200 to 6,000FF.

LE CORDON BLEU, 8 rue Léon-Delhomme (15th, M:Vaugirard), Tel. 01.53.68.22.50. Fees from 150 to 5,000FF.

ÉCOLE GASTRONOMIQUE BELLOUET CONSEIL, 304 rue Lecourbe (15th, M:Lourmel), Tel. 01.40.60.16.20. Fees from 1,600 to 6,500FF.

ÉCOLE LENOTRE, 48 avenue Victor-Hugo (16th, M:Victor-Hugo), Tel. 01.45.02.21.19. Fees from 450 to 1,200FF.

Diner (Dinner)

Some bistros and brasseries will serve dinner as early as 7:30 p.m., but most patrons arrive between 8:30 and 10:00 p.m.. Service continues up until close to midnight.

No matter when you arrive, your meal should be savored. Most French restaurants expect only one sitting per table per night, so don't feel as if you need to rush to make room for the next guy. Sit as long as you like.

Dinner in France can be akin to a religious experience – that is, if you choose your restaurants carefully and take time to study the menu so that you order what you think you're ordering.

Don't be rattled if the waiter comes by almost instantly to take your order. (The French often order very quickly.) Simply say, "*Pas encore. Deux minutes, s'il vous plaît.*" This means, "Not yet. Two minutes, please." "Two minutes" is not literal and simply means "in a little bit."

No matter how many French restaurants you've frequented in the US or Canada, you're going to come over here, sit down at a table in a nice restaurant, open the menu, and panic. Afraid to ask questions, you'll take your best guess and order what you think will be a tender veal medallion. Instead you'll get a plate of sizzling sweetbreads or a hulking veal kidney.

It's inevitable. Everyone we have ever met in Paris has a story like that. And, for the most part, guides just don't help much when it comes time to order a nice meal with a worthy bottle of wine. Until now, that is.

Below you will find what we think will be an indispensable Food Dictionary. French restaurants routinely invent names for new ways of preparing foods (or invent new names for old ways of preparing foods – good marketing), so you will still run across lots of mysterious words. When in doubt, ask for an explanation.

FOOD DICTIONARY

Our Food Dictionary includes vegetables, fruits, herbs, meat, fish, bird, seafood, game and desserts. We also explain terms, preparations, and dishes.

à la - in the manner of, indicating preparation style
abricot - apricot
abats - organs
agneau - lamb
aiguillettes - long thin slices
ail - garlic
aile - wing
aillé - with garlic

aïoli - mayonnaise suffused with garlic
Albert - sauce of cream and egg yolk with mustard and horseradish
ali baba - same as baba au rhum
alose - shad
alouette - lark
amandes - almonds
ananas - pineapple
anchoiade - anchovy paste with herbs, for fried bread
anchois - anchovy
andoillette - sausage of strips of pig's small intestines
anguille - eel
araignée - a long-legged crab
artichaut - artichoke
    coeurs d' - artichoke hearts
    fonds de - artichoke bottoms
    vinaigrette - cold artichoke with vinaigrette on the side
    violet - small red-tinged artichoke
asperges - asparagus
    d'Argenteuil - large white asparagus
    pointes d' - asparagus tips
assiette - a plate of something
assiette de crudités - plate of raw vegetables, such as tomato, shredded carrot
    (*carotte râpée*), celery root
assorti - assorted
aubergine - eggplant
aulx - plural of ail, or garlic
avocat - avocado
baba au rhum - small molded sponge cakes soaked in rum or rum flavoring
bacon - a Canadian-style bacon
baigné - bathed
bananes - bananas
bar - sea bass
barbue - brill, similar to sand dab or sole
barde - thin rasher of bacon
bardé - larded
baudroie - angler fish

bavette - flank steak

Béarnaise - creamy white sauce with egg yolk, butter, white wine, shallots, tarragon and other herbs

bécasse - woodcock

bécassine - snipe

béchamel - white sauce with butter, flour and milk

beignet - a fritter

belon - one of finest types of oyster

betterave - beet

beurre - butter

   blanc - butter sauce with shallots and vinegar

   noir - browned butter

bifteck - common steak

bigorneaux - spiral-shelled sea mollusk

biscuit - cookie

bisque - creamy soup, usually with seafood

   de crevettes - with shrimp

   de hommard - with lobster

blanquette - veal stew in heavy white gravy

blettes - Swiss chard

blini - small Russian-style pancake with sour cream, smoked salmon and caviar

boeuf - beef

bolet - wild mushroom

bombe - ice cream lined, molded frozen dessert

Bordelaise - brown sauce with pan juices, red wine, shallots, bone marrow, thyme, bay and other herbs

bouchée - mouthful

boudin - pork blood sausage

bouillabaisse - a fish stew rich with lots of olive oil, garlic, tomato and other herbs

bouilli - boiled

bouillon - broth, usually of beef or chicken

bouquet - large shrimp served cold

Bourguignon - beef cubes stewed in red wine sauce with bacon, onions, and herbs *boudin* - blood sausage

braisé - braised

brandade – usually a fish, especially cod, whipped with garlic, oil and cream

Brillat Savarin - hollow cake

brioche - a soft egg bread

brochet - pike

brochette - meat cubes grilled on a spit

brocoli - broccoli

cabillaud - codfish

cacahuète - peanut

caille - quail

calamar - squid

canapé - small round of toast, usually as a base to a topping of cheese, eggs, etc.

canard - duck

caneton - duckling

canette - small duck

câpres - capers

caramel - burned sugar

caramélisé(e)(s) - near-burned in a broiler

cardons - edible thistles

carotte - carot

carpe - carp

carré - ribs

   d'agneau - rack of lamb

carrelet - similar to a flounder

cassoulet - casserole with white beans and herbs, with duck, pork, sausage, and/or other meats

caviar - fish eggs

céleri - celery

céleri-rave - celery root

cendre chemisée - cloaked with ash, smoldering

cépe - wild mushroom

cerises - cherries

   jubilé - cherries poached and flamed with kirsch, often served with ice cream

cervelas - a balogna-like sausage
cervelle - brains
champignons - mushrooms
    croûte aux - mushrooms in a pastry shell
chanson aux pommes - flaky pastry with an apple filling
chanterelle - wild mushroom
chantilly - whipped cream used in toppings
chapon - capon, or castrated rooster
charcuterie - sampling of sausages
charlotte - pudding
Charolais - prized breed of French cattle
chasse - game
châtaignes - chestnuts
châteaubriand - beef tenderloin or Porterhouse cut
chaud(e) - hot
chausson - turnover
cheval - horse
chèvre - goat cheese
    fraîche - only a day to a few days old
    seche - dried somewhat with age
chevreau - baby goat
chevreuil - small deer, roebuck
    forestière - roasted with strips of pork fat, and served with onions, mushrooms and fried potatoes
chicorée - chicory
chiperons - squidlike cuttlefish
chipolatas - small-diameter sausage
choix - indicating you have a choice
chou - cabbage
chou à la crème - cream puff
chou-fleur - cauliflower
chou-frisé - kale
chou-rouge - red cabbage
chou de Bruxelles - Brussels sprouts
choucroute - sauerkraut, also referring to various types of pork served on a bed of sauerkraut
ciboulettes - chives

cigales - clam with distinctive long shell like a razor clam
citron - lemon
citron vert - lime
clafouti - a tart made by pouring batter over fresh fruit and then baking the
    mixture
claires - a good quality type of oyster
clémentine - kumquat
cochon - pig
cocotte - hen
coeur - heart
coeurs de palmier - hearts of palm
coings - quinces
colin - a whiting or hake
compote de fruits - stewed or poached fruits
concombres - cucumbers
confit - preserved meat
    de canard - preserved duck meat
    d'oie - preserved goose meat
confiture - preserves
consommé - usually meat stock
coq - rooster
coquelet - young rooster
coquillages - shellfish
coquilles - shells
coquilles Saint-Jacques - scallops
Cordon bleu - veal slices with slices of ham and Gruyère in between,
    breaded and fried in butter
cornichons - pickles
côte - rib or chop
côtelettes - chops
coulis - stewed meat juice
courgette - squash
couscous - steamed cracked wheat pilaf with lamb or chicken
crabe - crab
crème - cream
    Anglais - light custard sauce
    d'asperges - cream of asparagus soup

brulée - light custard with a very thin layer of burned sugar on top
caramel - custard prepared in a small mold with a light caramel sauce
champignons - cream of mushroom soup
fraîche - a very heavy cream commonly used instead of ice cream as a
    topping for tarts
glacée - ice cream
de poireaux - cream of leek soup
de poulet - cream of chicken soup
cramic - an egg bread with raisins
crêpe - a large thin pancake, served with a variety of fillings, including
    meats, cheeses or preserves
cresson - watercress
cressonière - watercress soup
crevettes - shrimp
croissant - crescent shaped flaky roll
croquant - crisp
croque madame - a croque monsieur with an egg cooked into the middle of
    the top slice of bread, or with chicken instead of ham
croque monsieur - a type of grilled cheese sandwich, often with a slice of ham
    inside
croustade - a pastry shell
    de champignons - mushrooms in a light pastry shell
croûte - crust
croûtes - croutons
cru - raw cured meat
crudités - cut and shredded raw vegetables
crustacés - shellfish
cuisse - thigh
cuit - cooked
datte - date
daube - a stew of beef in wine and vegetables
    Provençal - gravy laced with garlic, anchovies and capers
daurade - sea bream
déglacée - warmed up
délices - delights, meaning just about anything
demi - half

diable - brown meat sauce with pepper, shallots, herbs

dinde - turkey

dorade - sea bream

échalote - shallot

éclair - oblong puff pastry filled with chocolate or coffee custard and topped with icing

écrevisses - crayfish

effilé(e) - flaked (as in almonds), oven-ready

émincé(e) - cold roast meat reheated in a sauce

émulsionné(e) - liquefied

endive - endive

entier(e) - whole

entrecôte - common rib steak

entrées - appetizers

épaule - shoulder

éperlans - smelts

épices - spices

épinard - spinach

escalopes - thin slices of a meat

escargots - snails

escargots de mer - sea snails

escarole - green bitter lettuce

estouffade - stew of beef cubes braised in red wine, herbs, onions, bacon, mushrooms

estragon - tarragon

étuvé(e) - stewed

façon - in the manner of

faisan - pheasant

farci(e) - stuffed

fenouil - fennel

fermier - indicates poultry raised on farm

feuilles - leaves

feuilles de vigne - grape leaves

    farcies - grape leaves stuffed with rice and herbs

feuilleté - broad pastry leaf or shell

fèves - broad beans

figue - fig

filet - a tenderloin cut

fine herbs - fresh chopped parsley, tarragon, chervil

flageolets - beans resembling small green limas

flambé(e) - flamed

flétan - halibut

fleurette - small flower

Florentine - often a preparation using cooked spinach

foie - liver

    gras - goose liver, either whole or ground into a pâté

    de volaille - chicken liver

fondu(e) - melted

    Bourguignonne - cubes of meat cooked and eaten individually at table in a pot of hot oil

    Savoyarde - pot of melted cheese used as dip

forestière - often indicates sautéed mushrooms, sometimes with bacon and small potatoes

four (au) - baked

frais - fresh, cool

fraîche - fresh, cool

fraise - strawberry

    de bois - wild strawberry

fraboise - raspberry

fricassée - stew of meat, vegetables, and herbs in which the meat is partially cooked in butter before being added to stew

frit(e) - fried

frites - French fries

froid(e) - cold

fromage - cheese

    blanc - mild fresh cheese with heavy cream

    de tête - head cheese

fruits - fruits

fruits de mer - mixed seafood

fumé(e) - smoked

gambas - large Mediterranean prawns

garni(e) - garnished

garniture - garnishes

gâteau - cake

gelée - in aspic

genièvre - juniper berry

gibelotte - fricassee

gibier - wild game

gigot - leg

girolle - wild mushroom

glaces - ice cream

goujon - small carplike freshwater fish

gratin - a dish sprinkled with bread crumbs and grated cheese and then browned

gratin dauphinois - scalloped potatoes

gratiné - prepared with bread crumbs

gratinée - French onion soup with croutons

grenade - pomegranate

grenadine - pomegranate syrup

grenouilles - frogs

    Provencal - pan fried in olive oil, garlic, and tomatoes

grillades - grilled meats

grillé(e) - grilled

grive - thrush

groseilles - currants

    à maquereau - gooseberry

grumes - heavy skin or coatings

Gruyère - a Swiss-like cheese

hamburger - often a thin patty and little else

hareng - herring

    avec pommes à l'huile - salad with herring and potatoes on friseé lettuce vinaigrette

haricots - beans

    blanc - white lima beans

    rouge - kidney beans

    vert - green beans

hérissons de mer - sea urchins

hollandaise - white sauce with egg yolks, butter, lemon juice

hommard - lobster

hors d'oeuvres - appetizers

hot dog - a reheated foot-long dog of dubious pork stuffing, packed in a
   baguette with melted Gruyère on top

huile - oil

   d'arachides - peanut oil

   de noix - walnut oil

   d'olive - olive oil

huîtres - oysters

   douzaine d' - a dozen oysters

île flotant - floating island, an ice cream dessert

jambon - ham

   de Pari - cooked ham

   de Parme - Italian prosciutto

jambonneau - lower leg of ham, boned and usually cold

jeune - green, unripe

jour (du) - that day's offering

julienne - thin cut strips of vegetables

jus - juice

juteux - juicy

kebab - marinated meat and vegetables grilled on skewer

kramic - an egg bread with raisins

laitue - lettuce

lamelles - small strips, slivers

lamproie - lamprey

langouste - spiny lobster

langoustine - sea crayfish

langue - tongue

lapereau - young rabbit

lapin - rabbit

lard - with bacon

lardons - American-style bacon bits

léger - light

legumes - vegetables

lentilles - lentils

lièvre - wild hare

lotte - angler or frog fish

loup - sea bass

macarons - macaroons

macédoine de legumes - diced mixed vegetables cooked and served with
    mayonnaise

mâches - lamb's lettuce, corn-salad

madeleines - shell-shaped tea cakes

Madère - indicates sauce with Madeira wine

magrets - slices of breast meat, usually duck

mais - corn

maison (à la) - prepared in the house style

maître d'hôtel - creamed butter with parsley and lemon

mandarine - between an orange and a tangerine

maquereau - mackerel

marcassin - young wild boar

marennes - type of oyster

mariné(e) - marinated

marrons - chestnuts

    glacés - candied chestnuts

mateolote - fish stew with wine, onions and mushrooms

mayonnaise - mayonnaise

médaillon - round cut of meat

mélange - mix

melba - usually a poached fruit with syrup on ice cream

melon - melon

    de Cavaillon - like a cantaloupe

    d'eau - watermelon

    au porto - with Port

    a l'Italienne - with thin slices of Italian ham

menthe - mint

meringues - stiff shell of sweet egg white

merlan - a whiting

merlu - a type of hake

meunière - often flour-coated filets pan-fried in butter and served with
    parsley and lemon butter

meurette - poached eggs on toast rounds drenched with red wine sauce with shallots, garlic, and herbs

miel - honey

mignon - tenderloin cut

mijotè(e)(s) - simmered

mille feuille - flaky layered pastry with creamy filling

mirabelle - small yellow plum

moelle - beef bone marrow

Mont Blanc - small peak-shaped dessert of sweetened chestnut meat topped with whipped cream or powdered sugar

moka - coffee-flavored

morille - morel, a wild mushroom

mornay - white sauce with béchamel and grated Gruyère and Parmesan cheeses

morue - dried codfish

moules - mussels

   farcies - stuffed

moussaka - ground lamb mixture with eggplant and tomato

mousse - a whipped but creamy dessert usually made with egg and chocolate; also a rich meat pâté whipped with cream and egg whites

mousseline - hollandaise sauce with whipped cream

mousserons - small wild mushrooms

moutarde - mustard

mouton - sheep, mutton

mulet - mullet

museau - beef face or snout

myrtilles - bilberries

Napolitaine - slice of frozen ice cream with vanilla, chocolate, and strawberry

nappé - covered with gravy

natur - plain

navarin - lamb stew with potatoes, onions, tomatoes, herbs

navets - turnips

Newburg - creamy lobster and wine sauce

noisettes - hazelnuts, or small disks of tenderloin

noix - nuts, top round in veal, nuggets of something

   de coco - coconut

nougat - a burned sugar almond crunch

nouilles - noodles
oeufs - eggs
    a l'Americaine - fried
    brouillés - scrambled
    chemise - poached
    a la coque - soft-boiled
    durs - hard-boiled
    durs avec mayonnaise - hard-boiled with mayonnaise
    Florentine - with spinach and cheese sauce
    en meurette - poached on garlic toast with red wine sauce
    mollets - medium boiled eggs
    plat - fried
    poché - poached
    de saumon - salmon eggs
oie - goose
oignons - onions
oiseau - bird
olives - olives
    noires - black olives
    vertes - green olives
olivettes - type of grape
omble - a charr, similar to trout
omelette - plain omelet
    avec jambon - with ham
    avec fromage - with cheese, usually guyere
    complète - with ham and cheese
    et frites - with French fries
    natur - plain omelet
onglet - skirt steak
orange - orange
ortolan - small game bird
os - bone
oseille - sorrel
oursin - sea urchin
pain - bread
    d'epice - spice bread
    de campagne - country-style bread, usually with some wheat flour

pain au chocolat - flaky pastry with a small amount of chocolate in the middle

palombe - type of wild pigeon

palourdes - clams

pamplemousse - grapefruit

pané(e) - pan fried

papillote (en) - when something is marinated, then sealed in paper or foil and baked

parfum - flavor

parfumé(e) - flavored with

pâté - pate

pavé - tenderloin cut

pays (du) - a dish from the area

paysanne - mix of bacon pieces and cooked vegetables

pêches - peaches

perche - perch

perdreau - young partridge

perdrix - partridge

Périgueux - rich meat sauces with truffles

persil - parsley

persillé(e) - sprinkled with chopped parsley

petit salé - poached slightly salted meat

petits fours - tiny cakes

petits pois - peas

pied de cochon - pig's foot

pigeon - pigeon

pigeonneau - young pigeon

piments doux - pimentoes

pintade - Guinea fowl

pintadeau - young Guinea fowl

piquante - spicy

pistache - pistachio nut

plat - plate, dish of something

plateau - tray

    de fromage - cheese plate

plie - flat fish with brilliant orangish-red spots

poché(e) - poached

poèlé(e) - pan fried
poire - pear
   Belle Hélène - poached pear in syrup on ice cream with chocolate sauce
poireaux - leeks
pois chiches - garbanzos
poissons - fish
poitrine - chest
   fumée - American-style bacon rashers
poivre - pepper
   vert - green pepper
poivrons - bell peppers
pomme - apple
pommes de terre - potatoes
   allumettes - thin French fries
   chips - chips
porc - pork
porcelet - suckling pig
poularde - roasting chicken
pot au feu - a stew with beef, chicken and vegetables
potage - soup
poulet - chicken
poulpe - octopus
praline - roasted almonds in carmelized syrup
pré salé - refers to lamb fed on salt tidal grasses
profiteroles - small pastry balls filled with ice cream or custard, then doused
   with chocolate sauce
Provençal - indicates preparation with olive oil, white wine, garlic, tomato,
   anchovy and other ingredients
prune - plum
pruneau - prune
purée - mash, thick soup
quenelle - light dumpling with sauce
quetsche - small purple plum
queue - tail
queue de boeuf - oxtail
quiche - an egg pie, with various ingredients
   lorraine - with cream and bits of ham or bacon

râble - back, usually of rabbit
radis - radish
raie - stingray or skate
raifort - horseradish
raisin - grape
   sec - raisin
râpées - shredded, grated
ratatouille - a Provencal casserole with eggplant, squash, onions, tomatoes, garlic, and herbs
rémoulade - a mayonnaise sauce with mustard, capers, anchovies and herbs
rubarbe - rhubarb
rillettes - cold shredded meat pastes
ris de veau - veal sweetbreads
rissoles - breaded fritters stuffed and deep-fried
riz - rice
rognons - kidneys
rollmops - pickled herring wrapped around a piece of onion
romarin - rosemary
rosbif - roast beef
rosette - small round piece
rôti(e) - roasted
rôtis - roasts
rouget - Mediterranean red mullet
rouille (à la) - thick sauce of garlic, chili, pimento
rumsteack - sirloin cut
safran - saffron
salade composée - large lunch salad
   Niçoise - usually with tuna, egg, green beans, bell peppers, and anchovy on bed of lettuce, served vinaigrette
   verte - common green salad
Saint-Jacques - scallops
Saint-Pierre - John Dory fish of the mackerel family
salami - salami
sandre - a pike-perch
sandwich - baguette sandwich
   au jambon - with ham
   au jambon et fromage - with ham and Gruyère

au thon - with tuna

au thon et crudités - with tuna, lettuce, tomato and egg

sanglier - wild boar

sardines - sardines

saucisses - cooked sausage

saucisson - uncooked sausage

saumon - salmon

sauté(e) - sauteed

sauvage - wild

scampis - prawns

sec, sèche - dried

sèche - cuttlefish, a squidlike creature

sel - salt

selle - saddle, as in lamb

sirop - syrup

sole - sole, flat fish

sorbet - sherbet

soufflé - beaten egg whites suffused with various flavorings and baked in
   a mold

soupe - soup

   à l'oignon - French onion soup

   gratinée - French onion soup

   pêcheur - fish soup

spumoni - ice cream with candied fruit

steake - steak

   au poivre - with crushed peppercorns pushed into meat

sucre - sugar

suivant le marché - what's available and fresh at market

suprême de volaille - boneless chicken breast poached and served in cream
   sauce

tartare - mayonnaise sauce with egg, pickle, caper, parsley and herbs

tartare - raw meat, usually either beef or salmon

tarte - tart, open-faced pie

   à l'onion - onion and cream tart

   aux pommes - apple tart

   aux framboise - raspberry tart

citron - lemon tart
tartelette - individual-sized tarts
tartine - a small half baguette with butter
    avec confiture - with jam
    avec miel - with honey
terrine - strictly speaking, the vessel in which paté is made, but also refers to heavily ground meat with herbs
thon - tuna
thym - thyme
tiède - slightly warm
tiramisu - a bit of liqueur-soaked sponge cake topped with rich custard and chocolate powder
tomates - tomatoes
tortue de mer - turtle
    véritable - turtle soup
tournedoes - quality beef tenderloin
tourte - hot meat pie
tranche - a slice
tripe - stomach lining
triperie - tripe (stomach lining) shop
truffes - truffles
truffé - a dish with truffles mixed in
truite - trout
turbot - turbot, flounder-like fish
vanille - vanilla
vanneau - a small game bird
varié(e) - assorted
veau - veal
velouté - creamy white sauce with veal or fish stock
ventre - stomach
viande - meat
vichyssoise - light leek and potato cream soup, served cold
vigneronne - indicates a sauce or stuffing with grapes and wine
vinaigre - vinegar, literally soured wine
vinaigrette - a dressing of oil, vinegar and herbs
volailles - fowl, usually chicken
yaourt - yogurt

BEVERAGE DICTIONARY

apératif - before meal drinks
   Kir - mixture of white wine and crème de cassis
   Kir Royale - mixture of champagne and crème de cassis
   Pastis - a popular licorise-flavored drink
   Ricard - a Pastis
bière - beer
   à la pression - draft beer
   blonde - lager
   brune - dark beer
   légère - light
café - espresso
   café au lait - espresso with a pitcher of steamed milk
   café crème - espresso with steamed milk
   café filtre - an American coffee
chocolat chaud - hot chocolate
Calvados - alcoholic cider
Cassis - black currant liqueur
cidre - cider
citron pressé - lemon juice served with water and sugar
Coca - Coke
   Coca Light - Diet Coke
Cognac - Cognac
Cointreau - orange-flavored liqueur
eau - plain water
   avec gaz - with bubbles
   Château Chirac - tap water (named after former Paris mayor)
   de vie - very strong brandy-like liquor
   natur - tap water
   sans gaz - without bubbles
glace - ice
Grand Marnier - orange-flavored liqueur
jus - fruit jus
   d'orange - orange juice
   de pamplemousse - grapefruit juice
   de pomme - apple juice
   de tomate - tomato juice

kirsch - clear cherry brandy
lait - milk
limonade - a clear tart style of lemonade
Orangina - soft drink with tangerine and orange
Porto - port
rhum - rum
thé - tea
vin - wine (see following chapter on Wine)
    blanc - white
    de maison - house wine
    rosé - rosé
    rouge - red
whisky - Scotch
Williamine - pear brandy

FOOD GROUPS

fruits - fruits
herbs - herbs
légumes - vegetables
oeufs - eggs
pain - bread
pâte - pasta
patisseries - pastries
poissons - fish
viandes - meats

OBJECTS AT THE TABLE

assiette - plate
bouteuille - bottle
cendrier - ashtray
chaise - chair
couteau - knife
cuiller - spoon
fenêtre - window
fourchette - fork
nappe - tablecloth

sel et poivre - salt and pepper
serviette - napkin
table - table
verre - glass

COURSES OF A FORMAL DINNER
(in order)
entrée - *appetizer*
plat - *main course*
salade - *salad*
fromage - *cheese*
dessert - *dessert*
café - *coffee (only after, not during, dessert)*

8. THE WINES OF FRANCE

It sounds crazy to recommend that you drink wine when you visit France. Nothing could be more obvious. But then you'd be surprised how many Americans arrive in Paris and order Jack Daniels, neat, with a Bud back.

Most hard liquor is available, though bourbon is sometimes hard to find. But the price of a mixed drink will make your head spin long before the booze will. Why bother?

There is plenty of beer, some of which is quite good and some of which is truly awful. Kronenbourg, the Budweiser of France, is a refreshing, safe choice, and you should be able to afford a second glass.

But wine is an integral part of the national heritage in France. Check any bistro at lunch time and you'll find stuffy businessmen and grimy laborers alike quaffing — not sipping — wine with their midday meal. At home, even the children are given a small glass with the family feast.

And just as wine is part of any meal, so it is the economic and cultural backbone of communities throughout the country. Literally, grapes are grown and wine is made everywhere in France. There is even a tiny vineyard in Paris proper – see Chapter 11, *Seeing the Sights.*

The range of available wines is staggering, swinging wildly from bone dry to sickly sweet and from dirt cheap to impossibly expensive. Of course, that raises the question: How do you choose?

CHOOSING A WINE

- Drink what you think tastes good. Sounds dumb, but then so many people spend small fortunes drinking wines that snobs tell them they're supposed to like.
- When possible, drink the local wine. Regional French wines marry well with the local cuisine because they've grown up together over the past 2,000 years.
- Don't be afraid to ask for advice. Especially outside the major tourist regions, most restaurant owners and maîtres d'hôtels take pride in helping you find the right wine.
- Establish your price range. For the *crème de la crème*, you'll have to cash in your IRAs. There is, however, an unlimited number of outstanding wines at reasonable prices.
- Splurge occasionally. A great wine is a unique sensory pleasure. It comes at a price, but then so do so many memorable experiences.
- Match the wine with the food and the setting. A $75 bottle of Meursault would no doubt be a real treat on a picnic lunch. But then, if you're gazing across a golden valley to the river below and the mountains beyond, a $6 bottle of Muscadet would probably be just as good.
- Experiment. With the sea of wines available, you are sure to make some discoveries on your own, and those will probably be the most memorable wines of all.
- Have fun. Nothing ruins a good bottle of wine faster than a know-it-all who doesn't know enough to shut up and enjoy.

WINES IN A RESTAURANT

The nuts and bolts of what you're likely to see in a restaurant:

Red and white wine will be available in 25 and 50 centiliter carafes at most bistros and brasseries for anywhere from 30 to 60FF per 50 cl. carafe.

These wines will be the equivalent of jug wine and, on occasion, you'll wish it had come from another jug. But with an omelet or nondescript lunch steak, a carafe is a smart choice.

Brasseries and smaller restaurants usually stock a limited selection of bottled wine, with a list that indicates the type of wine (e.g. Burgundy, Bordeaux) but not necessarily the maker or the vintage. These won't be great wines, and are likely to be the same or slightly better than what you can order by the carafe.

The real fun begins when you're ready to spend nearly as much time choosing a wine as you do selecting your main course. The two are, in fact, usually chosen together so that they complement one another.

Wine lists run anywhere from a half page in your menu to a separate menu of twenty pages or more. For oenophiles, the wine lists of the top-ranked restaurants will be as engrossing as a good novel. But if you don't know wine well enough to request precisely what type you want and from what year, the longer lists can be mind-boggling. Whether the list is short or long, don't hesitate to ask for advice. We've discovered several memorable wines we never knew existed just by asking.

Several good restaurants offer bottled wine with a house label. It may not be the finest wine available, but it is often a safe and satisfying choice. After all, they know that unless they've picked a decent wine, the patrons won't come back.

IDENTIFYING FRENCH WINES

What follows here is a somewhat over-simplified description of French wines that should help you get started on what could easily become an obsessive new hobby.

To begin with, in France, the wines are usually named for the region they came from, not for the grapes used in the process (the exception is the Alsace region, where wines take the names of the dominant grape used to make the wine, as in California).

For instance, in the most general sense, a **Bordeaux** is any wine that comes from the Bordeaux region along the Atlantic Coast where the Gironde spills into the sea.

There are, however, many types of Bordeaux, each of which takes its name from the sub-section of Bordeaux where the grapes were grown. The micro-climates and soil content of each subregion can make two wines surprisingly different, even if they were made a couple of miles apart and from the same type of grape.

Several types of grape are grown in Bordeaux and other regions, and winemakers often blend juice from different grapes in varying proportions to give their wine its distinctive bouquet and flavor.

WHITE VERSUS RED
White Wines

White wines are usually drunk younger than red wines, are served chilled, and are generally thought to complement white meats, such as fish or chicken.

Made in the western end of the Loire Valley, **Muscadet** is a simple but refreshing dry white wine. It is so simple, in fact, you don't generally have to worry too much about when it was made or by whom.

Sancerre is another pleasant white, from the opposite end of the Loire. An **Entre Deux Mers** from the Bordeaux region is also a refreshing white wine that is usually drunk quite young.

The white **Rieslings** and **Gewurztraminers** from the Alsatian region of northern France are more carefully made. They are fuller and fruitier than a Muscadet. They are, in fact, vastly underrated by Americans, who usually assume they are the same syrupy sweet wine as is made from the same types of grapes in Germany. In fact, the Alsatian Rieslings are on the dry side and age well. Very good recent vintages were 1989, 1990, 1992, 1996, 1997 and 1998.

For the driest of the dry, try a white **Graves** from the Bordeaux region. Another fine dry white is the **Pouilly-Fuissé** from the Mâcon area of Burgundy.

White Burgundies are thought to be the finest white wines in France, maybe in the world. There is a range here, in part because the Burgundy region stretches south more than 100 miles, beginning roughly in the Chablis area southeast of Paris.

Chablis itself is quite good, and not at all like the mediocre wine called chablis that American restaurants served twenty and thirty years ago. **Meursault** is even better, and the **Puligny** and **Chassagne Montrachets** are thought to be the best white Burgundies of all. When made properly, these are wonderfully intense and flavorful dry wines. Excellent years include 1978, 1982, 1985, 1986, 1989, 1990, 1992, 1994, 1996, 1997 and 1998.

A word about **rosé**: We're not fans. In the grossest general terms, rosés too often taste to us like wimpy reds. The exception: **Tavel** from the Côtes du Rhône.

Red Wines

Ultimately, red wine is the greatest treat. There are larger differences among red wines than there are among whites. That means you'll also experience more surprises – good and bad.

Some reds are meant to be lightly chilled, but many are served at room temperature (though never warm). And generally reds will complement red meats, from beef and lamb to gamey birds or duck.

Beaujolais is probably the most delightfully fresh and fruity red wine, and is often served chilled. It's the standby of most bistros. The release of the **Beaujolais Nouveau** in mid-November is a big occasion throughout the country. It's the first wine produced in the current year, so it is very, very young. And it is very, very popular.

Bottles labeled simply Beaujolais or Beaujolais Villages can be good, but they are blends of juices and grapes from across the Beaujolais region. The better Beaujolais are the *crus*, which take their names from specific subregions, such as Juliénas, Fleurie, and Régnié.

The Languedoc region in the south and the Loire Valley produce a variety of inexpensive reds, many of which can be the perfect thing for a simple lunch. To generalize, however, they are mostly table wines with neither the bouquet nor the lasting power of the country's better wines.

The Côtes du Rhône in the south is noted for its outstanding **Côte-Rôtig Châteauneuf-du-Pape**, **Hermitage**, and **Saint-Joseph** wines, which boast a great deal of character. They may be too bold for some, but they're often a good value and once you get a taste for them, you'll wonder why you didn't always have some on hand. Wines bottled simply as a Côtes du Rhône can be a very good value. Good years were 1985, 1988, 1989, 1990, 1995, 1997 and 1998.

Unfortunately, really horrible cheap red Burgundies swamped American markets years ago. If you're one of those people who cringe at the memory, it's time to wipe the slate clean because you are missing some of the best wine around.

Genuine Burgundies, meaning the wines that come from Burgundy, are made exclusively from Pinot Noir grapes, age extremely well, and have a rich but rarely overpowering taste. The danger here is that the quality is all over the map. Even if something is labeled *Premier Cru*, that doesn't mean the wine is going to be any good.

In Burgundy, more than any other region in France, the growers are the key. We list several respected growers in the following charts.

In general, the best red Burgundies are thought to be the **Côte de Nuits**, which are a heavier, almost gamey wine, and the **Côte de Beaunes**, which are a bit lighter and softer.

Chambolle-Musigny, **Gevrey-Chambertin**, **Vougeot**, and **Vosne-Romanée** are considered the best subregions of the Côte de Nuits, and **Volnay**, **Pommard**, and **Savigny-lès-Beaunes** are the best of the Côte de Beaunes. Good years: 1978, 1979, 1983, 1985, 1988, 1989, 1990, 1993, 1995, 1996 and 1997.

Bordeaux is the accepted pride and joy of French wine. That is not to say that if you order a bottle labeled simply *Bordeaux* that it will be good. Judicious selection and a willingness to experiment and occasionally to loosen the purse strings are musts.

A complex ranking system was set in place more than a hundred years ago to identify the châteaux that consistently produced the best wines. The big, big names include **Château Margaux**, **Château Latour**, **Château Lafite-Rothschild**, **Château Haut-Brion**, **Château Pétrus**. A lot of experts scoff at the rating system, saying it's outdated. But it is still a good general indicator of the better producers.

You may not be able to afford the best of the Bordeaux, but there are many very good châteaux that produce excellent wines at reasonable prices. Again, don't hesitate to ask questions. If you want to make the choice yourself, you will want to weigh four factors: the subregion (the *Cru*, or vineyard) where the wine was made, the maker of the wine, the vintage, and the price.

Wines from the subregions of Margaux, Saint-Julien, and Pauillac are luxuriously rich and mellow when aged properly — and they can age well for decades. The **Graves** are particularly bold and the **Saint-Émilions** and **Pomerols** are wonderfully earthy. The more generic **Médocs** and **Haut-Médocs** are often rich and heavy, perfect for game. Good years: 1970, 1975, 1978, 1979, 1982, 1983, 1985, 1986, 1988, 1989, 1990, 1995 and 1996.

In the sections that follow, we've listed and reviewed the major French wines with selected vintages and producers.

BUYING WINE IN PARIS

L'Amour du Vin, 48 avenue de la Bourdonnais (7th, M:École Militaire), Tel. 01.45.55.68.63. Also, 94 rue Saint-Dominique (7th, M:École Militaire), Tel. 01.45.56.12.94. Very good wines at shockingly good prices chosen by owner Patrick Dussert-Gerber, author of "Le Guide Dussert-Gerber des Vins de France."

CCA, 128 rue Vieille du Temple (3rd, M:Saint-Sébastien), Tel. 01.48.87.55.67; 37 boulevard Malesherbes (8th, M:Saint-Augustin); and 51 avenue La Motte Picquet (15th, M:La Motte Picquet), 01.43.06.26.65. A small chain that offers a variety of smart recent vintage wines at reasonable prices. Look for several of the "second" wines produced by the major Bordeaux Châteaux.

Les Caves Augé, 116 boulevard Haussmann (8th, M:St-Augustin), Tel. 01.45.22.16.97. Literary giant Marcel Proust was said to frequent this, the oldest wine shop in Paris.

Caves du Marais, 64 rue Francois-Miron (4th, M:St-Paul), Tel. 01.42.78.54.64. Owner Jean-Jacques Bailly is often on hand and has sampled all his wares, so knows exactly what the best buys are.

Caves Estève, 10 rue de la Cerisaie (4th, M:Bastille), Tel. 01.42.72.33.05; 292 rue Saint-Jacques (5th, M:Port Royal), Tel. 01.46.34.69.78; and 32 avenue Félix Faure (15th, M:Lourmel), 01.44.26.33.05. A very good small chain that offers regular tastings and stocks of reasonably priced, carefully selected alternatives to the obvious Grand Crus. Popular with the locals.

Cave Jean-Baptiste Besse, 48 rue de la Montagne Sainte-Geneviève (5th, M:Maubert-Mutualité), Tel. 01.43.25.35.80. A trusted neighborhood wine shop for more than 60 years.

Les Caves Taillevent, 199 rue du Faubourg Saint-Honoré (8th, M:Saint-Philippe-du-Roule), Tel. 01.45.61.14.09. Though only open since 1987, this shop profits from its association with the famous restaurant by the same name.

Legrand Filles et Fils, 1 rue de la Banque (1st, M:Bourse), Tel. 01.42.60.07.12. Family nurtured variety.

Nicolas. A large chain with shops everywhere. Popular, though we've never been terribly impressed with their selection.

Tchin Tchin, 9 rue Montorgueil (1st, M:Les Halles), Tel. 01.42.33.07.77. In this newish shop, owner Antoine Bénariac breaks the rule by including wines from places other than France.

Au Verger de la Madeleine, 4 boulevard Malesherbes (8th, M:Madeleine), Tel. 01.42.65.51.99. A family-run enterprise since 1937, with a large selection of rare wines.

ALSACE

Alsatian winemakers complain that too many people confuse their wines with the sweet white wines the Germans make across the Rhine River from Alsace.

It's too bad because the comparison isn't fair. Yes, the Alsatian wines can taste fruity. But the good ones are dry and crisp — perfect to wash down the generally heavy Alsatian cuisine.

Alsace differs from other major French wine regions in two important ways. One, it is almost wholly dominated by white wine, producing a large share of the country's whites (the reds, in fact, are generally poor). Second, the wines are not named for the region or village where they are made. Instead, as in California, the wines are named for the grapes used to produce them.

Strong Vintages: *1976, 1981, 1983, 1985, 1988, 1989, 1990, 1992, 1993, 1996, 1997, 1998*

Types of Alsatian Wine

There are seven principal grape varieties used in Alsatian wines:

• **Gewurztraminer** - A spicy, flowery wine, the best of which ages extremely well.

• **Muscat** - A dry, heavily-scented wine that is not produced in much quantity. An acquired taste.

• **Pinot Blanc** - One of the less interesting wines, with much of it rising only to the level of acceptable table wine.

• **Pinot Noir** - It's hard to imagine this is the same grape that produces the best Burgundies, because here the wine is mostly a rosé. Still, these rosés often have good flavor.

• **Riesling** - In general, the best and most sophisticated of the Alsatian wines. Medium-dry with a solid finish.

• **Sylvaner** - You'll find lots of this available in pitchers in restaurants. Straight-forward, good taste, cheap.

• **Tokay** or **Pinot Gris** - A warm and rich wine, with more body than most regional wines and good aging prospects.

Vendage Tardives & the Grand Crus

In the last 20 years, Alsatian producers searched for ways to compete with other wine growing regions and came up with two effective ideas.

One, to promote their *vendage tardives* and, two, to establish a set of quality guidelines and to award *Grand Cru* status to those vineyards whose wine measures up.

"Vendage Tardive" translates essentially to "late harvest" and refers to wines that were made from grapes harvested unusually late in the season. That's good because the grapes are bursting with natural sugars, and that means more taste and more alcohol. The good ones also age especially well and are served as very sweet dessert wines. But, of course, because the weather must cooperate, vendage tardives don't come along very often.

There are about 50 vineyards whose wine and production standards measure up to *Grand Cru* guidelines. Producers who make wine from grapes in these vineyards can, and often do, add that vineyard's name to their label.

So the label would likely include: the grape from which the wine was made, the Grand Cru (or vineyard) where the grapes were grown, the words "Grand Cru," and the name of the producer. For example: Gewurztraminer, Altenberg de Bergheim, 1983, Lorentz (which is quite a nice wine).

Alsatian Grand Crus

Note: the nearby village is in parentheses in case you want to visit.

Altenberg de Bergbieten (Bergbieten)
Altenberg de Bergheim (Bergheim)
Altenberg de Wolxheim (Wolxheim)
Brand (Turckheim)
Eichberg (Eguisheim)
Engelberg (Dahlenheim)
Frankstein (Dambach-la-Ville)
Froehn (Zellenberg)
Geisberg (Ribeauvillé)
Gloeckelberg (Rodern)
Goldert (Gueberschwihr)
Hatschbourg (Hattsatt)
Hengst (Wintzenheim)
Kanzlerberg (Bergheim)

Kastelberg (Andlau)

Kessler (Guebwiller)

Kirchberg de Barr (Barr)

Kirchberg de Ribeauvillé (Ribeauvillé)

Kitterlé (Guebwiller)

Mambourg (Sigolsheim)

Mandelberg (Mittelwihr)

Markrain (Bennwihr)

Moenchberg Andlau)

Muenchberg (Nothalten)

Ollwiller (Wuenheim)

Osterberg (Ribeauvillé)

Pfersigberg (Equisheim)

Pfingstberg (Orschwihr)

Praelatenberg (Orschwiller)

Rangen (Thann)

Rosacker (Hunawihr)

Saering (Guebwiller)

Schlossberg (Kaysersberg)

Schoenenbourg (Riquewihr)

Sommerberg (Niedermorschwihr)

Sonnenglanz (Beblenheim)

Spiegel (Bergholtz)

Sporen (Riquewihr)

Steinbrubler (Wettolsheim)

Steinert (Pfaffenheim)

Steinklotz (Marlenheim)

Vorbourg (Rouffach-Westhalten)

Wiebelsberg (Andlau)

Wineck-Schlossberg (Katzenthal)

Winzenberg (Blienschwiller)

Zinnkoepflé (Westhalten-Soultzmatt)

Zotzenberg (Mittelbergheim)

Respected Alsatian Producers
Albert Boxler

Albert Mann

Alfred Wantz
André Thomas et Fils
Anstotz et Fils
Antoine Stoffel
Barmes-Buecher
Bernard et Robert Schoffit
Cave Vinicole de Hunawihr
Charles Schleret
Dirler
Einhart
Emile Schwartz
Ernest Burn
Gerard Wagner
Herbinger
Hugel
J.B. Adam
Jean Becker
Jean Huttard
Jean Schaetzel
Jean Sipp
Jean-Martin Spielmann
Jean-Pierre Dirler
Joseph Gsell
Josmeyer
Julien Meyer
Klein aux Vieux Remparts
Kuehn
Kuentz-Bas
Leon Heitzmann
Lucien Albrecht
Marc Kreydenweiss
Marcel Deiss
MaterneHaegelin et Ses Filles
Meyer-Fonne
Mittnackt Klack
Muré

d'Orschwihr
Ostertag
Paul Schneider
Paul Schwach
Pierre Arnold
Pierre Frick
Pierre Sparr
Pierre et Jean-Pierre Rietsch
Raymond Renck
Roland Schmitt
Rolly-Gassman
Schlumberger
Sick Dreyer
Sipp-Mack
de la Tour
Trimbach
Weinbach
Weingarten
Willy Rolli-Edel
Wittmann Fils
Zind-Humbrecht

BORDEAUX - RED

Bordeaux is no doubt the most famous of the French wines. That is due in part to the wizardry of the most accomplished châteaux and in part to the fact that a flood of table red and white wines are produced here and shipped all over the world.

Reports are that 500 million bottles of wine are produced out of the Bordeaux region's 100,000 hectares. The famous wines — the **Margaux**, **Pauillac**, **Saint-Julien**, and others — account for only a small pool of this sea of wine.

The most famous châteaux generally specialize in red wines, but Bordeaux is also well known for its whites. The **Graves** region produces some beautifully subtle and elegant dry white wines. And **Sauternes** are among the most famous sweet white dessert wines in the world. This embarrassment of riches constitutes a bit of a challenge for you. How do you pick a single bottle of Bordeaux from a wine list 20 pages long?

As we say in virtually every section here, you will need to weigh four factors: the producer of the wine, the subregion of Bordeaux where the vines were grown and the wine was made, the year or vintage that the wine was made, and the price.

As in most French wine regions, these wines take their names from the location (or *appellation*), not from the grape used in making the wine. The wines below are made mostly blends of Cabernet Sauvignon, Merlot, and Cabernet Franc grapes. In general, Cabernet Sauvignon is the dominant grape, though the wines from Saint-Émilion and especially Pomerol often focus on the Merlot.

The selection in the Bordeaux region is a wee bit simpler than in the Burgundy area. In Burgundy, a single vineyard may be divided among a dozen or more owners who produce wildly varying wines. In Bordeaux, châteaux often own large homogeneous vineyards.

Also unlike Burgundy, where a wine maker may produce wines from grapes grown in several vineyards scattered all over the Côte d'Or, the châteaux generally produce wine from a single large vineyard.

GRAVES

Location: The large area immediately to the west and southwest of the city of Bordeaux.

Type of Wine: A complex, but lighter red usually made with a blend of juices from the Cabernet Sauvignon (about half), Merlot, and small amounts of Cabernet Franc. Can be a bit overpowering for those who prefer the feathery touch of a good Margaux. The winemakers of Graves agreed on an independent quality control and rating system some time ago, and there are currently 13 red and 9 white Crus Classés.

Strong Vintages: *1975, 1978,1979, 1982, 1983, 1985, 1986, 1988, 1989, 1990, 1995, 1996*

The Graves Red Crus Classés

Bouscaut
Carbonnieux
Chevalier
Fieuzal
Haut-Bailly
Haut-Brion

Latour-Haut-Brion
Latour-Martillac
Malartic-Lagravière
Mission-Haut-Brion
Olivier
Pape-Clément
Smith-Haut-Lafitte

Other Respected Producers
Archambeau
Beau-Site
Bichon Cassignols
Brondelle
Chantegrive
Doms
Fleur Jonquet
Gravières
Louvière
Mission-Haut-Brion
Rahoul
Saint-Robert
Vieille France

MARGAUX
Location: About 20 kilometers (12 miles) north of Bordeaux.

Type of Wine: One of the most famous, sophisticated, and subtle reds. Though delicate, it has a full-bodied bouquet and taste. The Margaux are subject to the controls and rating system established for Médocs in 1855.

Strong Vintages: *1978, 1979, 1982, 1983, 1985, 1986, 1988, 1989, 1990, 1995, 1996*

The Margaux Grands Crus
See Grand Cru Médocs chart below.

Other Respected Producers

Berlande
Gurgue
Labergorce
Labergorce Zede
Larruau
Marsac Seguineau
Martinens
Monbrison
Pichecan
Rausan-Ségla
Siran
Tayac
Tour de Mons

PAUILLAC

Location: About 40 kilometers (25 miles) north of Bordeaux.

Type of Wine: Another highly sophisticated and rich red. Sometimes tannic, but rarely enough to intrude on the supple taste. The Pauillacs are subject to the controls and rating system established for Médocs in 1855.

Strong Vintages: *1975, 1978, 1979, 1981, 1982, 1983, 1985, 1986, 1988, 1989, 1990, 1995, 1996*

The Pauillac Grands Crus

See Grand Cru Médocs chart below.

Other Respected Producers

Baron Philippe
Becasse
Bellegrave
Bernadotte
Fleur Milon
Fleur Peyrabon
Fonbadet
Pibran
Tour du Roc Milon
Tourette

POMEROL

Location: Just to the east of the town of Libourne, about 30 kilometers (18 miles) east of Bordeaux.

Type of Wine: Made almost totally with Merlot, these reds can be richer and softer. Though they age well, they are often drunk younger than wines heavy with Cabernet Sauvignon. There is no formal Grand Cru status awarded Pomerols, though that should be seen more as a sort of political decision and should not reflect on your interest in the wine.

Strong Vintages: *1975, 1981, 1982, 1983, 1985, 1986, 1987, 1988, 1989, 1990, 1994, 1995, 1998*

Respected Pomerol Producers

Bon Pasteur
Certain de May
Clinet
Clos des Litanies
Conseillante
L'Eglise-Clinet
L'Evangile
Fleur Pétrus
Gazin
Grave-Trigant de Boisset
Gravette de Certan
Lafleur
Lagrange
Latour à Pomerol
Montviel
Petit-Village
Pétrus
Pin
Plincette
Rève d'Or
Trotanoy
Vieux Château Certan
Vray Croix de Gay

SAINT-ÉMILION

Location: Just a few kilometers east of the town of Libourne, about 35 kilometers (22 miles) east of Bordeaux.

Type of Wine: Sometimes infused with a larger percent of Cabernet Franc, these reds are generally heartier and fleshier, and are often drunk within a few years of production. Has its own ranking of 11 Premiers Grands Crus Classés and 61 Grands Crus Classés.

Strong Vintages: *1975, 1982, 1983, 1985, 1986, 1988, 1989, 1990, 1994, 1995, 1998*

Premiers Saint-Émilion Grands Crus

Ausone
Beauséjour
Belair
Canon
Cheval-Blanc
Clos Fourtet
Figeac
Gaffelière
Magdelaine
Pavie
Trottevieille

Other Respected Producers

Angelus
Belle Rose
Bernateau
Cadet-Bon
Canon-la-Gaffelière
Cantin
Carrillon de l'Angelus
Carteau Pin de Fleurs
Carteau-Matras
Clos Larcis
Commanderie
Corbin Michotte

Dassault
Dominique
Fleur Cardinale
Fonroque
Franc Pipeau Descombes
Grand Corbin Despagne
Grand Mayne
Grand-Pontet
Haut-Cadet
Haut-Nauve
Haut-Rocher
Jean Voisin
Lamarte
Larmande
Moulin Saint-Georges
Pavie Decesse
Petit Val
Robin des Moines
Rose Blanche
Saint-Hubert
Tertre-Roteboeuf
Tonnelle
Tour Figeac
Trolong-Mondot
Vieux Château l'Abbaye

SAINT-ESTÈPHE

Location: Just above the Pauillac subregion in the heart of what is called the Haut-Médoc, where many of the most famous wines are made.

Type of Wine: These may not have the class of other Bordeaux, especially those of neighboring Pauillac or Saint-Julien, but they are still rich and full of character. The Saint-Estèphe wines are subject to the controls and rating system established for Médocs in 1855.

Strong Vintages: *1975, 1978, 1979, 1981, 1982, 1983, 1985, 1986, 1988, 1989, 1990, 1995*

The Saint-Estèphe Grands Crus

See Grand Cru Médocs chart below.

Other Respected Producers

Andron Blanquet
Capbern Gasqueton
Chambert-Marbuzet
Crock
Domeyne
Haut-Marbuzet
Lavillotte
Lilian Ladouys
Marbuzet
Meyney
Ormes de Pez
Phelan Segur
Saint-Estèphe
Segur de Cabanac
Tronquoy-Lalande

SAINT-JULIEN

Location: About 35 kilometers (22 miles) north of Bordeaux in the Haut-Médoc region.

Type of Wine: A personal favorite of ours, with much of the seductive richness of the slightly more expensive Margaux and Pauillacs. Saint-Julien wines are subject to the controls and rating system established for Médocs in 1855.

Strong Vintages: *1975, 1978, 1979, 1981, 1982, 1983, 1985, 1986, 1988, 1989, 1990, 1995, 1996*

The Saint-Julien Grands Crus

See Grand Cru Médocs chart below.

Other Respected Producers

Bridane
Gloria
Lalande-Borie

Moulin de la Rose
Terry-Gros-Cailloux

THE GRAND CRU MÉDOCS

Way back in 1855, Napoleon III, wanting to promote his nation's fine wines, ordered the Bordeaux makers to devise a ranking system that would acknowledge the best producers of the great red wines of the region.

Judging as much by the price of the wines as any qualitative judgments, the makers came up with a five-tiered system: Premiers Crus, followed by Deuxièmes, Troisièmes, Quatrièmes, and Cinquièmes (which translates easily into First, Second, Third, Fourth and Fifth).

All the hotshots in the wine world agree that the rankings are woefully outdated. There are, they say, some producers who should have fallen from the list and many who should have been added. Still, the list is a formidable one, with the top two or three levels still cranking out one magnificent wine after another.

Over the past 10 years, almost all the ranked wines have begun producing what is called a "second" wine. The second wines are made from grapes on the same vineyard as the primary wine and are often similar to the primary wine. However, they can be purchased for half the price or less. (Remember, though, that the seconds are seconds because they don't quite measure up or come from younger vines, so it is possible to find an occasional dog.)

Premiers Crus
Haut-Brion (Graves)
    2nd: Bahans Haut-Brion
Lafite-Rothschild (Pauillac)
    2nd: Moulins de Carruades
Latour (Pauillac)
    2nd: Les Forts de Latour
Margaux (Margaux)
    2nd: Pavillon Rouge
Mouton-Rothschild (Pauillac)

Deuxièmes Crus
Brane-Cantenac (Margaux)
   2nd: Notton
       de Fontarney
Cos-d'Estournel (Saint-Estèphe)
   2nd: Marbuzet
Ducru-Beaucaillou (Saint-Julien)
   2nd: La Croix
Durfort-Vivens (Margaux)
   2nd: de Curé-Bourse
Gruaud-Larose (Saint-Julien)
   2nd: Sarget de Gruaud-Larose
Lascombes (Margaux)
   2nd: Segonnes
       La Gombaude
Léoville-Barton (Saint-Julien)
   2nd: Lady Langoa
Léoville-Las-Cases (Saint-Julien)
   2nd: Clos du Marquis
       Grand Parc
Léoville-Poferré (Saint-Julien)
   2nd: Moulin-Riche
Montrose (Saint-Estèphe)
   2nd: La Dame de Montrose
Pichon-Longueville-Baron (Pauillac)
   2nd: Les Tourelle de Pichon
Pichon-Longueville-Comtesse-de-Lalande (Pauillac)
   2nd: Réserve de la Comtesse
Rausan-Ségla (Margaux)
   2nd: Lamouroux
Rauzan-Gassies (Margaux)

Troisièmes Crus
Boyd-Cantenac (Margaux)
Cantenac-Brown (Margaux)
   2nd: Canuet
       Lamartine

Calon-Ségur (Saint-Estèphe)
    2nd: Marquis de Ségur
Desmirail (Margaux)
Ferrière (Margaux)
Giscours (Margaux)
    2nd: Cantelaude
d'Issan (Margaux)
    2nd: Candel
Kirwan (Margaux)
Lagrange (Saint-Julien)
    2nd: Les Fifes de Lagrange
Lagune (Haut-Médoc)
    2nd: Ludon-Pomiès-Agassac
Langoa-Barton (Saint-Julien)
    2nd: Lady Langoa
Malescot-Saints-Exupéry (Margaux)
    2nd: de Loyac
        du Balardin
Marquis d'Alesme-Becker (Margaux)
Palmer (Margaux)
    2nd: Réserve du Général

Quatrièmes Crus
Beychevelle (Saint-Julien)
    2nd: Amiral de Beychevelle
        Réserve de L'Amiral
Branaire-Ducru (Saint-Julien)
    2nd: Duluc
Duhart-Milon-Rothschild (Pauillac)
    2nd: Moulin de Duhart
Lafon-Rochet (Saint-Estèphe)
    2nd: Le Numéro 2 de Lafon-Rochet
Marquis-de-Terme (Margaux)
    2nd: de Gondats
Pouget (Margaux)
Prieuré-Lichine (Margaux)

2nd: Clairefont
Saint-Pierre (Saint-Julien)
   2nd: Clos de Uza
      Saint-Louis-le-Bosq
Talbot (Saint-Julien)
   2nd: Connétable de Talbot
Tour-Carnet (Haut-Médoc)

Cinquièmes Crus

d'Armailhac (Pauillac)
Batailley (Pauillac)
Belgrave (Haut-Médoc)
Camensac (Haut-Médoc)
Cantemerle (Haut-Médoc)
   2nd: Villeneuve de Cantemerle
Clerc-Milon (Pauillac)
Cos-Labory (Saint-Estéphe)
Croizet-Bages (Pauillac)
   2nd: Enclos de Moncabon
Dauzac (Margaux)
   2nd: Laborde
Grand-Puy-Ducasse (Pauillac)
   2nd: Artigues-Arnaud
Grand-Puy-Lacoste (Pauillac)
   2nd: Lacoste-Borie
Haut-Bages-Libéral (Pauillac)
Haut-Batailley (Pauillac)
   2nd: La Tour d'Aspic
Lynch-Bages (Pauillac)
   2nd: Haut-Bages-Averous
Lynch-Moussas (Pauillac)
Pédesclaux (Pauillac)
Pontet-Canet (Pauillac)
   2nd: Les Hauts de Pontet
du Tertre (Margaux)

OTHER RED BORDEAUX

Wines from these appellations are less well-known, but that doesn't mean you might not find some real gems at very reasonable prices (especially among the Haut-Médocs). In any case, there are scores of fine table wines bottled under these regional names:

Bordeaux AOC

Bordeaux Clairet (rosé)

Bordeaux Supérieur AOC

Bordeaux-Côtes de Castillon

Canon Fronsac

Côtes de Bourg

Côtes de Francs

Fronsac

Graves de Vayres

Haut-Médoc

Lalande de Pomerol

Lussac Saint-Émilion

Listrac

Médoc

Montagne-Saint-Émillion

Moulis

Moulis-en-Médoc

Parsac-Saint-Emillon

Premières Côtes de Bordeaux

Premières Côtes de Blaye

Sainte-Foy-Bordeaux

Saint-George Saint-Émilion

BORDEAUX - MAJOR WHITE & DESSERT WINES

Though the red Bordeaux receive most of the international praise, there are superior whites as well, especially those from the Graves and Sauterne regions. The Graves can be exceptionally light and dry. The Sauternes are famous sweet dessert wines.

ENTRE-DEUX-MERS

Location: Generally refers to the large delta-shaped region east of Bordeaux between the Dordogne and Garonne Rivers.

Type of Wine: True connoisseurs will take exception with us listing this as a major white Bordeaux. It's true that Entre-Deux-Mers is really a white table wine, but it is equally true that it is bright, reasonably priced, and exported in massive quantities.

Strong Vintages: Meant to be drunk quite young.

Respected Entre-Deux-Mers Producers

Bonnet
Candeley
Chevaux des Girondins
Ducla
Fleur
Gammage
Grangeneuve
Haut-Rian
Hauts de Fontaneau
Jamin
Launay
Peyrières
Reynier
Saint-Florin
Tour de Mirambeau
Tuquets

GRAVES

Location: Same general area as where the bold reds are made, immediately to the west and southwest of the city of Bordeaux.

Type of Wine: Some truly exquisite dry-as-a-bone white wines made from the Sémillon and Sauvignon Blanc grapes. No doubt the best of the non-Chardonnay dry whites made in Bordeaux. The Graves have an independent rating system identifying nine white and 13 red (see above) Crus Classés.

Strong Vintages: *1982, 1983, 1985, 1986, 1988, 1989, 1990, 1995, 1996, 1998*

The White Crus Classés
Bouscaut
Carbonnieux
Chevalier
Couhins
Couhins-Lurton
Latour-Martillac
Laville-Haut-Brion
Malartic-Lagravière
Olivier

Other Respected Producers
Belon
Brondelle
Caillou
Chantegrive
Clos Floridene
Fieuzal
Gravallas
Haut-Brion
Haut-Mayne
Louvière
Magneau
Millet
Pont de Brion
Pontac Monplaisir
Respide
Saint-Jean-des-Graves
Smith Haut Lafitte
Vieux Château Gaubert

SAUTERNES
Location: Generally, an area about 35 kilometers (22 miles) southeast of the city of Bordeaux.

Type of Wine: World-class sweet wines, made from a blend of Sémillon, Sauvignon, and Muscadelle grapes. (Also look for Barsac, another dessert wine made next door to the Sauterne area.) It is the sweet wine like a Sauterne in which the "noble rot" comes most into play. Noble rot is caused by the *Botrytis cinerea* fungus, which eats through the skin of a grape, ultimately turning the grape brown. The rot also concentrates the sugars. Sauternes are so valued that they, too, have a ranking system identifying the most highly prized vineyards (or crus). It has three tiers: Premier Crus Supèrieur, Premiers Crus, and Deuxièmes Crus.

Strong Vintages: *1975, 1976, 1980, 1981, 1983, 1985, 1986, 1988, 1989, 1990, 1995, 1996*

Premier Crus Supèrieur
d'Yquem

Premier Crus
Climens (a Barsac)
Clos Haut-Peyraguey
Coutet
Guiraud
Lafaurie-Peyraguey
Rabaud-Promis
Rayne-Vigneau
Rieussec
Sigalas-Rabaud
Suduiraut
Tour-Blanche

Deuxièmes Crus
d'Arche
Broustet
Caillou
Doisy-Daène
Doisy-Dubroca (a Barsac)
Doisy-Vèdrines
Filhot
Lamothe (Despujols)
Lamothe (Guignard)

Malle
Myrat
Nairac
Romer
Romer-du-Hayot
Suau

Other Strong Producers
Coutet-Cuvée Madame (Barsac)
Fargues
Gilette
Haut-Bergeron
Haut-Claverie
Liot
Raymond-Lafon
Remparts de Bastor
Suduirant-Cuvée Madame

OTHER WHITE BORDEAUX
   Like the minor red Bordeaux listed above, these are minor whites, meaning they're not the best of the lot. Still, you might discover a magnificent little wine under one of these labels:
Barsac (sweet)
Cadillac (sweet)
Cérons (sweet)
Côtes de Bourg
Graves de Vayres
Loupiac (sweet)
Premières Côtes de Blaye
Saint-Croix-du-Mont
Sainte-Foy-Bordeaux

BURGUNDY - RED
   Generally, a Burgundy is any wine produced in the Burgundy region of France, whether the wine is white, rosé, or red. Burgundy is the geographical region that snakes through four French *départements,* begin-

ning about 125 kilometers (77 miles) southeast of Paris and extending down the Yonne and Saône River valleys almost to Lyon, 460 kilometers (285 miles) southeast of Paris.

Many world-class white and red wines are produced in the region because controls are tight and growers try to maintain their reputation for quality (in part so they can justify the often screamingly-high prices).

In general, the best white Burgundies, all from the Chardonnay grape, are the **Chablis** from around the village of Chablis; **Meursaults**, **Puligny-Montrachets**, and **Chassagne-Montrachets** from the Côte de Beaune; and the **Pouilly-Fuissé** near Mâcon.

The best reds, all from the Pinot Noir grape, are said to be the **Gevrey-Chambertins**, **Vosne-Romanées**, and **Chambolle-Musignys** of the Côte de Nuits, and the **Pommards** and **Volnays** of the Côte de Beaune. The lighter and fruitier **Beaujolais**, made from the Gamay grape in the southern stretch of Burgundy, are the most affordable and internationally popular wines.

Choosing a Burgundy

Choosing a good Burgundy is a challenge, in part because there are umpteen different vineyards, growers, and producers.

Even if you recognize the name of a wine you like (for example, Meursault or Vosne-Romanée), that doesn't mean that just any Meursault or Vosne-Romanée will be good. There are just too many mediocre producers seeded through these valleys. And just because they're mediocre doesn't mean they won't charge you an arm and a leg.

So what do you look for on a label? Again, four things: one, the name of a respected producer; two, a good price; three, the words *Grand Cru* or *Premier Cru*; and, four, a good vintage.

Crus & Labels

In general, the Grand Crus are rated the best of the wines, and Premier Crus are the second rung. To earn either title, wines from those vineyards (*crus*) are tasted by regional panels of wine experts before being released.

Reading the labels can be a bit tricky. Again, the French generally define a wine by its point of origin (*appellation d'origine*). This is very much the case with good Burgundies. Here's why:

A bottle labeled merely "Burgundy" is probably not going to be very good. It may not even be a vintage wine. It may even contain juice from grapes grown in several regions and during different years.

A recognized Burgundy AOC (the abbreviation for *appellation d'origine contrôlée*), which has been found to meet several regional control standards, may add the region or even village name to their wine. For example, *Beaune* or *Nuits-Saint-Georges*, both of which are small towns.

Next on the ladder of quality Burgundy come the Premiers Crus and Grands Crus. The word *Cru* is essentially the same as *climat* and usually refers to a particular vineyard in a recognized and controlled region or village. For instance, in the Chablis region there are dozens of vineyards lining the valleys, but only seven vineyards (or Crus) are recognized as Grand Cru quality and another 12 are said to be of Premier Cru quality.

Back to reading the label: a Premier Cru can adopt a hyphenated name, combining the name of the village or subregion where the wine was produced (e.g. *Beaune*) with the name of the vineyard where the grapes were grown (e.g. *Cent-Vignes*). So you might find a wine that is labeled a *Beaune-Cent-Vignes, Premier Cru*.

To further complicate matters, each vineyard can be divided between several producers (e.g. **Château de Meursault**, **Michel Pont**, **Domaine René Monnier**, and others make wines from parcels of the Cent-Vignes vineyard). The name of the producer will also appear on the label.

So, to continue our example, you might see a Premier Cru whose label reads *Beaune-Cent-Vignes, Premier Cru, Château de Meursault* – which happens to be a very fine wine.

The few Grands Crus can take their names solely from the vineyard where they are produced, such as the famous **Clos-de-Vougeot**. But again, there are usually many producers making wines from parcels of Grand Cru vineyards, so it is still best to choose one of the better winemakers.

What all this boils down to is that there are hundreds of names of Burgundy wines. We try to simplify things below for each of the major regions so that you can spend more time enjoying the wine than in fretting over which to choose.

CÔTE DE NUITS

Location: The narrow northern section of the Côte d'Or, beginning just south of Dijon and extending 20 kilometers (12 miles) toward Beaune.

Type of wine: Almost exclusively heavier red wines produced from the Pinot Noir grape. The best age very well.

Strong Vintages: *1976, 1978, 1983, 1985, 1987, 1988, 1989, 1990, 1993, 1995, 1996, 1997*

Côte de Nuits-Villages

Wines made from grapes picked in the communes of Brochon, Comblanchien, Corgoloin, Fixin, and Prissey. Wines made strictly from grapes from Fixin can also include the name Fixin on the label.

Below you'll find the major red Côte de Nuits and a list of respected producers:

Chambolle-Musigny

Antonin Guyon
Barthod-Noèllat
Chambolle-Musigny
Christian Clerget
Christian Confuron
Comte Georges de Vogüé
Denis Mugneret
Faiveley
Georges Roumier
Ghislaine Barthod
Henri Perrot-Minot
Hudelot-Noèllat
Jacques-Frédéric Mugnier
Joseph Drouhin
Leymarie
Leroy
Lionel J. Bruck
Louis Jadot
Michel Serveau

Michelle Galley
Moine-Hudelot
Pierre Betheau
Robert Groffier et Fils

Fixin
Berthaut
Bruno Clair
Clavelier et Fils
Faiveley
Gelin-Moulin
Pierre Gelin

Gevrey-Chambertin
Alain Burguet
Armand Rousseau
Bernard et Pierre Dugat
Bourée Père et Fils
Charles Mortet et Fils
Chézeaux
Christian Serafin
Claude et Maurice Dugat
Denis Bachelet
Drouhin-Laroze
Dufouleur Pere et Fils
Faiveley
Geantet-Pansiot
Goillot-Bernollin
Humbert Frères
Jean et Jean-Louis Trapet
Lucien Boillot et Fils
Maume
Michel Esmonin et Fille
Pierre Damoy
Joseph Drouhin
Joseph Roty

Leroy
Louis Jadot
Lucot-Javelier
Philippe Leclerc
René Leclerc
Varoilles

Morey-Saint-Denis
Armand Rousseau
Bruno Clair
Dujac
Georges Bryczek
Guy Castagnier
Heresztyn
Hubert Lignier
Michel Serveau
Nicolas Rossignol-Trapet
Pierre Aimot
Ponsot
Robert Groffier et Fils
Truchot-Martin

Nuits-Saint-Georges
Alain Michelot
Caves des Hautes-Côtes
Chevillon
Clos de l'Arlot
Clos Frantin
Daniel Rion et Fils
Emanuel Rouget
Faiveley
Georges Chicotot
Henri Gouges
Hospices de Nuits
Jacques et Patrice Cacheux
Jean Chauvenet

Lecheneaut
Leroy
Lionel J. Bruck
Machard de Gramont
Max et Jean-François Ecard
Poulette

Vosne-Romanée

Arnoux Père et Fils
Bertrand Machard de Gramont
Château de Vosne-Romanée
Gerard Mugneret
Gros Frère et Soeur
Haegelen-Jayer
Henri Jayer
J. Confuron-Côtetidot
Jacques et Patrice Cacheux
Jean Faurois
Jean Grivot
Jean Méo-Camuzet
Jean Tardy
Leroy
Lupe-Cholet
Mongeard-Mugneret
Mugneret-Gibourg
Pascal Chevigny
Pernin-Rossin
René Engel
Robert Arnoux
Romanée-Conti
Vaucher Père et Fils

Vougeot

Chantal Lescure
Château de la Tour
Denis Mugneret
Drouhin-Laroze

Faiveley
G. Roumier
Gros
Henri Rebourseau
Hudelot-Noellat
Jean Grivot
Joseph Drouhin
Louis Jadot
Méo-Camuzet
René Engel

CÔTE DE BEAUNE

Location: Extends from just a couple of kilometers north of Beaune (the wine capital of Burgundy) south about 28 kilometers (17 miles) just past Santenay.

Type of Wine: Some of the Burgundy region's finest reds, from the Pinot Noir, and whites, from the Chardonnay grape.

Strong Vintages: *1976, 1978, 1983, 1985, 1988, 1989, 1990, 1993, 1995, 1996, 1997*

Côte de Beaune-Villages

Wines from the 16 communes of Auxey-Duresses, Blagny, Chassange-Monrachet, Cheilly-lès-Maranges, Chorey-lès-Beaune, Dézize-lès-Maranges, Ladoix, Meursault, Monthélie, Pernand-Vergelesses, Puligny-Montrachet, Saint-Aubin, Saint-Romain, Sampigny-lès-Maranges, Santenay, and Savigny.

Below you'll find the major red Côte de Beaunes and a list of respected producers:

Aloxe-Corton

Antonin Guyon
Cachat-Ocquidannt et Fils
Capitain-Gagnerot
Charles et Michelle Muller
Christian Gros
Maillard Père et Fils

P. De Marcilly
Robert et Raymond Jacob

Auxey-Duresses
Jean-Pierre Prunier
Jean-Pierre Diconne
Jessiaume Père et Fils

Beaune
Albert Morot Hospices de Beaune
Arnoux Père et Fils
Besancenot-Mathouillet
Château de la Velle
Coron Père et Fils
Charles Allexant et Fils
Jean-Marc Bouley
Jessiaume Père et Fils
Lois Dufouleur
Louis Jadot
Louis Violland
Moingeon
Mommessin
P. Misserey
Pierre Bouzereau-Emonin
Philippe Bouzereau
Prosper Maufoux
René Monnier
Xavier Bouzerand

Chassagne-Montrachet
Bernard Bachelet et Fils
Jean-Nöel Gagnard
Philippe Bouzereau
Prieur-Brunet
Roger Belland

Chorey-lès-Beaune
Château de Chorey-lès-Beaune

Guyon
Jacques Germain
Jean-Luc Dubois
Pascal Laboureau
Tollot-Beaut et Fils

Meursault
Comte Lafon
Doudet-Naudin
Jacques Prieur
Pierre Boillot

Pommard
A.F. Gros
André Mussy
Armand Girardin
Bichot
Caves des Hautes-Côtes
Comte Armand
Courcel
Crea
Cyrot-Buthiau
Gabriel Billard
Henri Delagrange et Fils
Hospices de Beaune
Jean Garaudet
Jean-Luc Joillot
Lahaye Père et Fils
Lejeune
Leroy
Michel Gaunoux
Michel Rebourgeon
Parent
Picard Père et Fils
Pothier-Rieusset
Rossignol-Fevrier Père et Fils

Saint-Aubin
Sylvain Langoureau
Vincent Prunier

Santenay
Buissière
Château de Mercey
Capuanao-Ferreri
Maison Jean Germain

Savigny-lès-Beaune
Camille Giroud
Capron-Charcousset
Cornu
Dubois d'Orgeval
Martin-Dufour
Maurice Ecard et Fils
Michel Gay
Rogert et Joel Remy

Volnay
Antonin Guyon
Boigelot
Doudet-Naudin
François d'Allaines
Jacques Prieur
Jean-Marc Bouley
Joseph Drouhin
Olivier Leflaive Frères
Pousse d'Or
Robert Ampeau et Fils

OTHER RED CÔTE DE BEAUNES
Minor wines that may include some bargains:
Cheilly-lès-Maranges
Monthélie

Pernand-Vergelesses
Saint-Romain
Sampigny-lès-Maranges

CHALLONAISE & MÂCONNAISE WINES

Location: Two very large regions extending 80 kilometers (50 miles) south from the town of Chagny just past the city of Mâcon.

Type of Wine: These two areas crank out an enormous amount of decent table wine. Most of the better wines are whites, but there are some reds, again from the Pinot Noir grape, but often lighter than the Côte de Beaune and Côte de Nuits reds.

Strong Vintages: Most of these reds here are meant to be drunk in the first few years.

Below you'll find a list of selected Challonaise & Mâconnaise reds and a list of respected producers:

Givry
François Lumpp
Gardin
Joblot
Michel Sarrazin et Fils
Sauleraie
Thenard
Thierry Lespinasse

Mercurey
Antonin Rodet
Bordeaux-Montrieux
Cellier Meix Guillaume
Chamerose
Charles Vienot
Château de Chamirey
Château de Mercey
Croix Jacquelet
Emile Juillot
Jeannin-Naltet Père et Fils

Maurice Protheau et Fils
Meix Foulot
Michel Briday
Michel Juillot
Michel Raquillet
Monette
Pierre Gruber
Renarde
Yves de Launay

Rully

Chapitre
Charles Gruber
Château de Davenay
Château de Rully
Eric Suremain
Folie
Jaffelin
Jean-Claude Brelière
Lheritier
Maurice Protheau et Fils
Michel Briday
Paul and Henri Jacqueson

BEAUJOLAIS

Location: Rhône *département* in the southern section of Burgundy region east of the Saône River, running about 35 kilometers (22 miles) from Mâcon almost to Lyon.

Type of Wine: Not really a Burgundy in that, geographically, it lies just outside the southern border of the Burgundy *départements*. Still, guides always include Beaujolais here, so we have followed suit. These fruity reds made from the Gamay grape are generally meant to be drunk within a few months to no more than four or five years.

Strong Vintages: *most are meant to be enjoyed in the first few years*

The Beaujolais Wines

Being such a young wine there are not the same complex rating systems as with other, more sophisticated red Burgundies. There are about 4,000 growers in the area, though many merely grow the grapes, then sell them to large producers. You will note below that Georges Duboeuf, a large company that generally makes very good wines, owns a piece of many of the better growers in the area.

- **Beaujolais AOC** – Probably grapes taken from various places in the southern stretch of Beaujolais country and used for a blended wine.
- **Beaujolais Supérieur AOC** – Also probably a blend made from grapes from various spots in the southern Beaujolais, but resulting in a wine with a slightly higher alcohol content than Beaujolais AOC.
- **Beaujolais Villages AOC** – Wines made from grapes scattered across 40 villages in the northern section of Beaujolais. Considered generally a bit better than the Beaujolais AOC.
- **Beaujolais Nouveau** – This wine is released by Beaujolais producers in increasingly enormous quantities on the third Thursday in November, when it is still as young as a kitten. Served chilled, it is fruity, delightful, and sinfully drinkable. (Keep aspirin handy.)

The Ten Crus

There are ten villages in Beaujolais that have been recognized for producing a higher quality wine — though it is still very reasonably priced. The experts tout **Moulin-à-Vent** and **Fleurie**, though we personally like **Juliénas** and **Brouilly** a great deal as well.

Brouilly

Château de Nervers (Duboeuf)
Grandes Vignes (J.C. Nesme)
Jean-Paul Ruet

Chénas

Benon
Brureaux
Charvet
Château Chévres
Combe-Remont (Duboeuf)

Darrous (Duboeuf)
Guy Braillon
Hubert Lapierre
Jean-Louis Santé
Louis Champagnon
Manoir des Journets (Duboeuf)
Robin

Chiroubles
Bouillard
Château de Javernand (Duboeuf)
Cheysson-Les-Fargues
Desmeures (Duboeuf)
Fourneau
Georges Boulon
Georges Passot
Raousset

Côte-de-Brouilly
Alain Bernillon
Château Delachanel
Château Thivin
Chavanne
Guy Cotton
J.C. Nesme
L. Bassy

Fleurie
Bachelard (Duboeuf)
Chapelle des Bois
Château de Fleurie
Château de Grand Pré (Pierre Ferraud)
Château des Deduits (Duboeuf)
Clos de la Roilette
Guy Depardon
Michel Chignard-lès-Moriers

Quatre Vents (Duboeuf)
René Berrod-Les Roches du Vivier

Juliénas
André Pelletier
Bottière Domaine de la Seigneuries de Juilénas (Duboeuf)
Château de Juliénas
Château des Capitans
Château des Vignes (Duboeuf)
Château du Bois de la Salle
Mouilles (Duboeuf)

Morgon
Aucoeur
Château de Bellevue
Château de Pizay
Desvignes
Georges Brun
Jacques Trichard
Janodet
Jean Descombes (Duboeuf)
Lapierre
Princess Lieven (Duboeuf)
Vatoux (Duboeuf)

Moulin-à-Vent
Bruyère
Château de Moulin-à-Vent-Jean (Pierre Bloud)
Château des Jacques
Chauvet (Duboeuf)
Diochon
Héritiers-Tagent (Duboeuf)
Jacky Janodet
René Berrod
Teppe (Chanut Frères)
Tour du Bief (Duboeuf)

Régnié
Georges Duboeuf
Jean Durand
Jean-Paul Ruet
Joel Rochette
Ponchon (J. Durand)
Potet (Duboeuf)

Saint-Amour
Champs Georges Trichard
Grilles
Janin
Pirolette (Duboeuf)

BURGUNDY - WHITE
CHABLIS
Location: Yonne *département* in the northwest section of Burgundy region east of the Yonne River.

Type of Wine: Dry, almost steely, white wines made from Chardonnay grape.

Strong Vintages: *1978, 1982, 1983, 1985, 1986, 1988, 1989, 1990, 1992, 1994, 1996, 1997, 1998*

The Different Chablis
• **Petit Chablis** – Inexpensive, light and meant to be drunk quite young. Not up to standards of the Crus.
• **Chablis AOC** --Wines that may be made from grapes grown in several different vineyards or in vineyards that have not earned Premier or Grand status. Still, they have been judged to meet various criteria and should be good wines.
• **Premier Crus** –There are 12 vineyards that have earned Premier Cru status.
• **Grand Crus** – There are seven recognized Grand Cru vineyards: Blanchots, Bougros, Les Clos, Grenouilles, Preuses, Valmur, and Vaudésir.

Respected Chablis Producers

Château Grenouilles
Château de Maligny
Château de Vivier
Colombier
Conciergerie
Cooperative la Chablisienne
Daniel Dampt
Denis Race
Durup
Duvergey-Taboureau
Edmond Chalmeau
Eglantière
Eglise
Etienne Defaix
François et Jean-Marie Raveneau
Guy Robin
Herve Azo
Jean Collet et Fils
Jean Goulley et Fils
Jean Dauvissat
Jean Defaix
Jean-Luc Aegerter
Jean-Paul Droin
Jean-Pierre Grossot
Laroche
Laurent Tribut
Long-Depaquit
Louis Michel
Maison Blanche
Malandes
Marcel Duplessis
Meulière
Michel Barat
Pascal Bouchard
Philippe Testut

Pierre André
Robert Vocoret et Fils
René et Vincent Dauvissat
Servin
William Fèvre

CÔTE DE BEAUNES

Location: Extends from just a couple of kilometers north of Beaune (the wine capital of Burgundy) south about 28 kilometers (17 miles) just past Santenay.

Type of Wine: Some of the Burgundy region's finest white wines from the Chardonnay grape, as well as red wines, from the Pinot Noir. The rich full-bodied whites are said to challenge any white wine in the world.

Strong Vintages: *1978, 1979, 1981, 1982, 1983, 1985, 1986, 1989, 1990, 1992, 1996, 1997, 1998*

Below you'll find the major white Côte de Beaunes and a list of respected producers:

Aloxe-Corton
Pierre Marey et Fils

Beaune
Château de Beaune
Château de la Velle
Goupil de Bouille
Joseph Drouhin
Louis Jadot
Louis Latour
Louis Violland
Remoissenet Père et Fils

Chassagne-Montrachet
Amiot-Bonfils
Bernard Moreau
Blain-Gagnard
Chartron et Trebuchet

Château de Chassagne-Montrachet
Colin-Deleger
Duc de Magenta
Fernand Coffinet
Fontaine-Gagnard
Georges Déleger
Jean Pillot et Fils
Jean-Nöel Gagnard
Marc Collin
Michel Niellon
Moillard-Grivot
Morey
Ramonet
René Lamy-Pillot

Meursault
Albert Grivault
Château de Meursault
Coche-Dury
Comte Lafon
François Jobard
Guy Roulot
Henri de Villamont
Lahaye Père et Fils
Latour-Giraud
Michel Bouzereau
Michel Dupont-Fahn
Michelot
Michelot-Buisson
Patrick Javillier
Pierre Boillot
Pierre Morey Robert Ampeau
Roger Caillot et Fils
Roux Père et Fils

Puligny-Montrachet
Charles et Paul Bavard
Coron Père et Fils
Leflaive
Etienne Sauzet
Gerard Thomas
Paul Pernot

Saint-Aubin
Maison Jean Germain
Roux Père et Fils

Santenay
Herve de Lavoreille
Olivier Père et Fils

OTHER WHITE CÔTE DE BEAUNES
Auxey-Duresses
Cheilly-lès-Maranges
Chorey-lès-Beaune
Pernand-Vergelesses
Saint-Romain
Sampigny-lès-Maranges
Savigny-lès-Beaune

CHALLONAISE & MÂCONNAISE
Location: Two very large regions extending 80 kilometers (50 miles) south from the town of Chagny just past the city of Mâcon.

Type of Wine: These two areas crank out an enormous amount of decent table wine. Most of the better wines are whites, again made from the Chardonnay grape.

Strong Vintages: Most wines here are meant to be drunk in the first few years.

Below you'll find a list of selected Challonaise & Mâconnaise whites:

Mâcon-Villages
André Bonhomme

Auvigue-Burrier-Revel
Bongrand
Bouchard Père et Fils
Cave de Prisse
Cave de Vivre
Château Berze
Château de Loche
Chenevière
Dominique Vaupré
Girard
Granges
Guffens-Heynen
Honoré Lavigne
Louis Jadot
Manciat-Poncet
Perelles
René Michel
Talmard
Valanges
Vieux Saint-Sorlin

Pouilly-Fuissé

André Forest
Cave de Chaintre
Chapelle
Château Fuissé
Daniel Barraud
Cordier Père et Fils
Corsin
Ferret
Gilles Noblet
Guffens-Heynen
Lorton et Fils
Manciat-Poncet
Plantes
Roger Lasserat

René Guerin
Soufrandise
Thibert Père et Fils
Vessigaud Père et Fils

Rully
André Lheritier
Château de Davenay
Folie
Michel Briday
Eric de Suremain
Henri et Paul Jacqueson
Jaffelin
Martial Thevenot
Rully Saint-Michel

CÔTES DU RHÔNE - RED

Wines from the **Côtes du Rhône** region, which begins just past Lyon and trails down both sides of the river to about Avignon, are among the best values you'll find in good French wines and are among the most underestimated by the average American consumer.

One obvious reason is that they are not available in the kinds of export quantity and variety as are the Bordeaux and Burgundies. But another reason is that some people, especially those who prefer the soft and refined qualities of a good Bordeaux, are a bit shocked by the relatively bold tastes of the **Hermitages** and even the **Châteauneuf-du-Papes**.

It's true that Hermitage is about as muscle-bound a wine as you're likely to find. Still, when it's good, it will knock your socks off. And the Châteauneuf-du-Papes, which range from rich and round to fruity and refreshing, are among our very favorites for just about any occasion. The robust **Gigondas** and especially the **Côte-Rôtie** wines also rank high in our books, and are well worth a try for anyone who enjoys a full-bodied, but rarely obnoxious, red.

This long region snaking along the river is almost completely dominated by red wines, with the dominant grape of the best products being the Syrah. Still, the supple and sophisticated whites from **Château Grillet** and **Condrieu** are said to be among the finest in all of France (they are hugely expensive as well). And you may be surprised at just how good the white Châteauneuf-du-Pape and Hermitage taste.

We even have to break our prejudice against rosés and recommend that you sample a **Tavel**, which many critics tout as the very best rosé around.

CHÂTEAUNEUF-DU-PAPE

Location: An area just south of the city of Orange and north of Avignon in the heart of the southern half of the Côtes du Rhône wine region.

Type of Wine: Probably the best known of the Côtes du Rhône wines. There is incredible diversity in the wines because 13 varieties of grapes are allowed. In general, the better wines are full-bodied, though rarely overpowering. They age well.

Strong Vintages: *1978, 1979, 1981, 1983, 1985, 1986, 1988, 1989, 1990, 1994, 1995, 1996, 1998*

Respected Châteauneuf-du-Pape Producers

Beaucastel

Beaurenard

Bosquet des Papes

Cabrières

Chante Cigale

Chante Perdrix

Chapoutier Barbe Rac

Charvin

Château de la Gardine

Château la Nerthe

Clefs d'Ors

Clos des Papes

Clos du Caillou

Clos du Calvaire

Clos du Mont-Olivet

Durieu

Eddie Féraud

Font de Michelle

Galet des Papes
Gardine
Gérard Charvin
Grand Jean
Guigal
Haut des Terres Blanches
Henri Bonneau
Janasse
Lucien Barrot
Lucien et André Brunel-Les Cailloux
Marcoux
Modorée
Moulin-Tacussel
Nerthe
Paul Autard
Pegau
Pierre André
Pierre Jacumin
Rayas
Rays Pignan
Reviscoulado
Roquette
Saint-Benôit
Solitude
Vieux Donjon
Vieux Télégraphe

CÔTES DU RHÔNE

Location: The growing region for this general wine extends over an enormous area through the Rhône River valley.

Type of Wine: All but a tiny percent are red, and there are many accepted grapes, meaning quality varies enormously. Generally hearty wines meant to be drunk young.

Strong Vintages: These are meant to be consumed within five years or so.

Respected Côtes du Rhône Producers
Amouriers
Andezon
Berthete
Bouche
Brezeme
Champ-Long
Château la Croix Chabrière
Château Saint-Estève d'Uchaux
Fuzière
Mordorée
Rigot
Romarins
Vieux Chàne
Vignerons d'Estezargues

CÔTES DU RHÔNE-VILLAGES

Location: Applies to 17 villages in the southern half of the Rhône Valley in the *départements* of Drôme, Gard, and Vaucluse.

Type of Wine: The next step up from the recognized Côtes du Rhônes, therefore with a bit more body and character.

Strong Vintages: *1985, 1986, 1988, 1989, 1990, 1993, 1995, 1996, 1998*

Respected Côtes du Rhône-Villages Producers
Brusset
Cabasse
Château du Grand Moulas
Coriancon
Parpaiouns
Presidente
Rabasse Charavin
Saint-Etienne
Sainte-Anne
Vieux Chêne

CÔTE-RÔTIE

Location: An area near Vienne, about 30 kilometers (18 miles) south of Lyons.

Type of Wine: At least 80 percent from the Syrah grape, the rest from the Viognier. Full-bodied and one of the very best, most prestigious of the Côtes du Rhône wines.

Strong Vintages: *1978, 1979, 1982, 1983, 1985, 1987, 1988, 1989, 1990, 1991, 1994, 1995, 1996, 1998*

Respected Côte-Rôtie Producers

Bernard Burgaud
Chapoutier
Clusel-Roch
Gilles Barge
Guigal
Henri Gallet
Jamet
Levet
Marius Gentaz-Dervieux
Michel Ogier
Pierre Gaillard
Pierre Barge
René Rostaing
Robert Jasmin
Vallouit Vagonier
Vidal-Fleury
Vincent Gasse

CROZES-HERMITAGE

Location: The area on the opposite side of the Rhône River from the city of Tournon.

Type of Wine: Another bold red made from the Syrah grape, though not as finished as the Hermitage. Ages moderately well, but you'd want to drink it before a decade passes.

Strong Vintages: *1978, 1979, 1982, 1983, 1985, 1987, 1988, 1989, 1990, 1991, 1994, 1995, 1996, 1997, 1998*

Respected Crozes-Hermitage Producers

Alain Graillot
Albert Belle
Château Curson
Entrefaux
Meysonniers
Pavillon-Mercurol
Paul Jaboulet
Thalabert
Vallouit

GIGONDAS

Location: In the Montmirail hills 16 kilometers (10 miles) east of the city of Orange.

Type of Wine: A personal favorite. A rich, potent, somewhat sassy and reasonably priced red made mostly from the Grenache grape with touches of Syrah and Cinsault to round out the taste.

Strong Vintages: *1978, 1979, 1981, 1983, 1985, 1986, 1988, 1989, 1990, 1993, 1995, 1998*

Respected Gigondas Producers

Cayron
Chapelle
Château du Trignon
Clos du Joncuas
Close des Cazaux
Daniel Brusset
Delas
Edmond Burle
Font-Sane
Gouberts
Gour de Chaule
Guigal
Longue-Toque
Moulin de la Gardette
Paul Jaboulet

Pesquiers
Piaugier
Raspail
Redoitier
Saint-Gayan
Santa Duc
Tourelles

HERMITAGE

Location: Around the town of Tain l'Hermitage in the central part of the Rhône Valley.

Type of Wine: Probably the boldest, toughest, most tannic wine of the region. Can be absolutely superb, unless you prefer more gentle wines. Made from the Syrah grape and needs a few years before you dip in.

Strong Vintages: *1978, 1979, 1982, 1983, 1985, 1987, 1988, 1989, 1990, 1991, 1994*

Respected Hermitage Producers

Albert Belle
Bernard Faurie
Cave de Tain l'Hermitage
Chapoutier
Chave
Henri Sorrel
Jaboulet
Vallouit Greffières

SAINT-JOSEPH

Location: A large area on the western banks of the Rhône around the city of Tournon.

Type of Wine: Though made entirely from the Syrah grape, the same as Hermitage, the Saint-Joseph reds are much lighter, fruitier, and less expensive. When good, these too are personal favorites.

Strong Vintages: *1988, 1989, 1990, 1994, 1995, 1997, 1998*

Respected Saint-Joseph Producers

Alain Graillot
André Perret
Bernard Faurie
Cave de Sarras
Chapoutier
Chave
Chêne
Cuilleron
Fauterie
Gachon
Grippat
Guy Veyrier
Jean Marsanne
Monteillet
Pascal Perrier
Paul Jaboulet
Pierre Gonon
Raymond Trollat
Roche Paradis
Vallouit

TAVEL

Location: Just a few kilometers northwest of Avignon, on the opposite side of the river from Châteauneuf-du-Pape.

Type of Wine: Okay, so we've included a rosé. In general, we're not fans, but these are very seductive.

Strong Vintages: Meant to be drunk in the first couple of years.

Respected Tavel Producers

Carabiniers
Château d'Aqueria
Maby
Mordorée
Vignerons de Tavel

OTHER RED CÔTE DU RHÔNE WINES

Cornas
Côteaux du Tricastin
Côtes du Luberon
Côtes du Ventoux
Côtes du Vivarais
Lirac
Muscat de Beaumes-de-Venise
Rasteau
Vin de Pays Côteaux de l'Ardèche
Vin de Pays Collines Rhodaniennes

CÔTES DU RHÔNE - WHITE
CHÂTEAU GRILLET

Location: A single vineyard located in the Condrieu area opposite the Rhône from Vienne.

Type of Wine: Said to be a remarkable dry white wine made only from the finicky Viognier grape. Supposed to be one of France's finest whites, made by the same family for three centuries. Probably overpriced. We're still looking for our first bottle. Experts recommend you drink this young.

Strong Vintages: *1976, 1978, 1979, 1981, 1982, 1985, 1986, 1987, 1988, 1989, 1994, 1997*

Respected Château Grillet Producers

Only the one, Château Grillet.

CHÂTEAUNEUF-DU-PAPE

Location: An area just south of the city of Orange and north of Avignon in the heart of the southern half of the Côte du Rhône wine region.

Type of Wine: Very few white Châteauneuf-du-Papes are made, and it's a shame because the best of them are a real treat. A fresh but textured wine made from Grenache Blanc and Clairette grapes.

Strong Vintages: Meant to be drunk within a few years.

Respected Châteauneuf-du-Pape Producers

Chante Perdrix
Charbonnière
Château de Vaudieu
Château la Nerthe
Château Mont-Redon
Font de Michelle
François Laget
Janasse
Juliette Avril
Paul Autard
Père Anselme
Saint-Benoit

CONDRIEU

Location: A small 57-acre area opposite the Rhône and southwest a few kilometers from Vienne.

Type of Wine: Like Château Grillet, the Condrieu wines are made from Viognier grapes and are very highly prized. They are often described as exotic and floral wines. We're still shopping for our first bottle of Condrieu as well.

Strong Vintages: Meant to be drunk within a few years.

Respected Condrieu Producers

André Perret
Côteau de Chery
Cuilleron
Delas Frères
Dumazet
Faviere
Georges Verney
Gilles Barge
Guigal
Herve Richard
Philippe Pichon
Robert Niero
Yves Cuilleron

CROZES-HERMITAGE

Location: The area on the opposite side of the Rhône River from the city of Tournon.

Type of Wine: A respectable white made from Marsanne and Roussanne grapes. Not much is produced and the white has nothing like the muscular flavor of the reds.

Strong Vintages: Meant to be drunk in the first few years.

Respected Crozes-Hermitage Producers

Château Curson
Remizières

HERMITAGE

Location: Around the town of Tain l'Hermitage in the central part of the Rhône Valley.

Type of Wine: As with the white Crozes-Hermitage wines, the Hermitage whites are made from the Marsanne and Roussanne grapes. These are generally richer and fuller than the white Crozes-Hermitages, though they still possess nothing like the aggressive character of the red Hermitages.

Strong Vintages: *stay on the younger side – just a few years*

Respected Hermitage Producers

Chante-Alouette
Chave

SAINT-JOSEPH

Location: A large area on the western banks of the Rhône around the city of Tournon.

Type of Wine: A light, fruity, and refreshing white wine made from Marsanne and Roussanne grapes.

Strong Vintages: Meant to be drunk in the first few years.

Respected Saint-Joseph Producers

Cave de Saint-Desirat
Cave de Tain l'Hermitage
Chapoutier

Delas
Jean-Louis Grippat
Maurice et Dominique Courbis
Pierre Gonon
Vallouit

OTHER WHITE CÔTE DU RHÔNE WINES
Clairette de Die (sparkling)
Côtes du Rhône
Côtes du Rhône-Villages
Lirac
Saint-Péray (sparkling)

THE WINE EXPERTS
We've compiled a lot of information for you, but we're still not experts. If you want to dig really deep, turn to the genuine gurus. Here are just a handful of invaluable resources to help you along in your newfound hobby. Parker and Johnson, both mentioned below, have several very smart books on various facets of the wine trade.

• Anglade, Pierre (ed.) **Larousse Wines and Vineyards of France** *(New York: Arcade Publishing, translation).*

• Barbey, Adélaide (ed.), **Le Guide Des Vins** *(French only), (Paris: Hachette, updated annually).*

• Johnson, Hugh, **Pocket Encyclopedia of Wine** *(New York: Fireside Books, Simon & Schuster Inc., updated annually).*

• Millon, Marc and Kim, **The Wine Roads of France** *(London: Grafton Books, Harper Collins Publishers).*

• Parker, Jr., Robert M., **Wine Buyer's Guide** *(New York: Fireside Books, Simon & Schuster).*

• **Wine Spectator** *magazine, P.O. Box 50462, Boulder CO 80322-0462; Tel. 800/752-7799.*

9. WHERE TO STAY

Your first challenge is to decide where to stay. To make that decision, you need to know a bit about the various central neighborhoods of Paris — which has more character, which has better restaurants or more sights to see, which is historic and which is relatively new, that sort of thing.

Choosing a hotel recalls the old rule of thumb about the three most important things in shopping for a house. Answer: location, location, location.

So what follows here are what we think of as the seven primary neighborhoods in central Paris and an accompanying list of hotels. Each neighborhood is home to several very pleasant hotels.

For the most part, the hotels we've included here are ones in which any American would feel comfortable. For instance, unless otherwise noted, all have private bathrooms. Virtually every room also has a

APARTMENT RENTALS

If you are looking for an apartment all your own, whether long- or short-term, there are a number of agencies eager to help. This works out pretty well for business types, as well as families who might want to have a kitchen. Some agencies will rent by the week, some only by the month; some will lead you to residence hotels and some are subletting apartments belonging to private owners. Fees vary wildly and the level of assistance is mixed, but there are many decent deals to be found. Agencies you might try include:

- *Inside Paris, Tel. 01.56.24.38.20*
- *Guest Apartment Services, Tel. 01.44.07.06.20*
- *Apalachee Bay, Tel. 01.42.94.13.13*
- *France Appartements, Tel. 01.56.89.31.00*

television (most with cable) and a direct dial phone, and, in many cases, a hair dryer, a minibar, and a small safe for your valuables.

Even in the better hotels, rooms are usually on the small size by American standards. But that is rarely a problem because you won't spend much time in the room anyway. But if you do want something larger, you'll probably want a junior suite. It will be slightly larger than the average double and will have a small sitting area with a love seat or sofa. A full suite, called an *appartement*, will have a separate sitting room. Either are likely to cost anywhere from twenty percent more to twice the rate of a double.

The management and reception staff at the better hotels (most three stars and all four stars) are university trained. Hotel management is a respected profession in Europe and the men and women who practice it

THE FAB FIVE

Some call them palaces. These are the places a fairytale princess would stay, or an industry giant, or a major movie star on a promotional tour for his latest release. They are sumptuous and chic in every way. Fit for a fantasy, if you can foot the bill. Personally, we just stop by for a glass of wine every now and then; each has a lovely bar area where you can sit for hours if you like.

Rates are for the least expensive single to the most costly double. Suites run from 10,000 to 50,000FF.

LE BRISTOL, *112 rue du Faubourg Saint-Honoré (8th, M:Miromesnil). Tel. 01.53.43.43.00, Fax 01.53.43.43.01. Rates: 3,100 to 4,200FF.*

LE CRILLON, *10 place de la Concorde (8th, M:Concorde). Tel. 01.01.44.71.15.00, Fax 01.01.44.71.15.02. Rates: 3,400 to 4,400FF.*

FOUR SEASONS GEORGE V, *31 avenue George V (8th, M:George V). Tel. 01.49.52.70.00, Fax 01.49.52.70.10. Rates: 3,000 to 4,200FF.*

LA PLAZA ANTHENÉE, *25 avenue Montaigne (8th, M:Franklin-Roosevelt). Tel. 01.53.67.66.65, Fax 01.53.67.66.66. Rates: 3,000 to 4,800FF.*

THE RITZ, *15 place Vendôme (1st, M:Tuileries). Tel. 01.43.16.30.30, Fax 01.43.16.31.78. Rates: 3,300 to 4,500FF.*

are quite serious about providing quality service. You may have heard lots of horror stories about the rudeness of the French, but you shouldn't run into that at your hotel. If you do, you might want to consider changing hotels.

There are some hotels so grand they're referred to as palaces. We list those separately in case your visit marks an extra special occasion. But our advice is to choose one of the nice, mid-sized hotels near the neighborhoods you most want to visit.

In general, the Right Bank hotels are more expensive, even though most are no better (and some are worse) than the Left Bank hotels we list. You should be able to enjoy comfort and convenience for about $125 a night. For an added touch of class, figure on spending closer to $200 a night.

THE ISLANDS
Îles de la Cité & Saint-Louis

This is where it all began – on the **Île de la Cité** with a primitive people who sought proximity to the water and the fish, and who wanted to profit from the busy north-south trade route that crossed the Seine at this spot.

Today, the two islands are still at the very heart of Paris. Geographically, they are almost dead center. They have also remained important politically. Though City Hall is across the river on the Right Bank, the **main police headquarters** and the **Palais de Justice** are still located on the Île de la Cité. And culturally, though there's not much in the way of art museums, nightclubs, or even great restaurants, there is **Notre-Dame**, arguably the single most inspiring church in the land.

An appropriate spot to begin any tour of Paris, whether this is your first trip or your fiftieth, is **Ground Zero**, a marker in the square facing Notre-Dame from which all mileage counts to Paris are measured. From here, on foot, you can reach most of Paris proper within 30 minutes.

The **Île Saint-Louis**, which began as a residential real estate venture centuries ago, is much more hospitable for overnight stays than the area around Notre-Dame, which is crawling with tourists night and day. You'll also find better food and some tiny shops and galleries worth visiting along the main street that divides Saint-Louis east to west.

1. HÔTEL DE LUTÈCE, *65 rue Saint-Louis-en-l'Île (4th, M:Pont-Marie). Tel. 01.43.26.23.52, Fax 01.43.29.60.25. Rooms: 23. Rates: 890FF. Breakfast: 45FF. No restaurant.*

The Lutèce is owned by the same people who own the Deux-Îles a few doors down (see our next entry). Like the other, it is small, having been carved out of a 17th-century apartment house, and is well-located for both Left and Right Bank expeditions.

This is not as bright and cheery as its sister inn, though there is a warming, well-used fireplace in the entry. A cozy three-table breakfast nook is also located off the main foyer.

The hallways are quite narrow, most rooms have beamed ceilings, and bathrooms come either with a somewhat cramped shower or a tub with hand-held shower (request the latter). The staff is friendly and English is spoken here.

2. HÔTEL DES DEUX-ÎLES, *59 rue Saint-Louis-en-l'Île (4th, M:Pont-Marie). Tel. 01.43.26.13.35, Fax 01.43.29.60.25. Rooms: 17. Rates: 760-890FF. Breakfast: 45FF. No restaurant.*

A delightful little hotel set among the small shops that line the main street of the Île Saint-Louis, the Deux-Îles is a cheery and warm hotel fashioned out of a 17th-century apartment building. It offers a very good location (close to Left and Right Bank attractions and restaurants) at a reasonable price.

The lobby, with its glass-enclosed garden, is the most colorfully decorated space in the hotel, though the smallish rooms are comfortable and pleasing. There is plenty of closet space, and bathrooms are outfitted sometimes with showers and sometimes with tubs equipped with hand-held showers. English spoken here.

3. JEU DE PAUME, *54 rue Saint-Louis-en-l'Île (4th, M:Pont-Marie). Tel. 01.43.26.14.18, Fax 01.40.01.46.02.76. Rooms: 32. Rates: 950-1,600FF. Breakfast: 80FF. No restaurant.*

Only eight years old, this fascinating hotel was once an indoor tennis court, where members of Louis XIII's royal entourage thrashed out a few sets in the mid-1600s. You can still see the loft where friends and fans watched the matches in progress.

Enter off of the shop-lined rue Saint-Louis-en-l'Île, through a short stone passageway, past a small garden, and into a captivating lobby with a beamed ceiling, red-tiled floor, leather couches and a small bar. Beyond

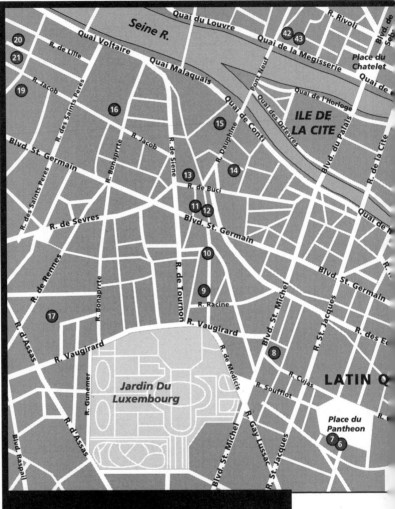

PARIS HOTELS (Southeast)

1. Hôtel de Lutèce
2. Hôtel des Deux-Îles
3. Jeu de Paume
4. Hôtel de Notre-Dame
5. Hôtel des Grandes Écoles
6. Hôtel des Grands Hommes
7. Résidence du Panthéon
8. Hôtel de la Sorbonne
9. Odéon Hôtel
10. Hôtel Le Relais Saint-Germain
11. Hôtel de Fleurie
12. Left Bank Hôtel
13. Hôtel Buci Latin
14. Relais Christine

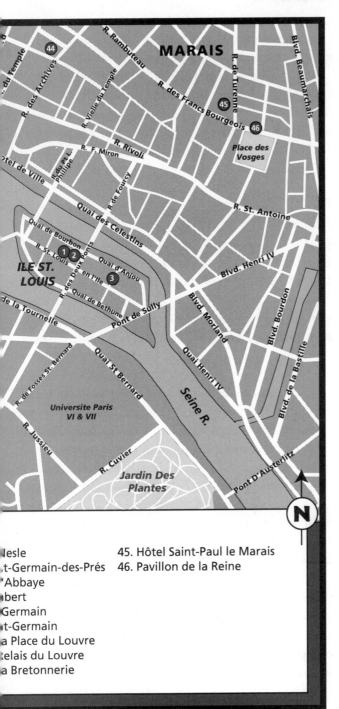

a glass elevator that takes you up to your room is the breakfast area, with glass-topped wrought-iron tables, original rough stone walls, and a lattice of timbers that support both walls and ceiling.

Rooms are a decent size, with blond wood furnishings, fabric-covered walls, beamed ceilings, minibars and gray marble bathrooms. If you're worn out by your flight or a few days of energetic sightseeing, relax in the free hotel sauna. The closets are disappointingly small.

Book long in advance.

LEFT BANK
The Latin Quarter
5th Arrondissement

The **Latin Quarter** is just like you would imagine it to be. This is where the Romans expanded the early city of Lutetia, building arenas, baths, and homes up the slopes of the hill which later became known as **Mount Sainte-Geneviève**, and where today stands the gravely majestic **Panthéon**, a last resting place for many of France's greatest artists and politicians.

Roman and medieval remains can still be seen here, both at the **Arènes de Lutece** and the **Cluny museum**. The **rue Mouffetard** with its colorful open market was once the primary Roman road to the south.

It was also on these slopes that the **Sorbonne** and **University of Paris** were established. Stuffy students and scholars once walked these streets with their noses in the air speaking Latin — thus Latin Quarter.

Today, there are even more schools, students, and professors, often lending the narrow old streets the gaiety of their youth and enthusiasm. Bookstores, cafés, small clubs, and restaurants abound and are among the more affordable in the city. There is a dash of elitism as well: The 5th arrondissement is also home to the famous **Tour d'Argent** restaurant and the late President François Mitterand.

4. HÔTEL DE NOTRE-DAME, *19 rue Maître-Albert (5th, M:Saint-Michel or Maubert-Mutualité). Tel. 01.43.26.79.00, Fax 01.46.33.50.11. Rooms: 34. Rates: 750-820FF. Breakfast: 40FF. No restaurant.*

As its name suggests, the Notre-Dame is just a block from the river just opposite the Notre-Dame cathedral. Though this hotel is near the heart of the busy Latin Quarter, it is on a tiny street that doesn't get much traffic. As a result you have a pretty and tranquil hideaway.

The rooms are, as with most hotels here, on the small side. They have been redecorated in the past four years in a kind of unobtrusive contemporary style, with blond wood desks, fabric wall coverings, and beige faux-marble bathrooms, which are separated from the bedrooms by frosted glass partitions. Bathrooms all have tubs, many of which are the three-quarter length variety, where you sit rather than lay yourself out.

Minibars and cable television are the rule. A tiny breakfast room is just past the front desk, and the staff is very friendly and speaks good English.

5. HÔTEL DES GRANDES ÉCOLES, *75 rue du Cardinal Lemoine (5th, M:Cardinal Lemoine). Tel. 01.43.26.79.23, Fax 01.43.25.28.15. Rooms: 50. Rates: 550-720FF. Breakfast: 45FF. No restaurant.*

Charming with a capital 'C.'

The Grandes Écoles, built as a private home back in 1760, takes its name from the quarter, which is liberally seeded with schools of all kinds for all ages. Though the hotel is just a stone's throw from the Panthéon and the busy but charming Place de la Contrescarpe, it is set off the street in a garden courtyard that is unusually tranquil for this neighborhood.

The three main buildings, three stories high, flank the cobbled courtyard, where many of the visitors take breakfast or sip an afternoon drink. Most rooms, which are smallish to average size, look out on the courtyard and reflect the garden motif in floral and pastel decor.

In fact, tranquillity is considered so important here that though the owners outfitted every room to receive cable television, guests said they wanted no such thing. Result: no televisions at all.

The Grands Ecoles could use a splash of paint here and there, but the ambiance and the staff are very welcoming. Book at least a month in advance because regulars quickly claim all the rooms.

6. HÔTEL DES GRANDS HOMMES, *17 place du Panthéon (5th, M:Luxembourg or Sorbonne). Tel. 01.46.34.19.60, Fax 01.43.26.67.32. Rooms: 32. Rates: 800-1,200FF. Breakfast: 45FF. No restaurant.*

The Grands Hommes offers elegance and a stunning location at a relatively reasonable price. The hotel dates back to the 18th century and looks directly out onto the majestic Panthéon, the handsome City Hall for the 5th *arrondissement*, and the expansive place du Panthéon. In fact, rooms on the second, fifth and sixth floors have small terraces where you can gaze transfixed or, in some cases, even take your breakfast.

Rooms are all decorated differently, though many have the same type of beamed ceiling, brass beds, antique (and newly antiqued) armoires, and colorful prints covering the walls. Minibars, radios, and television with cable come with each room. Bathrooms have tubs and are tiled.

The breakfast room is the converted wine and storage cellar downstairs from a well-lit, warmly decorated lobby and sitting area. Very well located, near the Luxembourg Gardens, and popular with business types. Book ahead. If you find the hotel booked, see Résidence du Panthéon below.

7. RÉSIDENCE DU PANTHÉON, *19 place du Panthéon (5th, M:Luxembourg or Sorbonne). Tel. 01.43.54.32.95, Fax 01.43.26.64.65. Rooms: 34. Rates: 800-1,000FF. Breakfast: 45FF. No restaurant.*

The same owner and largely the same hotel as the Grand Hommes detailed above.

8. HÔTEL DE LA SORBONNE, *6 rue Victor-Cousin (5th, M:Luxembourg or Sorbonne). Tel. 01.43.54.58.08, Fax 01.40.51.05.18. Rooms: 37. Rates: 485-550FF. Breakfast: 35FF. No restaurant.*

A no-frills kind of place, but very reasonably priced, clean, and well located for Latin Quarter adventures.

The Sorbonne is on a tiny street facing one of the many entrances to, yes, you guessed it, the Sorbonne. If you stay here, you should go around the corner to the square fronting the Sorbonne entrance and have a coffee at one of the small cafés — it's great people watching as you spy on the life of a French student.

The hotel has small rooms outfitted in a kind of nondescript contemporary style, and small bathrooms, many with showers. All rooms have cable television.

The breakfast nook off of the entry on the main level has but four tables and a somewhat intimidating African totem. But again, it's perfectly serviceable and the staff is well used to foreigners.

Saint-Germain & Montparnasse
6th & 14th Arrondissements

An interesting blend of student, commercial, and residential interests, this quarter is at the center of the Left Bank and is probably best known to Americans as the favored stomping grounds for Lost Generation literary giants such as Hemingway and Fitzgerald.

HOTEL FINDS & FAVORITES

Of the spots we review in this chapter, we'd recommend the following hotels to those who want something special without signing away the farm.

3. JEU DE PAUME, *54 rue Saint-Louis-en-l'Ile (4th, M:Pont-Marie). Tel. 01.43.26.14.18, Fax 01.40.01.46.02.76.*

5. HÔTEL DES GRANDES ÉCOLES, *75 rue du Cardinal Lemoine (5th, M:Cardinal Lemoine). Tel. 01.43.26.79.23, Fax 01.43.25.28.15.*

6. HÔTEL DES GRANDS HOMMES, *17 place du Panthéon (5th, M:Luxembourg or Sorbonne). Tel. 01.46.34.19.60, Fax 01.43.26.67.32.*

10. HÔTEL LE RELAIS SAINT-GERMAIN, *9 carrefour de l'Odéon (6th, M:Odéon). Tel. 01.43.29.12.05, Fax 01.46.33.01.45.30.*

15. HÔTEL DE NESLE, *7 rue de Nesle (6th, M:Odéon or Saint-Michel). Tel. 01.43.54.62.41. Fax 01.43.54.31.88.*

23. DUC DE SAINT-SIMON, *14 rue de Saint-Simon (7th, M:Rue du Bac). Tel. 01.44.39.20.20, Fax 01.45.48.68.25.*

28. LA TRÉMOILLE, *14 rue de la Trémoille (8th, M:Alma-Marceau). Tel. 01.47.23.34.20, Fax 01.40.70.01.08.*

32. SAINT JAMES PARIS, *43 avenue Bugeaud (16th, M:Victor Hugo), 01.44.05.81.81, Fax 01.44.05.81.82.*

35. EBER MONCEAU, *18 rue Léon Jost (17th, M:Courcelles), 01.46.22.60.70, Fax: 01.47.63.01.01.*

37. HÔTEL BRIGHTON, *218 rue de Rivoli (1st, M:Tuileries), 01.47.03.61.61, Fax 01.42.60.41.78.*

01.46. PAVILLON DE LA REINE, *28 place des Vosges (3rd, M:Chemin Vert), 01.40.29.19.19, Fax 01.40.29.19.20.*

Their old haunts are still very much alive — the cafés especially still profit from the Lost Generation mystique. Along the boulevard Saint-Germain and, further south, the boulevard du Montparnasse, you'll find such familiar sounding places as **Le Deux Magots**, the **Café Flore**, **Le Select**, **La Coupole**, **Le Polidor**, and **La Closerie des Lilas** (see "Literary Legacies" sidebar in Chapter 10, *Where to Eat*.)

The **Luxembourg Garden** in this quarter is Paris's favorite, and rightly so. The grounds are beautifully kept with brilliantly colored flower beds, tranquil hideaways, and a busy central pool where children push toy sailboats with long sticks. The **Saint-Germain-des-Prés** and **Saint-Sulpice** churches are also in this quarter.

Between the boulevard Saint-Germain and the river is a bustling commercial neighborhood that includes dozens of galleries with original art — much of it overpriced, but still worth a look.

There are several very good hotels here, allowing you to profit from the variety of the neighborhood, its many restaurants and clubs, and its proximity to the rest of the city. In fact, if you're a Left Bank type, this is probably what you're looking for.

9. ODÉON HÔTEL, *3 rue de l'Odéon (6th, M:Odéon). Tel. 01.43.25.90.67, Fax 01.43.25.55.98. Rooms: 33. Rates: 700-1,500FF. Breakfast: 60FF. No restaurant.*

The Odéon Hotel is in a terrific location and would be a dream come true for those whose vision of early Parisian architecture is beamed ceilings. The 16th-century building was renovated a few years ago and, though the beams are a nice touch, the designers might have done something to enlarge the narrow hallways and tiny rooms.

The rooms do, however, have plugs adaptable to American computers and two telephone lines so you won't have to miss that important client while you're on the phone with your partner.

Rooms are air-conditioned, which is uncommon in Paris despite the summer humidity. English is spoken.

10. HÔTEL LE RELAIS SAINT-GERMAIN, *9 carrefour de l'Odéon (6th, M:Odéon). Tel. 01.43.29.12.05, Fax 01.46.33.01.45.30. Rooms: 22. Rates: 1,280-1,930FF. Breakfast included. No restaurant.*

This is hotel heaven.

If you want good taste, style, elegance, period furniture, big rooms, huge closets and storage space where you can keep your luggage and purchases, breakfast any time of the day in a sunny setting that allows for lots of people-watching, great service, and even a small library in case you finish the book you brought, then you definitely want to be one of the lucky people to get a reservation at the Hôtel Le Relais Saint-Germain. Some rooms even have terraces.

The hôtelier, Monsieur Laipsker, is justifiably proud of his creation, which he continues to improve all the time. If you love charm and have some money to spend, this is a marvelous spot to settle in.

11. HÔTEL DE FLEURIE, *32-34 rue Grégoire de Tours (6th, M:Saint-Germain-des-Prés). Tel. 01.53.73.70.00, Fax 01.53.73.70.20. Rooms: 29. Rates: 800-1,400FF. Breakfast: 50FF. No restaurant.*

This is a charming hotel on the other side (away from the river) of the boulevard Saint-Germain. Its location makes it much quieter than other hotels in the area, but it is still just steps away from the action. The 18th-century building was completely renovated in 1989 and the result is a lovely setting with many modern and practical features (such as individual room controls for heat and air conditioning).

A light touch in the traditional furnishings is matched by the light color of the textured fabric wall covering and the marble in the baths, which come with mounted towel warmers (the less expensive rooms have more modest bathrooms with showers only). Each room also has a valet-pants presser.

The staff is friendly and English is spoken.

12. LEFT BANK HÔTEL, *9 rue de l'Ancienne Comédie (6th, M:Odéon). Tel. 01.43.54.01.70, Fax 01.43.26.17.14. Rooms: 31. Rates: 1,100-1,350FF. Breakfast: 30FF. No restaurant.*

Just a few doors up from Le Procope (one of the oldest restaurants in Paris), the Left Bank Hôtel welcomes you into a lobby that is pure charm. Although the decorators were somewhat heavy-handed in their application of the Empire style, many of the rooms are good sized and a few come with day beds that would be ideal for a couple traveling with a child. Some of the rooms have a delightful roofline view of Notre-Dame.

A fun location, where English is spoken and service is as important to the staff as it is to you. And surprise: this is part of the American Best Western chain.

13. HÔTEL BUCI LATIN, *34 rue de Buci (6th, M:Mabillion). Tel. 01.43.29.07.20, Fax 01.43.29.67.01.44. Rooms: 27. Rates: 1,100-1,300FF. Suites available. Breakfast included. Restaurant: coffee shop open until 6 p.m.*

Designed with a capital 'D' from top to bottom by a young Frenchman, Alain Perrier (whose work echoes that of Philippe Stark), the Buci Latin seems to have been created on the principle that both fun and form follow function.

The stairway is painted floor to ceiling with graffiti and the door to each room has its own distinctive paint job. Inside, the rooms are a nice size with lots of beautiful light wood and Haitian cotton spreads and wall hangings. The rooms on the street side are air conditioned (so you can close the windows on hot, noisy nights), but those on the rear courtyard are not.

The duplex and the junior suite are something to write home about. The upstairs bathroom in the duplex has a clawfooted tub, a gorgeous tiled stall shower, a double sink and a rattan vanity that will make you feel as if you're spending quality time in the tropics. All this on a mezzanine that overlooks the king size bed downstairs. The junior suite has a huge bedroom, a large circular whirlpool bath, and a tiny private terrace.

The English-speaking staff prides itself on offering excellent service, and the hotel is well-located in the beating heart of the neighborhood surrounding the Saint-Germain-des-Prés church.

The Buci also offers something very rare in Paris: rooms accessible to people in wheelchairs. Although management failed to install the rails that would make the shower and toilet areas of the bathroom safer, the rooms are larger, they're on the ground floor, they have extra wide doors and the showers are completely open.

14. RELAIS CHRISTINE, *3 rue Christine (6th, M:Odéon). Tel. 01.40.51.60.80, Fax 01.40.51.60.81. Rooms: 51. Rates: 2,000-2,400FF. Breakfast: 95FF. No restaurant.*

On a quiet street in one of Paris's most historic and picturesque Left Bank neighborhoods, the Relais Christine offers guests comfort, style, and top quality service — for a price, of course.

The building, a 16th-century cloister, has been transformed into a contemporary four-star luxury hotel without losing its historic charm. Each room is decorated slightly differently in a charming mélange of traditional French styles. In addition, each looks out onto a flower-filled courtyard.

The marble bathrooms are fit for royalty, which seems only appropriate since the street and the hotel are named for the second daughter of Henri IV and Marie de Medici. (Be sure to ask for the brochure — available in English — relating the history of the neighborhood, the street, and the hotel.)

The breakfast room, a converted basement with stone walls, vaulted ceiling, and suit of armor, vibrates with a sense of history. And bacon (or ham) and eggs are available for those on special high cholesterol diets.

The staff speaks English and is extremely eager to help. A suite and a duplex are available, as is a private garage.

15. HÔTEL DE NESLE, *7 rue de Nesle (6th, M:Odéon or Saint-Michel). Tel. 01.43.54.62.41. Fax 01.43.54.31.88. Rooms: 20. Rates: 400-600FF. Breakfast: included. No restaurant.*

The Hôtel de Nesle is not for everyone. For one thing, they don't take reservations (just show up around 10:30 a.m.), they don't speak English, and not a single member of the staff has benefited from a degree in hotel management.

But what the hotel does have are happy, satisfied customers who have enough money left over after they pay their hotel bill to enjoy Paris as they see fit. The hotel is located in as chic a neighborhood as the Left Bank offers. (Indeed, it's a stone's throw from the four-star Relais Christine.) The street is quiet, some of the rooms look out on a rose garden (populated by two live ducks at no extra charge), and the sheets on the freshly made beds are immaculately white.

The place is charming but funky. Almost all of the rooms are painted with nearly life-sized murals depicting various scenes from French history. All have sinks, and many also have toilets and tubs and showers. It's possible to share a two-bed room with a stranger and pay only 130FF per night, breakfast included. A couple of large rooms will accommodate four people for only 450FF.

If you're young or young at heart and on a shoestring budget, you'd feel at home.

16. HÔTEL SAINT-GERMAIN-DES-PRÉS, *36 rue Bonaparte (6th, M:Saint-Germain-des-Prés). Tel. 01.43.26.00.19, Fax 01.40.01.46.83.63. Rooms: 30. Rates: 780-1,350FF. Breakfast: 50FF. No restaurant.*

Just steps away from Les Deux Magots and the lively center of Saint-Germain, this pleasant hotel has a lovely, antique-filled lobby to welcome you and a cozy breakfast room to help you start each day. The reception staff is English-speaking and, while not warm and fuzzy, they are efficient and clearly want to be of service.

The rooms are generally small, but are bright and gay thanks to the color schemes and patterns of the wallpaper, rugs, and bedspreads. The large armoires have enough space for clothes and suitcases. While the sitting rooms of the suites (1,300-1,600FF) are on the small side, the bedrooms are spacious and comfortable.

Many guests are repeat customers, so clearly the Hôtel Saint-Germain-des-Prés is doing something right.

17. HÔTEL DE L'ABBAYE, *10 rue Cassette (6th, M:Saint-Sulpice). Tel. 01.45.01.44.38.11, Fax 01.45.48.07.86. Rooms: 01.46. Rates: 1,100-1,700FF. Suites available. Breakfast included. No restaurant.*

This 18th-century residence gets more and more charming as time goes by. The standard rooms are not huge, but the suites are very comfortable and the four duplex suites come with private terraces. Room number four, a large one, has its own lovely private garden. And the view from the terraces of the suites is quintessentially Parisian. In fact, you can see the top of Saint-Sulpice's bell towers.

In good weather, you can enjoy breakfast in the slate courtyard at the center of the hotel. Or you can order room service for breakfast or light meals any time you like.

The decor of the rooms is not wildly distinctive — no antiques, for example — but they are quietly elegant. The real draw, aside from the charm of the common areas and the extremely friendly and helpful staff, is that the Hôtel de l'Abbaye, while situated in the heart of Saint-Germain, offers an oasis of tranquillity in one of the world's most frenetic cities.

18. HÔTEL LE SAINT-GRÉGOIRE, *43 rue de l'Abbé-Grégoire (6th, M:Saint-Placide). Tel. 01.45.48.23.23, Fax 01.45.48.33.95. Rooms: 20. Rates: 900-1,500FF. Suite available. Breakfast: 60FF. No restaurant.*

Although in the heart of Paris and near many of the 6th *arrondissement's* most famous attractions, the Hôtel Le Saint-Grégoire is tucked away in a quiet corner where few tourists (other than hotel guests) venture.

The decorating style in the larger-than-average rooms relies on a pleasant mix of antiques and modern pieces. Some rooms have wonderful private terraces. The junior suite (excellent for a party of three, at 1,390FF) has a small terrace on the courtyard. When asked what made his hotel different from all the others, François de Bene, the manager, replied that "the Saint-Grégoire is more like a home than a hotel." Given his friendliness and eagerness to please, it's an apt description.

An added advantage is that the hotel is near a few bargain-priced retailers. Look for the words *stock* and *dégriffé* in the windows — they are akin to American stores that offer brand name and last season's discontinued designer clothes at cut rates.

Near the Eiffel Tower
7th Arrondissement

At a little more than 27,000FF per square meter, this is the priciest real estate in the city. It's surprising in a way because so much is residential and because the character is not nearly as stuffy or snooty as some of the Right Bank neighborhoods.

Maybe in part because of the real estate, this neighborhood is safe, clean, attractive, and less crowded than others — though there is a large enclave of government agencies that clog up the eastern half of the *arrondissement* with walled-off buildings, official cars, and intimidating well-armed guards.

The **Eiffel Tower** (*La Tour Eiffel*) is here, of course, as is the **Hôtel des Invalides**, which is the massive complex that includes a gigantic golden dome under which you will find Napoleon's tomb. The **Musée Rodin**, dedicated to the sculptor, and the **Musée d'Orsay**, the converted rail station where the best of the country's Impressionist works are housed, are must-sees on any itinerary.

This is also where many of the enormous barge-like tour boats leave on their hour-long trips up and down the river. Taking a boat may sound a bit touristy, but the experience is well worth the price (see Chapter 6, *Basic Information*).

There are a handful of very good restaurants and some trendy hotels near the Musée d'Orsay and the Tour Eiffel. And, whether it's for better or worse, you're likely to bump into a bunch of Americans here — and not just tourists. This is where a large part of Paris's American population has nested.

19. MONTALEMBERT, *3 rue de Montalembert (7th, M:Rue du Bac). Tel. 01.45.49.68.68, Fax 01.45.49.69.49. Rooms: 48. Rates: 1,750-2,300FF. Suites available. Breakfast: 100FF. Restaurant.*

It's your honeymoon, your anniversary, your special gift to yourself. Whatever the occasion, the Montalembert will make it memorable and make you feel special.

This well-located luxury hotel offers a range of services not usually found outside the grand hotels such as the Ritz or Crillon. The Montalembert also has the added benefit of being less stuffy ... er, *formal*, than the deluxe hotels.

The special pluses include 24-hour room service, air conditioning, VCRs and a video library, valet service, two private rooms which can be used for meetings or private dining, and convenient parking. These pluses make up for the less-than-huge (but not small) rooms.

In addition to the special services, an energetic and English-speaking staff is available to respond to your every need.

The one warning here involves the choice between rooms appointed in what management calls "the traditional French style" or the modern style. Go traditional. If you do, you'll feel like you're living a Parisian dream. If you choose modern, you might as well be at a Hilton in any city in the world.

20. BAC SAINT-GERMAIN, *66 rue du Bac (7th, M:Rue du Bac). Tel. 01.42.22.20.03, Fax 01.45.48.52.30. Rooms: 21. Rates: 590-890FF. Breakfast: 79FF. No restaurant.*

Don't be put off by the unimposing entrance of this well-located small hotel (virtually on the corner of rue du Bac and boulevard Saint-Germain). Take the elevator up one flight to the reception and lobby area and you'll be in good hands with the friendly staff that speaks excellent English.

The rooms are good sized and the double-paned windows dampen the street noise. The real prize here is the eighth-floor terrace, part of which is glass enclosed and which offers a classic view of the Paris roofline.

Breakfast is served on the terrace and the staff is amenable to its use by guests at virtually any hour. Stop at a local wine store, make a special selection, and take the elevator to the top. Pop the cork, settle in, and you'll feel like a native in no time.

21. HÔTEL SAINT-GERMAIN, *88 rue du Bac (7th, M:Rue du Bac). Tel. 01.49.54.70.00, Fax 01.45.48.26.89. Rooms: 29. Rates: 550-900FF. Breakfast: 40FF. No restaurant.*

Apparently there are more than a dozen hotels with this same name in Paris, so if you want to avoid ending up somewhere other than here, memorize your address. This particular Hôtel Saint-Germain combines a reasonable price and good location with a welcoming touch of elegance. The best bets are the rooms on the courtyard. This isn't because they're quieter (double panes on all the windows take care of that problem), but because all these bathrooms have been renovated and are quite stunning.

The baths in the other rooms are cramped and, by American standards, old-fashioned.

This Hôtel Saint-Germain has been a hotel for thirty years, and the building has been in the same family for two hundred years. English, Spanish, and German are spoken – probably even some French.

22. HÔTEL LIBERTEL BELLECHASSE, *8 rue de Bellechasse (7th, M:Solférino). Tel. 01.45.50.22.31, Fax 01.45.51.52.36. Rooms: 41. Rates: 965-1,250FF. Breakfast: 75FF. No restaurant.*

If you plan to make an extensive visit to the Musée d'Orsay (which we score as the city's most architecturally interesting large art museum), this is the hotel for you. It's half a block down from that bright jewel in Paris's cultural crown.

Recently renovated, the hotel's public areas offer lots of glass and chrome. The rooms are small and, if you happen to get one of those decorated in a deep gray wallpaper, a little on the dark side. Ask for a yellow room and your visit will seem sun-filled even if the weather doesn't cooperate (which it frequently doesn't).

The staff is friendly and English is spoken, which is helpful because most guests are American.

23. DUC DE SAINT-SIMON, *14 rue de Saint-Simon (7th, M:Rue du Bac). Tel. 01.44.39.20.20, Fax 01.45.48.68.25. Rooms: 29. Rates: 1,400-1,550FF. Suites available. Breakfast: 70FF. No restaurant.*

More than half of the Duc de Saint-Simon's guests are American, so it's hardly undiscovered. But that fact also attests to how exquisite this small hotel is.

Although the rooms are not large, they are decorated in style. Each bedstead and dresser appears to have been personally selected, as if it were meant to decorate the home of an individual with discerning taste. Indeed, the sitting rooms of the suites are very impressive.

Four regular rooms (numbers 14, 24, 25, and 42) come with private terraces that would be the ideal spot for a romantic rendezvous.

You can enjoy breakfast in your room, or in what was, in the 17th century, a coal and wine cellar. Room service is also available for light meals all day. The reception staff speaks excellent English. Reservations as much as a month in advance are necessary in peak season.

If you're lucky, one of the Americans you will run into will be one of America's most famous actresses. We're told she stays at the Duc de Saint-

Simon frequently. At first, you may not see her. You may just hear that unforgettably husky voice that recalls film classics such as *To Have and Have Not.*

24. HÔTEL LATOUR-MAUBOURG, *150 rue de Grenelle (7th M:Latour-Maubourg). Tel. 01.47.05.16.16, Fax 01.47.05.16.14. Rooms: 10. Rates: 950-1,200FF. Suite available. Breakfast included. No restaurant.*

This tiny hotel, once a residence, was completely renovated inside and opened in 1994 to guests — among the more famous past visitors being the late Allen Ginsberg. As its owners like to say, it does combine "yesterday's charm and the convenience of tomorrow." Its mansards and high ceilings are typical of 19th-century Parisian architecture, and they have outfitted the rooms with extra telephone plugs for your laptop or fax machine.

Most of the rooms look out on the magnificent golden dome of Invalides, as well as its grassy, popular esplanade leading to the Seine and across the river to the Grand Palais. In the other direction, you are within easy reach of the rue Cler street market and the Tour Eiffel.

The rooms are of a good size and feature full-length mirrors, color TV, mini-bars, good closets, and feather duvets. Rooms on the courtyard side are remarkably tranquil for a hotel near the heart of the city.

25. HÔTEL LE TOURVILLE, *16 avenue de Tourville (7th, M:École Militaire). Tel. 01.47.05.62.62, Fax 01.47.05.01.43.90. Rooms: 30. Rates: 900-2,000FF. Suites available. Breakfast: 60FF. No restaurant.*

The owners of the Hôtel Le Tourville are committed to making their hotel the best it can be, and their quest for quality shows. The average-size rooms are warmly decorated in soft colors (yellow, sand, or pink schemes), and the well-outfitted bathrooms have classy marble touches. Antique armoires and dressers add a touch of elegance to the modern bed and nightstand arrangements.

Easily the nicest double rooms are the four with private terraces. But at these prices, they're not exactly a bargain, especially if you happen to come during a stretch of wet or cool weather. The two junior suites are good for families, with beds enough to sleep four. They also have whirlpool baths, stall showers, and double sinks.

The Tourville, which was renovated in 1993, is charming, the staff seems eager to help, and the location is very good (near sights, the Métro, and a cab stand). But it seemed a wee bit overpriced. Perhaps that reflects

PARIS HOTELS (Southwest)

Key

18. Hôtel Le Saint-Grégoire
22. Hôtel Libertel Bellechasse
23. Duc de Saint-Simon
24. Hôtel Latour-Maubourg
25. Hôtel Le Tourville
26. Hôtel Splendid
27. Hôtel La Bourdonnais

the fourth star the hotel was granted from the national hotel board in 1994.

26. HÔTEL SPLENDID, *29 avenue de Tourville (7th, M:École Militaire). Tel. 01.45.51.29.29, Fax 01.44.18.94.60. Rooms: 48. Rates: 630-990FF. Suites available. Breakfast: 55FF. No restaurant.*

Of all the hotels we visited, the newly renovated and spiffy Splendid is the only one that conceded up front that it would negotiate its rates. So, if you hate to pay full price, here's your chance to bargain.

Located in the heart of the 7th *arrondissement*, the Splendid offers guests an excellent example of a "Haussmann" style building (Haussmann was the brilliant city planner who redesigned the city in the late 1800s and whose name is often used to describe the classic architectural style the city is best known for) with the most modern of interiors.

Renovated in 1992, the Splendid's furnishings are reproductions of simple Art Deco pieces. The feel of the hotel is very new, so if you're after Old World charm you might want to consider another place.

If a room with a view of the Tour Eiffel is something you've dreamed of, then you'll want Room 307. There are also three suites, two of which have views of the Tower, that are well-suited for the business traveler who needs a fax and computer-adaptable plugs. The Splendid's staff is friendly and ready to serve.

27. HÔTEL LA BOURDONNAIS, *111 avenue de al Bourdonnais (7th, M:École Militaire). Tel. 01.47.05.01.45.42, Fax 01.45.55.75.54. Rooms: 60. Rates: 600-800FF. Breakfast: 35FF. Fine restaurant.*

A popular home-away-from-home for many of its returning American guests, La Bourdonnais is less than elegant but is still homey and cozy. It is a short walk from the Tour Eiffel, Invalides, and the market street Rue Cler. It also boasts La Cantine des Gourmets, a restaurant that has earned a prized Michelin star for its cuisine that features everything from light seafood dishes to the hearty fare of Southwestern France.

Many enjoy the interior garden for breakfast, afternoon tea, or just sitting. The rooms, many of which have recenlty been renovated, are reasably priced and of average size and decor. Double-pane windows keep street noise to a minimum — though this is a relatively quiet neighborhood in the evening anyway. There are minibars in some rooms, and most have good-sized closets.

On the down side, there is no air conditioning, which in the dead of summer can be a real drawback.

RIGHT BANK
Near the Champs-Élysées
8th & 16th Arrondissements

Chic and historic. And often expensive.

First for the chic. Just south (toward the river) of the famous Champs-Élysées is the **Golden Triangle**, formed by the **Champs-Élysées, avenue George V**, and **avenue Montaigne**. Here are several of the very finest and most expensive upper crust hotels. And along **François 1er**, the street that cuts the triangle in half, are many of the clothing designers you've read about in the fashion mags.

Window-shopping is a passionate pastime here, and the largely residential avenues themselves are some the most handsome in all of Paris.

Above the Champs-Élysées, the streets are a bit less grand, but still affluent, with lots of restaurants and clubs that are generally trendier with the tourists than they are with the locals.

Unfortunately, the Champs-Élysées itself can be a bit of a disappointment, with overpriced shops, fast food outlets, car dealerships, and largely unthinking, unfriendly crowds. Still, at either end of the avenue, you will find some of the city's most memorable sights — the **Arc de Triomphe** to the west and the **Place de la Concorde** to the east.

The nearby grand **Trocadéro**, always humming with rollerskaters, mimes, artists, and strollers, is also in this quarter, as is the **Grand Palais des Beaux Arts**, the magnificent **Madeleine church**, the **American Embassy** and even the US Ambassador's residence.

28. LA TRÉMOILLE, *14 rue la Trémoille (8th, M:Alma-Marceau). Tel. 01.47.23.34.20, Fax 01.40.70.01.08. Rooms: 107. Rates for a double: 2,300-3,400FF. Breakfast: 100FF. Restaurant.*

If you have four legs, a tail, ears that fold over and you answer to the name of Norton, then you have stayed at this dream-come-true four-star luxury hotel. Yes, this is where *The Cat Who Went to Paris* stayed. The hero of Peter Gethers' charming (to cat lovers, that is) book is fondly remembered here.

In the heart of the ultra-rich Golden Triangle area of the ritzy Right Bank, the Hôtel de la Trémoille seems to have everything a four-star luxury hotel should have without the snooty formal atmosphere that permeates some others. The rooms are enormous and beautiful and each one is different. The suites are quite literally breathtaking.

The common areas of the hotel are the very definition of elegance, the restaurant offers a varied menu at surprisingly low prices (relative to the cost of the rooms), and the hotel has full conference facilities.

But it is the staff that truly distinguishes the Trémoille. Management and reception teams are graduates of Europe's finest hotel management programs. Each and every person who works here strives to learn the names, as well as the tastes of each guest.

29. HÔTEL ÉLYSÉES RÉGENCIA, *41 avenue Marceau (16th, M:Georges V). Tel. 01.47.20.01.42.65, Fax 49.52.03.01.42. Rooms: 41. Rates: 800-,1050FF. Breakfast: 80-120FF. No restaurant.*

This is a very chic neighborhood, filled with dramatic apartment buildings, expensive restaurants and, along nearby François 1er, some of the most dazzling fashion boutiques in the world. It is also a short stroll to the Arc de Triomphe a few blocks to the north and the Seine a few blocks to the south.

Though the Régencia might seem a bit steep in price, it is actually quite reasonable for this area, where the *grandes dames* of hotels charge two or three times as much. Though there are classic touches in the arched lobby area and even in some of the furnishings, this hotel has a contemporary feel to it. Fittingly, it also boasts all the modern conveniences — air conditioning, double-paned windows to keep the noise out, marble baths, a laundry service, private safe, fax service, cable TV, etc. The rooms are even somewhat larger than average.

30. HÔTEL MAJESTIC, *29 rue Dumont d'Urville (16th, M:Kléber). Tel. 01.45.00.83.70, Fax 01.45.00.29.48. Rooms: 30. Rates: 1,070-1,550FF. Suites available. Breakfast: 60FF. No restaurant.*

The Hôtel Majestic is unlike any other hotel we visited. Having said that, we will note that what distinguishes it from the competition may or may not be your cup of tea.

Both the common areas and the rooms in this four-star hotel seem more like the bedrooms and salons of a private home than a place where strangers stop off briefly. The furnishings, the carpeting, even the color schemes reflect a personal rather than a calculating professional eye.

Of course, that's exactly what many travelers prefer. The caveat is that the Majestic's rooms look like they were decorated by one's formal, affluent, and old-fashioned French aunt. They're charming, but in a way that may not be to everyone's taste.

What would be to everyone's liking is the size of the rooms. The standard doubles are roomy, the doubles with a "lounge combined" are spacious, the suites are enormous, and the Penthouse, which also has a big balcony, is out of this world.

The reception staff speaks English, the street is extremely quiet but is still close to the action.

31. HÔTEL ALEXANDER, *102 avenue Victor Hugo (16th, M:Victor Hugo). Tel. 01.45.53.64.65, Fax 01.45.53.12.51. Rooms: 62. Rates: 900-1,590FF. Breakfast: 75FF. No restaurant.*

Just off of the charming Victor Hugo circle, the Hôtel Alexander is something of a surprise. From the looks of the tasteful, but tiny lobby, the Alexander doesn't seem quite as grand as many other four stars. Although it's in a chic neighborhood, it's nothing like the Trémoille, for example, or even the Relais Christine on the Left Bank.

But it does have advantages. The rooms are a good size and are tastefully decorated. The bathrooms are enormous and each shower/tub combination has a shower curtain. This isn't really the petty thing it might seem. Very few French shower/tubs have curtains and most Americans, unfamiliar with how to use a hand-held shower without something protecting the rest of the bathroom, end up swimming from the tub to the door after they've bathed.

The curtain, we're told, is also evidence that the management aims to please and knows what Americans expect. In addition to the large bathrooms, the Alexander offers large televisions and roomy armoires. Another small plus is the courtyard where you can take your breakfast in good weather and onto which some of the rooms face.

The reception staff speaks excellent English. Well-located if you prefer the Right Bank.

32. SAINT JAMES PARIS, *43 avenue Bugeaud (16th, M:Victor Hugo).*
Tel. 01.44.05.81.81, Fax 01.44.05.81.82. Rooms: 48. Rates: 1,900-2,300FF.
Suites available. Breakfast: 115FF. Restaurant.

First rate — a hotel for a special occasion. The Saint James, owned by
the French family that manages Le Relais Christine and Le Pavillon de la
Reine, is a magnificent converted château built in 1892 in memory of
Adolphe Thiers, the French president from 1852 through 1857. Initially
it housed scholars, then was made into a private club, before it was
transformed in 1991 into a hotel.

Inside a grand staircase rises from the large, but clearly clubby styled
lobby with its groups of leather chairs. The Library Bar continues the feel
of the grand club, with more groups of leather chairs and two stories
worth of bound volumes, leading right up to the coffered ceiling.The
restaurant continues the theme of exclusivity and elegance, and, in good
weather, guests can dine on the terrace under the huge canvas umbrellas.

There is a gym and conference room — in case this is a business trip
for you. And the rooms themselves are mostly spacious, with double-sink
bathrooms, floor-to-ceiling mirrors, and all of the amenities you would
expect of a first-rate hotel.

The location is both a plus and a minus. This is a lovely and expensive
neighborhood about midway between the Bois de Boulogne and the Arc
de Triomphe. It is also tranquil and there's plenty of window-shopping to
be done nearby. The down side is that the Saint James is a bit on the edge
of the city, so might not have the convenience wanted by visitors seeking
a central location where most of the major sights are within short walking
distance. Still, this is the kind of place that fond and romantic memories
are made of.

33. HÔTEL CENTRE VILLE ÉTOILE, *6 rue des Acacias (17th,
M:Argentine). Tel. 01.43.80.56.18, Fax 01.47.54.93.01.43. Rooms: 16. Rates:
690-890FF. Breakfast: 55FF. No restaurant.*

This small hotel is pleasant and appears to be well-managed, but really
doesn't have a whole lot to distinguish it. The common areas and the
rooms are so modern that you could be anywhere and, because not a
single room faces the street, you can't even soak up Parisian ambiance
staring out the window.

The fact that all the rooms are on a courtyard also tends to keep them
pretty dark throughout the day.

PARIS HOTELS (Northwest)

Key

28. La Trémoille
29. Hôtel Élysées Régencia
30. Hôtel Majestic
31. Hôtel Alexander
32. Saint James Paris
33. Hôtel Centre Ville Étoile
34. Hôtel Cécilia
35. Eber Monceau
36. Hôtel Mayfair

The location, however, is not bad if you like the Right Bank. The Arc de Triomphe, for instance, is right around the corner — as is one of the main Air France bus terminals, from which you can be quickly whisked away to the airports.

34. HÔTEL CÉCILIA, *11 avenue MacMahon (17th, M:Charles-de-Gaulle). Tel. 01.43.80.32.10, Fax 01.40.53.05.96. Rooms: 48. Rates: 780-880FF. Breakfast: 50FF. No restaurant.*

Just around the corner from the Arc de Triomphe, the mid-sized Cécilia is ideally located for those folks who want to browse the shops of the Champs Élysées (or better yet the chic boutiques that line nearby avenue François 1er). It's also quite reasonably priced, which has made it popular with business people who come to town for the remarkable annual Paris air show, as well as the seasonal fashion shows.

The lobby has hints of elegance in its wood paneling, mosaic-tiled floor, and carved steeds the size of horses on a merry-go-round. The rooms themselves are unexceptional but clean and comfortable, featuring double-glazed windows to reduce noise, double sinks in some rooms, and better-than-average closet space. There are also color TVs and hair dryers in each room.

35. EBER MONCEAU, *18 rue Léon Jost (17th, M:Courcelles). Tel. 01.46.22.60.70, Fax: 01.47.63.01.01. Rooms: 18. Rates: 550-850FF. Breakfast: 50FF. No restaurant, but an arrangement with a restaurant a couple of doors down allows for full room service until 10 p.m.*

Maybe you've always dreamed of coming to Paris but you've put it off because you don't speak French or you get lost in big cities. If that's the case, this is the hotel for you. Jean-Marc Eber, the owner, lives to ensure that his guests have the most outstanding Parisian vacation possible. He maintains a library of guide books which he loans out. He recommends restaurants, makes reservations, and runs interference with the more difficult locals because he genuinely likes his guests.

The standard doubles are fine without being exceptional. The three *appartements* and the two suites are ideal for families. Some rooms have terraces, some skylights. All have a French-style sofa bed in the sitting room that is called a *clic-clac* and makes a surprisingly comfortable fold-out bed. In addition, they have enormous closet space for stashing luggage as well as hanging clothes.

Not far from the Arc de Triomphe and the lovely Place des Ternes, the Hôtel Eber is a real find.

Near the Louvre
1st & 2nd Arrondissements

This quarter is steeped in monuments to French history and culture, led, naturally, by the **Musée du Louvre**. We're still not great fans of I.M. Pei's glass pyramid and the shallow surrounding fountains that hose down visitors at the slightest breeze. But the new **Richelieu wing** is a great triumph, as are the below-ground shops where you can find everything from Lalique glass to affordable antique prints.

The freshly restored **Jardin des Tuileries**, with its many fountains and statues guarding bright patches of green lawn, is here, of course, running west out of the mouth of the Louvre. The **Palais Royal**, with its enormous enclosed garden, is just north of the Louvre, and the truly elegant **Place Vendôme** is a few blocks west. The fabulously sumptuous **Opéra Garnier** is also just north of the Vendôme.

Lots of Americans stay in the high end hotels on and just off the **rue de Rivoli** here, and there's no question they are elegant, usually with fine dining no further than the lobby. You'll have no trouble finding jewels, antiques, and *haute couture* here either.

On the down side, this is largely a business quarter (in fact, this was the first neighborhood in the city to be dominated by commerce), made even more congested by zillions of tourists. And the prices of just about everything are unusually steep.

36. HÔTEL MAYFAIR, *3 rue Rouget-de-Lisle (1st, M:Tuileries). Tel. 01.42.60.38.14, Fax 01.40.15.04.78. Rooms: 53. Rates: 1,100FF. Suites available. Breakfast: 85FF. No restaurant.*

The Mayfair has some of the feel of a palace-style hotel. Huge Oriental rugs and plush green furnishings greet you in the reception area. The salon/bar has a parquet floor and red leather-tiled ceiling. The small elevator is nicely appointed with fabric wall coverings.

The rooms are also quite nice, with fabric wall coverings, king-sized beds, and roomy off-white marble bathrooms. Safes, minibars, cable television, towel-warmers, and air-conditioning are standard. Two floors are also designated non-smoking floors, which is daring for a hotel in Paris, where many locals still smoke like fiends.

The service is attentive and the location is convenient to most of the major Right Bank sights. On the down side: for a hotel of this stature and at this price, it could do with a little sprucing up. Some of the common areas especially are beginning to look a bit overused and tired.

37. HÔTEL BRIGHTON, *218 rue de Rivoli (1st, M:Tuileries). Tel. 01.47.03.61.61, Fax 01.42.60.41.78. Rooms: 70. Rates: 700-950FF. Breakfast included. No restaurant.*

The rooms on the rue de Rivoli side of this large hotel overlook the Tuileries gardens and open up onto a view that stretches from I.M. Pei's glass pyramid at the center of the Louvre to the Arc de Triomphe and, on clear days, the Grande Arche of La Défense beyond. At night, the view gets even better, with the Tour Eiffel across the river bathed in light.

A Japanese firm bought the Brighton a few years ago and refinished the lovely salon with its striking marbled columns and coffered ceiling off of the entry. Many of the rooms have also been spruced up.

In general the rooms are especially large, with high ceilings, lots of period furnishings, chandeliers, and ample closet space. And most of the rooms with views have a small balcony. Room 216 is particularly grand.

The bathrooms, too, are enormous by Paris standards. Though often done in a rather sterile white tile reminiscent of a health club, they feature large tubs with hand-held showers, sometimes double sinks, bidets, and convenient small benches.

Even the location is good — especially for a Right Bank hotel. True, the rue de Rivoli is a mob-scene of tourists, but you can easily stroll to just about any Right Bank attraction from here.

Remember to request a room with a view.

38. HÔTEL VENDÔME, *1 place Vendôme (1st, M:Tuileries). Tel. 01.55.04.55.00, Fax 01.49.27.97.89. Rooms: 22. Rates: 2,300-3,200FF. Suites available. Breakfast included. Small restaurant.*

A very well-known hotel with a stunning address, just a few paces off the magnificent Place Vendôme. If you want to shop for a few expensive baubles, maybe a diamond tiara or two, this is the perfect neighborhood.

The hotel puts on a show of elegance as well, with high ceilings, elaborate molding on the ceilings and walls, and several period pieces and chandeliers in the rooms. Even brass beds and marble fireplaces are available in some rooms. And some bathrooms have double sinks and most are about as roomy as you'll find in Paris.

Still, the common areas could use a little freshening up. And the salon, where you can grab a sandwich, sip a cocktail, or even dine on various unimaginative pasta dishes, seems a bit grim with its black leather banquettes and aging red carpet. An amusing historical detail: this building, constructed in 1699 by the architect to Louis XIV, housed the Republic of Texas Embassy in 1842–1843!

39. HÔTEL DES TUILERIES, *10 rue Saint-Hyacinthe (1st, M:Tuileries). Tel. 01.42.61.04.17, Fax 49.27.91.56. Rooms: 26. Rates: 990-1,400FF. Breakfast: 50FF. No restaurant.*

Located just above the Tuileries, near the Louvre, the Opéra Garnier, the Place Vendôme, and other Right Bank sights, this hotel is a bit like someone's private residence. Each room is decorated differently (wallpapers change room to room). Sometimes the concept is a great success; sometimes you wonder what the decorator was thinking.

Still, this is a very friendly hotel converted from an 18th-century residence. It is run by an attentive staff and boasts several extra features — air conditioning, a trouser press in every room, large closets and space underneath to stow your bags, and double-glazed windows to subdue the noise. Room number 1 even has a jacuzzi-tub.

Pleasant common areas, with a small sitting area on the main floor and a breakfast room in the former basement.

40. LE STENDAHL, *22 rue Danielle Casanova (2nd, M:Opéra). Tel. 01.44.58.52.52, Fax 01.44.58.52.00. Rooms: 20. Suite available. Rates: 1,580-2,000FF. Breakfast: 95FF. No restaurant.*

Let's start with the bad news: this hotel is extremely expensive. In every other way, it is a magnificent small hotel.

The location on an uncrowded street near the elegant Place Vendôme is just a few blocks from the Opéra Garnier, the Madeleine, the Place de la Concorde, and the Tuileries. Every room is immaculate and filled with light, and the general decor is stylish and classy — down to the matching curtains and bedspreads and the sophisticated tile chosen for the bathrooms (bathrobes are also included). The hotel even offers wooden hangers in its large armoires, which are also fitted out with drawers for your socks and other items.

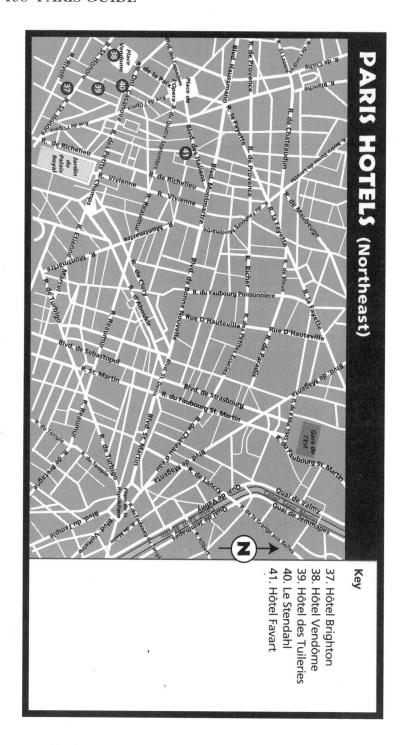

PARIS HOTELS (Northeast)

Key

37. Hôtel Brighton
38. Hôtel Vendôme
39. Hôtel des Tuileries
40. Le Stendahl
41. Hôtel Favart

Air conditioning, minibars, cable television, and small safes are standard. A folder in each room advises guests where to eat and shop, as well as how to get around and use the public telephones. Last but not least: the inviting salon/bar has been decorated as a small library featuring copies of every volume Stendahl ever wrote.

41. HÔTEL FAVART, *5 rue Marivaux (1st, M:Richelieu-Drouot). Tel. 01.42.97.59.83, Fax 01.40.15.95.58. Rooms: 37. Rates: 510-625FF. Breakfast: 20FF. No restaurant.*

A plaque affixed beside the entrance to this hotel proudly proclaims that the master Spanish painter Francisco Goya stayed here in the summer of 1824. The Favart also faces the historic Opéra Comique, a fabulous classic performance hall.

The Favart was redecorated only five years ago, and the entry area still looks fresh and welcoming. The *trompe l'oeil* behind the reception desk and another up the staircase, which also has a handsome wrought-iron railing, are extremely well executed.

The rooms are rather large, with beamed ceilings, fabric on the walls, good-sized closets, and bathrooms with tubs equipped with hand-held showers. The furnishings aren't exactly chic, but neither are they dowdy.

The location is just a few blocks above the Opéra Garnier and the Madeleine. Up sidestreets to the north, you'll spot the imposing elongated onion domes of Sacré-Coeur. The Métro stop is a few doors away, giving you easy access to the rest of the city.

42. HÔTEL DE LA PLACE DU LOUVRE, *21 rue des Prêtres Saint-Germain l'Auxerrois (1st, M:Louvre). Tel. 01.42.33.78.68, Fax 01.42.33.09.95. Rooms: 20. Rates: 540-880FF. Breakfast: 45FF. No restaurant.*

In honor of its proximity to the Louvre, this hotel has named each room for a famous French painter and decorated each room with prints of that painter's work (though the painters are from the modern era, which is poorly represented at the Louvre). The hotel's proximity to the Louvre is one of its big selling points. Rooms in the front of the building can get a glimpse of the Louvre and look out on a sideview of the Saint-Germain l'Auxerrois church.

The hotel occupies a tiny street located virtually in the heart of Paris, so the Île de la Cité, the Musée d'Orsay, the Opéra Garnier, the Pompidou Center and other attractions are a short walk away.

The decor, redone in 1988, is *très* modern. The foyer is dominated by a pastel mural along one rippling stone wall. The faint colors suggests Cubist shapes and shadows. Even the decor of the downstairs breakfast room, the 14th-century Cellar of the Musketeers, is mod.

Rooms are on the smallish size and have minibars and televisions (no cable). Bathrooms are also a bit small, but are comfortable and have tubs with hand-held showers.

43. HÔTEL LE RELAIS DU LOUVRE, *19 rue des Prêtres Saint-Germain l'Auxerrois (1st, M:Louvre). Tel. 01.40.41.96.42, Fax 01.40.41.96.01.44. Rooms: 20. Rates: 650-1,500FF. Breakfast in your room only: 60FF. No restaurant.*

This is a gay and charming little hotel located on a tiny street directly behind the Louvre. Though the street itself is a bit dull, its central location puts you within an easy walk of several major monuments and museums — Notre-Dame, the Palais Royal, and Pont Neuf among them. The famous Samaritaine department store, with its rooftop terrace, is just a few doors away as well.

Only a few years old, the Relais du Louvre has a fresh, bright and welcoming feel about it. The foyer is decorated in salmon pink, with forest green doors, a large Oriental rug, and colorfully-upholstered furnishings. The rooms themselves follow that lead.

Each room is decorated slightly differently, though they all have bright, light color schemes and floral patterns on the beds, sofas, and curtains. They have good-sized closets, which can come in very handy. Bathrooms all have tubs with hand-held showers.

The Marais & Bastille
3rd, 4th, & 11th Arrondissements

This is a fascinating area steeped in history and dripping with character. Long, long ago the area around the elegantly restored **Place des Vosges** was a marshy tract. It's hard to picture today because any stroll along tiny neighborhood streets just north of the rue de Rivoli uncovers an endless number of hip art galleries, coffee houses, and clothing shops.

There is also a thriving Jewish quarter, with all the wonderful food you might imagine, and a popular gay neighborhood, with all the clubs you might imagine.

A few blocks further east, you'll find the **Place de la Bastille**, site of the prison that played so formidable a symbolic role in the Revolution. That square is now home to the palatial **Bastille Opera House**, which opened in 1989 on the 200th anniversary of the Revolution. That opening also helped bring about a transformation in the blocks to the east of the opera house. This area has become the Soho of Paris, with increasingly popular clubs and small restaurants.

First- time visitors might find this area a little bit off the beaten track. Still, it is so easy to get around on the Métro that location shouldn't be a concern.

44. HÔTEL DE LA BRETONNERIE, *22 rue Sainte-Croix-de-la-Bretonnerie (4th, M:Hôtel de Ville). Tel. 01.48.87.77.63, Fax 01.42.77.26.78. Rooms: 24. Rates: 660-830FF. Breakfast: 45FF. No restaurant.*

The Bretonnerie is a popular hotel in the middle of the 4th *arrondissement*, not far from the Georges Pompidou Center, the Place des Vosges, and the Île de la Cité. Lots of small shops and clubs dot the immediate neighborhood, which is also quite near the Jewish quarter and such fabulous eateries as Jo Goldenberg's.

The hotel itself, with its stone walls, ceiling beams, and period furnishings, was a 17th-century residence. The decor of the common areas, dominated by heavy browns and a sort of startling turquoise, is a bit grim.

The rooms, however, are somewhat brighter (still too much brown) and are of a decent size — many have especially high ceilings, which is somewhat unusual for Paris hotels in this quarter. Bathrooms come with tubs and hand-held showers and give you plenty of room to maneuver.

45. HÔTEL SAINT-PAUL LE MARAIS, *8 rue de Sévigné (4th, M:Saint-Paul). Tel. 01.48.04.97.27, Fax 01.48.87.37.04. Rooms: 27. Rates: 690-890FF. Suite available. Breakfast: 45FF. No restaurant.*

This five-year-old hotel is just down the street from the Place des Vosges and about three blocks from the marvelous Musée Picasso. A few blocks south, you run into the Seine.

The owners chose a contemporary decor, with some touches of the original 16th-century frame showing through, such as the beams in the foyer and the exposed stone in the cellar where breakfasts are now served.

There is a small bar on the main floor and a small patio in back, away from the noise of rue de Sévigné.

Overall, the accommodations are adequate and the furnishings are generic contemporary stained woods. Cable television and safes for your belongings are available in all rooms.

46. PAVILLON DE LA REINE, *28 place des Vosges (3rd, M:Chemin Vert). Tel. 01.40.29.19.19, Fax 01.40.29.19.20. Rooms: 55. Rates: 1,900-2,200FF. Suites available. Breakfast: 95FF. No restaurant.*

Just off the Place des Vosges, one of most elegant historic squares in Paris, the Pavillon is likewise one of the most elegant hotels in Paris – especially at the price, which is expensive, but is still half the cost of the snooty *grandes dames* near the Champs-Élysées. And this is a much more interesting neighborhood.

Built only in 1986 – and owned by the same people who run the Relais Christine (reviewed above) – the Pavillon is set in a private courtyard with a vibrant garden and blends flawlessly into its historic surroundings. A large sitting room off the foyer is outfitted with huge leather couches and chairs, massive Oriental rugs, and various artworks recalling the 1600s when the Place des Vosges was built as residences for various royal families. A marvelous detail: the *trompe l'oeil* concealing the elevator.

Rooms are generous, with varying decors, though almost all have fine fabric walls, king-sized beds, air conditioning, minibars, large closets and spacious bathrooms (comfy bathrobes included). There is even a private garage.

The company motto: "Know How to Live." Book months in advance.

10. WHERE TO EAT

In our view, dining out in Paris is one of the great pleasures in life.

No doubt, part of that attitude comes from the sheer romance of the idea. But there's more to it than starry-eyed visions of clinking crystal goblets and gazing across the table toward the Seine and the illuminated Tour Eiffel beyond.

In France, food isn't just fuel meant to be burned off quickly at the office the next morning. It's one of the foundations of French culture. A good meal is equal, if not superior, to a profitable day at work.

That's been so for centuries. Cuisine is revered in France more so than in just about any other country in the world (with Italy, in our opinion, following as a close second).

And it's not just *haute cuisine* that tantilizes the French. In fact, we'd say most of the locals prefer traditional, country-style cooking. But whether the restaurant specializes in roast chicken and boiled potatoes or boned quail breast in a light pastry served with grilled baby squash, French patrons give the meal their undivided attention.

The dining table is also where they catch up on all the local gossip. And it would never occur to them to leave the table until not only all the food has been vacuumed up, but until all their tales are told. That table is theirs and theirs alone for the night.

Dining in Paris is also a pleasure because of the extraordinary variety that you can find in local restaurants. Corner bistros offer a blend of neighborly boisterousness and simple country cooking. Or you can settle into an intimate booth at one of the elegant three-star establishments where the presentations on the plate are as artful as anything you've seen on a canvas.

And don't forget that you can find some marvelous Vietnamese, Italian, Lebanese, and other ethnic restaurants. There are even American-style steak houses if you're dying for a T-bone or a decent bowl of chili.

Our choices below try to capture that variety, both in terms of ambiance and cuisine. Again, most restaurants on the main boulevards, such as the Champs-Élysées or Saint-Germain, are likely to be disappointing. Those places tend to toss together mediocre meals at high prices, then quickly show you the door.

Be patient, look around, and be willing to walk a few blocks or grab a cab.

GOOD FOOD DOESN'T COME CHEAP

You may lose your appetite when you see some of the prices. In fact, you might consider every restaurant but the corner crêperie to be expensive.

However, don't forget that the 15 percent tip and 19.6 percent tax are included. Also, unlike in North America, where restaurants profit by two or three seatings per table per evening, French restaurants expect patrons to linger as long as they like.

At the better restaurants your bill will never appear before you request it. At smaller bistros, the waiter may drop off a register receipt for each course or round of drinks you order, then tally them up at the end when you ask to pay.

For our purposes here, we created three price categories for meals, not including wine: inexpensive, for meals costing less than 150FF per person; moderate, for 150 to 300FF per person; and expensive, for more than 300FF per person. You'll note a couple of "very expensive" restaurants as well. It's quite easy to spend 1,000FF per person.

And don't forget to call ahead to find out if the restaurant is open (many close on Sundays or Mondays, and sometimes all of August) and to make reservations.

Finally, you'll notice that quite a few of our reviews use French for the dishes you'll see on the menu. We refer you to our extensive Food Dictionary in Chapter 8, *The Cuisine of France*, for specific food and dining terms you'll see throughout this chapter.

Bon appétit!

THE ISLANDS
Îles de la Cité & Saint-Louis

1. LE CAVEAU DU PALAIS *(traditional/moderate), 19 place Dauphine (1st, M:Pont Neuf). Tel. 01.43.26.04.28.*

While plumbers were remodeling (read: ripping to shreds) our apartment near Invalides, we borrowed a friend's flat on the Île de la Cité overlooking Pont Neuf. We tried all the little restaurants surrounding the historic Place Dauphine, named after the Dauphin, the future Louis XIII. The small tree-blanketed square is really a triangle and is found through an unremarkable cobbled entry off Pont Neuf between a wine bar and an Italian restaurant. In general, the little bistros were dreadful and we were beginning to despair when we dropped into Le Caveau. It was magnificent. The ingredients were clearly fresh and some of the plates were adventurous without being foolishly daring.

The interior, as you might expect, is somewhat cave-like, with a handful of smallish, white-washed rooms. Tables outside take up a good portion of the width of the small sidewalk, but since there is little foot traffic and the tables look out onto the age-old square, the seating is a delight. Our favorite dishes included a green salad with sautéed lamb's brain in a raspberry vinaigrette (don't cringe, this was very good), a plate of sliced dry sausages laced with a variety of herbs, roast filets of tuna with a purée of fresh tomatoes, grilled leg of lamb with rosemary, preserved duck legs in garlic, filet of rouget with a rhubarb-based sauce, and quick grilled duck breast with orange sauce.

2. AUBERGE DE LA REINE BLANCHE *(traditional/inexpensive), 30 rue Saint-Louis-en-Ile (4th, M:Pont-Marie). Tel. 01.46.33.07.87.*

A tiny bistro for a tiny island — appropriately decorated with miniature pieces of furniture hanging from the walls. The reasonable prix fixe offers an unusually wide range of choices. Some examples: a leek tart, mussels in garlic, grilled quail, saddle of lamb, veal scallops with a cream and mushroom sauce. The food here is quite decent, but, in part, we include this spot because it's cute and the crowd, though touristy, is often friendly.

3. BERTHILLON *(ice cream), 31 rue Saint-Louis-en-Ile (4th, M:Pont-Marie). Tel. 01.43.54.31.61.*

Ice cream and sorbets — guava (wow!), pink grapefruit, pear, tea, Grand-Marnier (excellent), glazed chestnut, and on and on and on. Even vanilla, but the kind of vanilla that could lead to serious addiction. Though this is the main shop, several places on the Île Saint-Louis sell Berthillon now. Just look for long lines.

LEFT BANK
The Latin Quarter
5th Arrondissement

4. CHEZ HENRI, LE MOULIN A VENT *(traditional/moderate to inexpensive)*, *20 rue des Follés-Saint-Bernard (5th, M:Jussieu), Tel. 01.43.54.99.37.*

By the ambiance it is easy to tell that people (mostly locals) have been coming here for years. Much of the staff has worked there even longer than that–what's more, they seem even to love their jobs.

Tiny, but joyous, Chez Henri is a real treat. It is warm and friendly and genuine. It is also a perfect stop on a chilly evening. Anything but delicate, the dishes here are robust and filling. Tender red meat and hearty red wine are the order of the day–though the frog legs are brilliantly garlicy and the snails tender and hot. And you can try to order one of the more expensive bottles from their modest wine list, but likely as not the waiter will shake his head and insist that the Beaujolais is best–a Juliénas or Morgon. Chilled. And for dessert, you could have a tart, and it would be great. But then, consider indulging your waistline with the freshly made mousse au chocolat.

5. TOUR D'ARGENT *(haute cuisine/very expensive)*, *15 quai de la Tournelle (5th, M:Maubert-Mutualité). Tel. 01.43.54.23.31, Fax 44.07.12.04.*

Everyone who knows anything about fine dining in Paris has heard of Tour d'Argent, the Michelin two-star restaurant that sits on the top floor of a riverside building on the Left Bank just a half dozen blocks east of Notre-Dame. This is the home that Claude Terrail built, and, though some snooty critics say he caters too much to tourists, it is a brilliant restaurant with very, very fine food, an army of attentive waiters, and a view of the Seine and Notre-Dame to die for.

Try the house specialty, pressed duck, with a *crêpe Suzette* for dessert. Tour d'Argent (which means Silver Tower — though *argent* also means money, which is an equally appropriate translation) also boasts the most extensive wine list in all of France. Ask for a tour of its cellar. And brace yourself for the tab. Think of it as an investment in your memories.

6. RÔTISSERIE DU BEAUJOLAIS *(traditional/moderate), 19 quai de la Tournelle (5th, M:Maubert-Mutualité). Tel. 01.43.54.17.47.*

Like a handful of his colleagues in town, Claude Terrail, owner of the Tour d'Argent across the street, invested in a "baby bistro," the Rôtisserie du Beaujolais. Opened on July 14, 1989, the 200th anniversary of the French Revolution, the Beaujolais is a classic affordable bistro with simple wooden chairs pushed up to small tables covered in green and white or red and white checked tablecloths. There are two small rooms, the second of which gives you a view of the kitchen and the roasting chickens.

The food isn't fancy, but it's still no easy trick to make *coq au vin* as good as this. Other worthwhile dishes include roast pigeon, roast duck, Lyon sausage with roasted apples, duck breast or preserved duck legs, stuffed pig's feet, grilled sole, snails, goat cheese salads, and a daily fruit tart for dessert slathered with *crème fraiche*. And sample one or two of the refreshing Beaujolais on hand. Try a Juliénas or Fleuri. Both are crisp and fruity.

7. AL DAR *(Lebanese/moderate), 8 rue Frédéric-Sauton (5th, M:Saint-Michel). Tel. 01.43.25.17.15. Also 93 avenue de Raymond Poincaré (16th, M:Victor Hugo). Tel. 01.45.00.96.64.*

Marvelous Lebanese. The only way to fly is to order the combinations of twelve, twenty, or twenty-six dishes. The quality and quantities are good for the money. And sometimes, if you've really stuffed yourself, they'll bring a bit of baklava at the end for free. If you're hunting for a snack or quick lunch, the Al Dar in the Latin Quarter has a takeout deli (some seating) next door.

8. LE BISTRO D'A COTÉ *(traditional/moderate), 16 boulevard Saint-Germain (5th, M:Maubert-Mutualité). Tel. 01.43.54.59.10.*

This delightful stop is another of master chef Michel Rostang's successful "baby bistros". For those who can't afford the steep prices at his two-star palace in the 17th *arrondissement* or for those who just don't feel like tugging on their Armani suits, these bistros offer a warm and casual atmosphere and better than traditional bistro fare at reasonable rates.

Rostang allows each local chef leeway in the daily specials, but he consults regularly on the standing menu and the preparations to insure that the food is up to his high standards. Another plus: given the hustle and bustle of Saint-Germain, this bistro is far enough east (almost to the river) that the setting is thankfully peaceful.

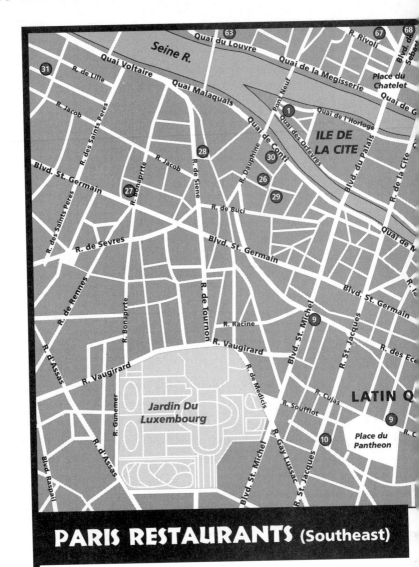

PARIS RESTAURANTS (Southeast)

1. Le Caveau du Palais
2. Auberge de la Reine Blanche
3. Berthillon
4. Chez Henri, Le Moulin a Vent
5. Tour d'Argent
6. Rôtisserie du Beaujolais
7. Al Dar
8. Le Bistro d'a Coté
9. Brasserie Balzar
10. Perraudin
11. L'Epoque
12. Chez Lena & Mimile
13. Brasserie Mouffetard
14. Le Saint Médard

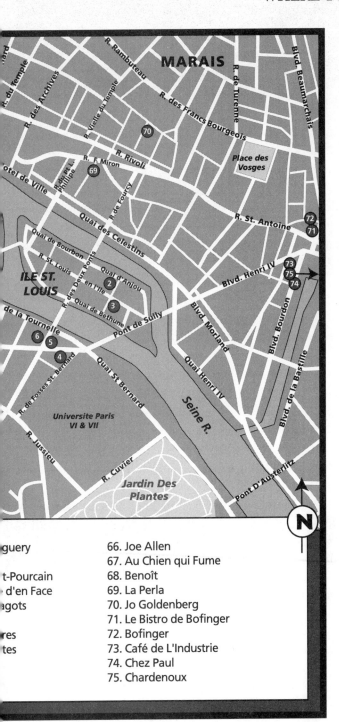

9. BRASSERIE BALZAR (*traditional/moderate*), *49 rue des Écoles (5th, M:Cluny-Sorbonne). Tel. 01.43.54.13.67.*

A lively brasserie that is as popular with locals as it is with tourists. Daily specials are often best, featuring such simple dishes as sliced leg of lamb, fresh asparagus with a vinaigrette, snails steeped in garlic butter, and hot apple tart with *crême fraiche*. The people-watching here is as good as any floor show. It's the real thing.

10. PERRAUDIN (*traditional/inexpensive*), *157 rue Saint-Jacques (5th, M:Luxembourg). Tel. 01.46.33.15.75.*

One of the best of the very casual old-style bistros. The Perraudin looks pretty much like it always has. You're not quite sure if the walls were painted that kind of musty yellow, or whether it's just the patina of age showing through.

Still, this tiny place is big on charm. The seating is tight, but the atmosphere so friendly that you're likely to get to know your neighbors. Chances are they're students or professors from the nearby Sorbonne. We've even seen professors digging through stacks of papers between bites.

The food is as basic as the decor, which means that some dishes are very hearty and rich with flavor, and a few are a bit dull. The better ones include artichoke hearts in a vinaigrette, seafood salad mixing shrimp and mussels, onion tarte, herring filets in cream, hard-boiled eggs in freshly made mayonnaise, leg of lamb with scalloped potatoes, rumpsteak with pepper sauce, poached salmon in sorrel, and, probably the best, *boeuf bourguignon*.

No reservations, but if you have to wait in line you'll be treated to a free Kir and some olives.

11. L'EPOQUE (*traditional/inexpensive*), *81 rue du Cardinal Lemoine (5th, M:Cardinale Lemoine). Tel. 01.46.34.15.84.*

Just off the picturesque Place de la Contrescarpe, this small bistro is an undiscovered gem, serving hearty standards such as pork *salé* with lentils or roast chicken with tarragon in a casual atmosphere at un-Parisian low prices. The staff is friendly and willing to explain the menu or just chat about the neighborhood. After dinner, stroll around the corner to the Contrescarpe, sit at one of the cafés, and watch the world go by.

SEEING STARS

Haute cuisine at its very finest – at least that's what the esteemed Michelin Guide says. These are the seven restaurants in Paris that have earned three Michelin stars. Bring your Platinum credit card.

L'AMBROISIE, *9 place des Vosges (4th, M:Chemin Vert). Tel. 01.42.78.51.45. Closed Sunday and Monday. Chef Bernard Pacaud's Florentine villa.*

ALAIN DUCASSE, *59 avenue Raymond Poincaré (16th, M:Trocadéro). Tel. 01.47.27.12.27, Fax 47.27.31.22. New home for a world-famous chef. Art nouveau chic.*

LUCAS-CARTON, *9 place de la Madeleine (8th, M:Madeleine). Tel. 01.42.65.22.90, Fax 01.42.65.06.23. Closed Sunday. A Belle Epoque belle.*

TAILLEVENT, *15 rue Lamennais (8th, M:George V). Tel. 01.44.95.15.01, Fax 01.42.25.95.18. Closed Saturday and Sunday. Some say the very best.*

ARPÈGE, *84 rue Varenne (7th, M:Varenne). Tel. 01.45.51.47.33, Fax 01.44.18.98.39. Closed Saturday. Young chef Alain Passard's modernistic dream.*

GRAND VEFOUR, *17 rue Beaujolais (1st, M:Palais Royale). Tel. 01.42.96.56.27, Fax 01.42.86.80.71. A much revived 18th-century café in the Palais Royale, and said by some to be the most romantic dining spot in all of Paris.*

PIERRE GAGNAIRE, *Hôtel Balzac, 6 rue Balzac (8th, M:George V), Tel. 01.44.35.18.25, Fax 01.44.35.18.37. Not the most visually elegant, but still stunning dining.*

12. CHEZ LÉNA & MIMILE *(traditional/moderate), 32 rue Tournefort (5th, M:Censier-Daubenton). Tel. 01.47.07.72.47.*

A tiny and wonderfully homey bistro tucked away in a corner that most tourists will never find. Good standards are culled from all the wonderfully fresh foods of the open market on the nearby rue Mouffetard. The service is so easygoing you'd think you were a friend of the family, and frequently there will be a piano player and a young songstress singing

Edith Piaf classics and rock ballads. A fixed price menu that includes dessert and a half bottle of respectable wine per person.

13. BRASSERIE MOUFFETARD *(traditional/inexpensive), 116 rue Mouffetard (5th, M:Censier-Daubenton). Tel. 01.43.31.42.50. Closed Monday.*

This is the quintessential Left Bank café in the heart of one of Paris's most famous open markets. Locals and workers from the market gather here in the early morning and argue about current events over wine and coffee before setting out to tackle the day's chores. On a sunny day, the café spills out onto the tiny street, where singers, dancers, and jugglers add to the carnival atmosphere. Baked-on-the-premises croissants are heavenly. Good for lunch too.

14. LE SAINT MÉDARD *(café food/inexpensive), 53 rue Censier (5th, M:Censier-Daubenton). Tel. 01.43.31.32.99.*

Another modest student quarter café, Le Saint Médard is named for the church of the same name just across the street. The outdoor tables along the sidewalk that bends around this corner café also look out on the pretty Place Médard, a cobble-stoned circle with a garden and fountain in the center. And just opposite the circle are the last few vegetable stands and fish markets of the famous Rue Mouffetard street market.

The Saint-Médard church dates back 800 years and possesses a somewhat gruesome past. In the mid-1700s, a Jansenist novice famed for epic levels of self-sacrifice on behalf of the poor died and was buried on the church grounds. Shortly afterward, word got around that his grave site possessed miraculous curative powers. Young women were drawn by the dozens, then the hundreds, eating the dirt surrounding the grave site and having themselves viciously tortured until they fell in what were described as "rapturous" states of semiconsciousness. The crown, disturbed that a tombstone was exhibiting such magnetism, closed the grounds, posting a sign that read: "By order of the king, God is forbidden to perform miracles in this place."

15. LE PETIT MARGUERY *(traditional/moderate), 9 boulevard de Port-Royal (13th, M:Gobelins). Tel. 01.43.31.58.59.*

An absolute favorite, Le Petit Marguery combines the best of all possible ingredients: an inventive menu, attention to seasonal specials, affordable prices, friendly service, and a classic turn-of-the-century environment. Not to gush, but there are really no appreciable flaws to the Marguery. The Marguery is also known as Les Frères Cousin, in tribute

PARIS RESTAURANTS (South)

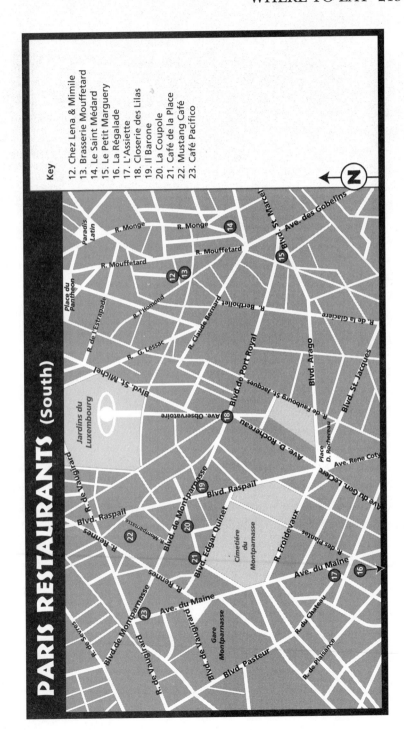

Key

12. Chez Lena & Mimile
13. Brasserie Mouffetard
14. Le Saint Médard
15. Le Petit Marguery
16. La Régalade
17. L'Assiette
18. Closerie des Lilas
19. Il Barone
20. La Coupole
21. Café de la Place
22. Mustang Café
23. Café Pacifico

to the Cousin Brothers: Alain, Jacques, and Michel, who own and run the restaurant — further evidence that owners who also run a bistro try harder to please their customers.

Drawing a large and very loyal crowd of Parisians and foreigners who pass through town regularly, the Marguery is probably best known for its skillful preparation of game dishes. The season extends from about late October through to the end of January. Few bistros handle venison, young deer, wild boar, and pheasant and other game birds so well. The meats are tender and succulent, and the sauces heighten but never overwhelm.

Other dishes: Greek salad with ginger and asparagus, warm salad with slices of smoked duck breast and foie gras, cèpe mushrooms sautéed in butter and garlic, green salad with generous hunks of lobster, raviolis stuffed with crayfish, veal liver in a cherry sauce, young Guinea fowl in mushrooms and garlic, duck leg that has been steeped in salt and then slightly poached, roast young deer, dessert soufflé suffused with Grand Marnier, fresh-baked pastries stuffed with strawberries

The wine list is also one of the most adept at finding special offerings from Burgundy and the Côtes du Rhône that will enrich your meals without breaking your bank.

Saint-Germain & Montparnasse
6th & 14th Arrondissements

16. LA RÉGALADE (*traditional/moderate*), *49 avenue Jean Moulin (14th, M:Porte d'Orléans). Tel. 01.45.45.68.58.*

This is a truly fabulous place. It is rare that a bistro with such spectacularly well-prepared dishes remains largely a neighborhood phenomenon. Still, that doesn't mean it's easy to get in. Well-dressed locals routinely book as much as three weeks in advance to insure that they get a table.

It isn't the decor that has won such a following. Tucked away on the very southern border of the city, La Régalade (which means "roaring fire") is somewhat plain inside. The nondescript, bargain-basement lighting fixtures could use changing, for instance. But once the food arrives, you quickly forget the lack of ambiance.

The moment you've selected your meal, an enormous crock of freshly made paté arrives on the table with a basket of chewy bread. The paté is

RESTAURANT FINDS & FAVORITES

Our very favorites, these restaurants have pretty much everything we look for: ambiance, a friendly staff, a good wine list, value for the money, and inventive food made with fresh ingredients.

9. BRASSERIE BALZAR (traditional/moderate), 49 rue des Écoles (5th, M:Cluny-Sorbonne). Tel. 01.43.54.13.67.

15. LE PETIT MARGUERY (traditional-game/moderate), 9 boulevard de Port-Royal (13th, M:Gobelins). Tel. 01.43.31.58.59.

16. LA RÉGALADE (traditional/moderate), 49 avenue Jean Moulin (14th, M:Porte d'Orléans). Tel. 01.45.45.68.58.

17. L'ASSIETTE (traditional-haute cuisine/moderate-expensive), 181 rue du Château (14th, M:Gaîté). Tel. 01.43.22.64.86. Closed Monday.

25. AU BON SAINT-POURCAIN (traditional/inexpensive to moderate), 10bis rue Servandoni (6th, M:Saint-Sulpice). Tel. 01.43.54.93.63. Closed Sundays. No credit cards.

29. MARIAGE FRÈRES (a real tea salon/inexpensive to moderate), 13 rue des Grands-Augustins (6th, M:Odéon). Tel. 01.40.51.82.50. Open daily. Best brunch.

30. LES BOOKINISTES (modernized traditional/moderate), 53 quai des Grands Augustins (6th, M:Saint-Michel). Tel. 01.43.25.45.94.

33. MICHEL COURTALHAC RESTAURANT (traditional/inexpensive to moderate), 47 rue de Bourgogne (7th, M:Varenne). Tel. 01.45.55.15.35. Closed Sunday.

35. LE BISTRO DE BRETEUIL (traditional/inexpensive), 3 place de Breteuil (7th, M:Duroc). Tel. 01.45.67.07.27. Open daily.

40. AUBERGE D'CHEZ EUX (southwest French traditional/moderate-expensive), 4 avenue de Lowendal (7th, M:École Militaire). Tel. 01.47.05.52.55. Closed Sunday.

44. AU BON ACCUEIL (traditional/inexpensive), 14 rue de Monttessuy (7th, M:École Militaire). Tel. 01.47.05.46.11.

52. LE BISTRO D'À CÔTÉ (traditional/moderate), 10 rue Gustave-Flaubert (17th, M:Charles-de-Gaulle). Tel. 01.42.67.05.81.

56. L'ECLUSE (traditional/moderate), 15 place de la Madeleine (8th, M:Madeleine). Tel. 01.42.65.34.69. For lunch.

63. CAFÉ MARLY (international/moderate), Cour Napoléon, Palais du Louvre (1st, M:Louvre). Tel. 01.49.26.06.60.

71. LE BISTRO DE BOFINGER (traditional/inexpensive), 6 rue de la Bastille (4th, M:Bastille). Tel. 01.42.72.05.23.

75. CHARDENOUX (traditional/moderate), 1 rue Jules-Vallés (11th, M:Charonne). Tel. 01.43.71.49.52.

like everything else here: the ingredients are chosen at the marketplace that morning. Everything is screamingly fresh, as reflected by the ever-changing and inventive menu. Dishes include: a delicious tart made with blood sausage, apple and potato; risotto zipped up with squid ink and pan-fried calamari; a salad of lentils, foie gras, and chicken wings; a thick potato soup with roasted beef's tail; scallops with tomato, mozarella and basil; leg of lamb steeped in garlic; a Grand Marnier dessert soufflé; a gazpacho of strawberries with a bit of tomato; rice pudding with marmalade, and a dessert crêpe stuffed with raspberries.

17. L'ASSIETTE (*traditional/moderate-expensive*), *181 rue du Château (14th, M:Gaîté). Tel. 01.43.22.64.86.*

When chef and owner Lucette Rousseau is on her game, this restaurant is truly outstanding. Lucette blends much of the best of traditional and haute cuisine. Plates of marinated salmon or foie gras are enormous. Or start with a lobster salad with garlic, or asparagus with truffles, or smoked duck breast sliced thin and stacked on frisée lettuce. Main dishes are generous as well, with a blanquette of sea scallops, tender and juicy saddle of rabbit, perfectly roasted pigeon, and a petit *salé* of duck that is sinfully rich and flavorful.

The wine list is as thoughtfully composed as the menu, with lots of Bordeaux and Burgundy from the best of the 1980s (prices are a bit steep). The setting is unspectacular and the neighborhood a bit removed, but don't let that get in the way of a memorable meal.

18. CLOSERIE DES LILAS (*nouvelle-seafood/moderate*), *171 boulevard du Montparnasse (6th, M:Port Royal). Tel. 01.40.51.34.50.*

This one-time country inn, which is now quite stylish, is a sort of monument to the arts and letters community. Former regulars include Baudelaire, Verlaine, Beckett, Joyce, and, of course, Hemingway, who seems to have enjoyed a glass in every conceivable Left Bank café. The bar area even has engraved plaques commemorating some of its past literary glory. Request a table in the garden side of the restaurant, though the bar area has its charm as well.

Dishes include lobster bisque, endive salad with real Roquefort, oysters Florentine, the house steak tartare, and medallions of lamb with fresh herbs in pastry.

19. IL BARONE *(Italian/moderate), 5 rue Léopold Robert (14th, M:Vavin). Tel. 01.43.20.87.14.*

Though this restaurant is unassuming visually, the food is good and the portions generous. Mostly neighborhood folks drop by for starters like marinated sardines, *prosciutto di Parma* or carpaccio, then follow up with veal scallops with ham and grated parmesan, spaghetti with butter and anchovies, or *falioline alla carbonara*. For dessert, try a plate of profiteroles or a mixed selection of rich gelati. The back room is the lively one.

20. LA COUPOLE *(traditional-seafood/moderate), 102 boulevard Montparnasse (14th, M:Vavin). Tel. 01.43.20.14.20.*

This showplace of a bistro has been fully renovated since it was a haunt to Jean-Paul Sartre and the Americans before him. It is chic, spacious, brightly lit, and noisy – a perfect place to see (be prepared to gawk at the young and beautiful) and be seen. There's a downstairs ballroom for those who want to kick up their heels to a bit of jazz. The menu offers lots of fresh seafood, as well as filling staples such as a steak and fries. The food is nothing to rave about, but the overall experience is memorable.

21. CAFÉ DE LA PLACE *(traditional/inexpensive), 23 rue d'Odessa (14th, M:Edgar-Quinet). Tel. 01.42.18.01.55.*

Just a block below the often chaotic boulevard de Montparnasse, you'll find this homey little café run by a friendly group of young folks who welcome you as if you were a regular from the neighborhood. The food is very simple. Just salads, omelets, steaks and fries, and that sort of thing. But it's properly prepared and is quite satisfying. And they offer an inexpensive and usually very decent wine *du jour*. All in all, this warm and woody café with outdoor seating under shady trees is a comfortable little sanctuary where you can refuel in peace and quiet.

22. MUSTANG CAFÉ *(Tex-Mex/moderate), 84 boulevard du Montparnasse (14th, M:Vavin). Tel. 01.43.35.36.12.*

A new hot spot with one of the best Happy Hour deals in town from 4 to 8 p.m. The café draws a young (sometimes very young) French and American crowd throughout the afternoon and evening. Lots of ogling, nursing beers for hours, smoking, and chattering, all at the same time. The second shift begins at about 8 p.m., when diners arrive for taco combinations, grilled shrimp, barbecue pork ribs, a turkey-bacon club, and Haagèn Dazs for dessert.

LITERARY LEGACIES

Start with the premise that Hemingway drank everywhere – even places that opened after his death. These are a few of the famous places where the literary giants drew inspiration from caffeine and entrecote (cheap steak).

CAFÉ LES DEUX-MAGOTS, 170 boulevard Saint-Germain (6th, M:Saint-Germain-des-Prés). Tel. 01.45.48.55.25. The big daddy of them all. Ghosts include: Simone de Beauvoir, Malcolm Cowley, Hart Crane, Gore Vidal, Christopher Isherwood.

CAFÉ DE FLORÉ, 172 boulevard Saint-Germain (6th, M:Saint-Germain-des-Prés). Tel. 01.45.48.55.26. Ghosts: everyone who ever stopped at the Deux Magots next door.

BRASSERIE LIPP, 151 boulevard Saint-Germain (6th, M:Saint-Germain-des-Prés). Tel. 01.45.48.53.91. Waverly Root, Thornton Wilder, Harold Loeb. Did we mention Hemingway?

LA CLOSERIE DES LILAS, 171 boulevard du Montparnasse (6th, M:Port-Royal). Tel. 01.40.51.34.50. Baudelaire, Verlaine, James Joyce, John Dos Passos, F. Scott Fitzgerald, Archibald MacLeish.

LA COUPOLE, 102 boulevard du Montparnasse (14th, M:Vavin). Tel. 01.43.20.14.20. Henry Miller, Lawrence Durrell, Françoise Sagan, Gabriel Garcia Marquez.

LE SELECT, 99 boulevard du Montparnasse (6th, M:Vavin). Tel. 01.42.22.65.27. Isadora Duncan, Hart Crane, Harold Stearns. Did we mention Hemingway?

POLIDOR, 41 rue Monsieur-le-Prince (6th, M:Odéon). Tel. 01.43.26.95.34. James Joyce, Rimbaud, Verlaine, Richard Wright.

23. CAFÉ PACIFICO (*Mexican/inexpensive*), 50 boulevard Montparnasse (15th, M:Montparnasse or Duroc). Tel. 01.45.48.63.87.

Okay, so it's a small chain, with restaurants in London and Amsterdam as well. But the Pacifico is one of the few Mexican restaurants in Paris where you'll find pretty much what you think of as conventional Mexican fare: enchiladas, burritos, and tacos, with lots of refried beans and tangy rice. The prices are right (except for the 300FF pitchers of Margueritas), and there are six tables in a tranquil outdoor patio in back. The bar sizzles at night, when patrons tank up on Dos XX and carbohydrates.

24. POLIDOR *(traditional/inexpensive)*, *41 rue Monsieur-le-Prince (6th, M:Odéon). Tel. 01.43.26.95.34.*

One of the many former Hemingway haunts, this bustling bistro brings French country cooking to the heart of the Left Bank. Most seating is elbow to elbow at long tables packed with hungry students and tourists trying to choose between rabbit in mustard sauce or veal kidneys. No reservations. Arrive early for a decent seat and be prepared to get to know your neighbors.

25. AU BON SAINT-POURCAIN *(traditional/inexpensive to moderate), 10bis rue Servandoni (6th, M:Saint-Sulpice). Tel. 01.43.54.93.63. Closed Sundays. No credit cards.*

This fabulously genuine corner bistro a block from Saint-Sulpice (and from Catherine Deneuve's apartment) has a well-used feel to its faded tile floor, red banquettes, lace curtains, and chalkboard menus. The food is also superb, prepared by chef and owner Daniel Pesle, the tall distinguished-looking gentleman who wanders from table to table with a welcoming smile on his face. Dishes are simple and run a bit on the heavy side, so come with a hearty appetite and be ready to dig into escargots, *coq au vin*, tender beef with olives, *blanquette de veau*, and the cake or tart of the day. The house Gamay is especially light and refreshing.

26. LA RÔTISSERIE D'EN FACE *(nouvelle/moderate-expensive), 2 rue Christine (6th, M:Odéon). Tel. 01.43.26.40.98.*

On a tiny street near the river, this what is known as a "baby bistro," which means it's a place owned by a high-rung chef from a pricey nearby restaurant. In this case the chef is Jacques Cagna, whose two-star is "en face," which is to say, across the street. Comfortable contemporary-country setting with lots of imaginative dishes. Though the food was very good, the service was a bit hurried and the prices a tad too high.

27. LES DEUX MAGOTS *(coffee-lunch/moderate), 170 boulevard Saint-Germain (6th, M:Saint-Germain-des-Prés). Tel. 01.45.48.55.25.*

Said to have been one of the favorites for literati before and after World War II, the Deux Magots is directly across from the Saint-Germain-des-Prés cathedral. It is an ideal place to sip espresso or a fine whiskey on a sunny day and watch the beautiful people go by. The food is nothing to write poetry about. And in case you were worried about the name, Magots refers to the statues of Chinese merchants that flank the front door, not to bugs.

28. LA PALETTE (*café/inexpensive*), *43 rue de Seine (6th, M:Mabillon).* *Tel. 01.43.26.68.15.*

La Palette, as in the small board used by painters to mix oils, is a bit tough to find. But that's part of this café's special charm — its location provides visitors with relative tranquillity in the heart of an *arrondissement* famous for pushy crowds. That, and the sense that you're sipping inky coffees with local artists taking a breather from garrets stuffy with the smell of linseed oil.

Located at the corner of rue de Seine and rue Callot, a tiny lane no more than 50 yards long located one lengthy block north toward the river from bustling rue Buci, La Palette is itself a work of art. The interior, with a cozy back room for rainy days and a classic zinc-topped bar up front, boasts pillars and walls decked out with murals depicting bucolic glades, sea-ravaged ships, and other classic subjects. Tacked up along the rafters are also rows of palettes, caked with inky and vibrant colors.

29. MARIAGE FRÈRES (*a real tea salon/inexpensive*), *13 rue des Grands-Augustins (6th, M:Odéon). Tel. 01.40.51.82.50.*

All over Paris you will see what looks like a bistro with an awning that insists that the establishment is a tea salon. Well, that bit of advertising is almost always a complete sham. However, Mariage is the real thing, with a tea shop downstairs where you can choose from a couple hundred teas and purchase all the proper *accoutrements* (tea balls, pots, cups, etc.).

Upstairs is an airy warm salon with bushy palms, crisp tablecloths, and eight tables where you can sample any of the teas offered on the main floor (hot or iced), and dig into great brunches and salads – who can resist the "Snob Salad" with foie gras, smoked salmon, and artichoke hearts?

The Mariage family, by the way, has been in the tea business for 140 years, and they offer a book filled with family history and recipes.

They also have another location, which some folks favor over this one. It is tucked into the heart of the Marais in the 4th arrondissement at 30 rue du Bourg-Tibourg (not terribly far from the Hôtel de Ville). If you want to call ahead for a reservation, phone *01.42.72.28.11.*

30. LES BOOKINISTES (*modernized traditional/moderate*), *53 quai des Grands Augustins (6th, M: Saint-Michel). Tel. 01.43.25.45.94.*

Les Bookinistes, named after the book sellers who line the Seine in this part of Paris, is another of master chef Guy Savoy's "baby bistros." In fact, we enjoy Bookinistes infinitely more than Butte Chaillot, Savoy's bistro in the 16th *arrondissement*, which is far too touristy, too cute by half and too busy for the harried wait staff.

Les Bookinistes, like all of Savoy's establishments, is decked out in a contemporary design, with a handsome hardwood floor, potted plants, tastefully "mod" paintings, and green leather and metal-backed chairs. The setting is roomy and comfortable, and the service attentive and informative. And, after dinner, you can walk off the calories along the river facing the Île de la Cité.

The food is not quite as adventurous as you would find in Savoy's flagship restaurant in the 17th *arrondissement* (which goes by the name of Guy Savoy), but it does offer nouvelle-like flourishes to some hearty French standbys. Ingredients are very fresh, and the seasoning is thoughtful and subtle. Some of the finer dishes: a salad of asparagus and avocados, a country paté with lamb sweatbreads, marinated sardines with coriander, tuna sautéed Basque-style with basil, braised sole with green olives and lemon juice, a veal rib cut stuffed with sausage.

Near The Eiffel Tower
7th Arrondissement

31. TAN DIHN *(Vietnamese/expensive), 60 rue de Verneuil (7th, M:Rue du Bac). Tel. 01.45.44.04.84.*

This smallish restaurant tucked away on an off-the-beaten-track street is a delightful find. The food is extremely good – rich but delicate, with specialties such as ravioli stuffed with goose, tender strips of marinated lamb and beef, and on and on. The wine list is truly impressive, with one of the largest collections of Pomerol around. And the owners, the Vifians, are ever present, like a roving floor show, commenting on the food, stopping to discuss their strategy for finding fine wines at bargain prices, or just gossiping.

32. BRASSERIE LE BASILIC *(traditional/inexpensive), 2 rue Casimir Perier (7th, M:Solferino). Tel. 01.44.18.94.64. Open daily.*

Tucked behind the picturesque, though little known Sainte-Clotilde church, the Basilic is a warm, welcoming neighborhood brasserie that prides itself on its lamb dishes. Other dishes include cold artichokes, *confit de canard*, veal chops, medallions of salmon with basil, foot-long eclairs, and the renowned Berthillon sorbets. The restaurant has a pleasant patio section, where there is often a refreshing breeze, and a cozy interior of hardwoods and potted palms.

33. MICHEL COURTALHAC RESTAURANT *(traditional/inexpensive to moderate), 47 rue de Bourgogne (7th, M:Varenne). Tel. 01.45.55.15.35. Closed Sunday.*

You can watch Michel cook through the smallish opening into the kitchen from the back section downstairs. This tiny family restaurant makes you feel as if you've dropped by a good friend's house for some dinner. It fills up quickly with neighborhood residents who've grown to know and love Michel's dedication to fresh ingredients in everything from the salads to the main courses.

The menu is limited to a handful of main dishes, but Michel makes sure that there is true variety in those choices – such as offerings of tender beef stew in Bordeaux, a roast sea bream with coriander, and a salad stacked with preserved duck breast. The selective wine list also includes a recommendation, which is usually a wonderful wine that Michel has recently discovered at a good price and wants to share with his customers.

34. AU PIED DE FOUET *(traditional/inexpensive), 45 rue de Babylon (7th, M:Sevres-Babylone), Tel. 01.47.05.12.27. Closed Sunday.*

This tiniest of cafes is probably no bigger than your living room—maybe smaller. And it has certainly been around longer than your living room.

Aristocrats from the nearby government buildings, as well as local shopkeepers and the like, make this a favorite lunch stop. You wait at the bar for a table to open up, choosing your meal from a chalk board with limited but satisfying standards such as *confit de canard*, grilled trout, veal stew, even hard-boiled eggs and apple compote. Once you've sopped up the last drop of rich sauce with a hunk of chewy baguette, you return to the bar for your coffee.

A true local hangout, this can be a bit of a challenge if you don't have at least a passable facility with French. Still, this warm local family-owned bistro is sure to provide you with a vacation tale you'll pass along to friends when you return home.

35. LE BISTRO DE BRETEUIL *(traditional/inexpensive), 3 place de Breteuil (7th, M:Duroc). Tel. 01.45.67.07.27.*

The neighborhood crowd is drawn here by the dozens every night. The repeat customers, us included, love the reasonable prices, the generous helpings of good food, the friendly service, and the spacious outdoor dining area facing the striking white statue of Louis Pasteur and the colorful garden that occupy the center of the place de Breteuil. A reasonable prix fixe includes a half bottle of wine and choices of a tasty salmon tartare, escargots steeped in garlic butter, a goat cheese salad, rack of lamb, veal medallions with blue cheese, and *confit de canard*. The wines that accompany the meal aren't exactly the finest, but they are quite passable table varieties.

36. AUX DELICES DE SZECHUEN *(Chinese/moderate)*, *40 avenue Duquesne (7th, M:Saint-François Xavier). Tel. 01.43.06.22.55.*

The first time we ate here, Lauren Bacall came in with her son and a friend and dined at the table next to us. Need we say more? Friendly service and fine food with standard offerings and such specials as grilled ravioli with ginger and smoked duck in tea. Afterward take a refreshing stroll down the striking avenue de Breteuil toward the illuminated dome of Invalides.

37. LALLEMENT *(lunch/inexpensive), 37 avenue Duquesne (7th, M:École Militaire). Tel. 01.47.05.03.87.*

This cheery local bakery, with seating for about twenty people, is one of the rare establishments where you feel instantly at ease and welcome. The menu offers great lunches, with all sorts of salads, quiches, and tarts, and hearty daily specials that have yet to disappoint. No wonder the locals crowd in at midday. Check out the chocolates counter if you dare.

38. CASA PASTA *(Italian/moderate), avenue Duquesne (7th, M:École Militaire). Tel. 01.45.55.43.43.*

Room enough for twenty people at most, this cozy spot lists a respectable range of dishes, including baked eggplant with parmesan, duck ravioli with capers and truffles, linguine with shellfish, veal scallops doused in lemon and butter – all prepared just seconds before the dishes are served by the owner.

39. LES OLIVADES *(Provencal/inexpensive), 41 avenue de Ségur (7th, M:École Militaire), Tel. 01.47.83.70.09.*

A funny little storefront of a restaurant, this new gem is the loving product of Flora Mikula, trained both in New York and at the Michelan three-star l'Arpege. Anything but stuffy, it is the quintessential neighborhood spot with a modest decor, but a wonderful menu of specialties from Provence and the south of France (she is from Avignon, so knows exactly what she's doing). She serves up an impressive variety that ranges from turbot and rouget to pheasant, quail and rabbit—many of the dishes enriched with artichokes, olives, red pepper, capers, eggplant and other staples of the south. Her desserts are equally varied, with a stunning *moelleux au chocolat* (a light miniature chocolate cake with a center of melted chocolate) and a dish we have never seen anywhere else—lavender ice cream. Sounds a bit strange, but it was truly wonderful and refreshing.

40. AUBERGE D'CHEZ EUX (*southwest French traditional/moderate-expensive*), *4 avenue de Lowendal (7th, M:École Militaire). Tel. 01.47.05.52.55. Closed Sunday.*

No dainty nouvelle portions here. These are massive, country-sized meals. The minute you settle into one of the tables draped with a red-and-white checkered cloth, a waiter brings you Kir poured out of a magnum bottle and slabs of meat cut from one of the dozen or so sausages sticking

---

LEGUME LOVERS

All is not flesh and bone in Parisian cuisine. Venues for vegetarians, all of which are priced very reasonably, include:

AQUARIUS, 54 rue Sainte-Croix de la Bretonnerie (4th, M:Hôtel de Ville). Tel. 01.48.87.48.71. Closed Sunday.

AQUARIUS, 40 rue de Gergovie (14th, M:Pernety). Tel. 01.45.41.36.88. Closed Sunday.

AU GRAIN DE FOLIE, 24 rue de La Vieuville (18th, M:Abbesses). Tel. 01.42.58.15.57. Open daily.

PICCOLO, 6 rue des Ecouffes (4th, M:Saint-Paul). Tel. 01.42.72.17.79. Closed Monday and Tuesday.

LA TRUFFE, Restaurant 'Nature,' 31 rue Vieille du Temple (4th, M:Saint-Paul). Tel. 01.42.71.08.39. Open daily. May be the best.

LE GRENIER DE NOTRE DAME, 18 rue de la Bucherie (5th, M:Maubert-Mutualité), Tel. 01.43.29.98.29. One of the oldest in town, established in 1978. Offers a prix fixe that will give you all the veggies you will ever need.

LA PETITE LÉGUME, 36 rue des Boulangers (5th, M:Jussieu), Tel. 01.40.46.06.85. Off the beaten track, but said to be one of the city's best haunts for vegans.

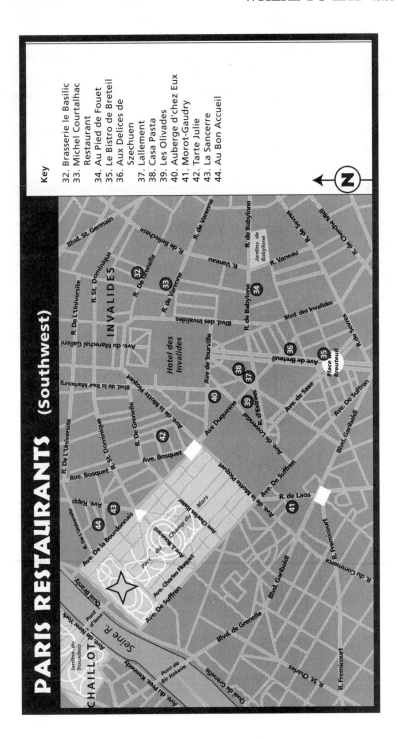

PARIS RESTAURANTS (Southwest)

Key

32. Brasserie le Basilic
33. Michel Courtalhac Restaurant
34. Au Pied de Fouet
35. Le Bistro de Breteil
36. Aux Delices de Szechuen
37. Lallement
38. Casa Pasta
39. Les Olivades
40. Auberge d'chez Eux
41. Morot-Gaudry
42. Tarte Julie
43. La Sancerre
44. Au Bon Accueil

up like baguettes out of a large woven basket. If you're really hungry, pick the salad cart for your appetizer. They leave the cart in case you want another helping. Or maybe you'd prefer a whole pan of garlic-fried frog legs for an appetizer. Next: main courses of rack of lamb, thick succulent chops, bubbling cassoulet with duck, or the better part of a rabbit bathed in mustard sauce. And finally the dessert cart with fresh fruit, ice cream, custard, chocolate mousse, and more and more and more. Plan a long walk afterward.

41. MOROT-GAUDRY *(haute cuisine/expensive)*, *8 rue de la Cavalerie (15th, M:La Motte-Picquet). Tel. 01.45.67.06.85.*

Notable mostly for its eighth-floor view of the Tour Eiffel and its stunning wine list. Many of the big-name wines are here – Haut-Brion, Lafite-Rothschild, Latour. There is even an impressive list of *vendage tardives* (superior Alsatian wines made from grapes harvested especially late in the season). The ambiance is a bit too hotel-like for our taste; the food is good, but not exceptional. Pigeon surrounded by baby artichokes and the appetizer of rougie and langoustino with avocado and tomato in a saffron sauce are notable.

42. TARTE JULIE *(quiches-tarts/inexpensive)*, *28 rue Cler (7th, M:École Militaire). Tel. 01.47.53.91.55.*

The window display alone will drive you crazy. Set in the heart of one of Paris's finest market streets, Tarte Julie creates a fabulous variety of quiches and tarts to munch on right there or take home. Combinations include salmon with spinach, tomato, feta, and basil; tomato, eggplant, and red pepper pineapple, nuts, and coconut; pears and chocolate. Julie's also makes a few salads and pizzas.

43. LA SANCERRE *(lunch/inexpensive)*, *22 avenue Rapp (7th, M:École Militaire). Tel. 01.45.51.75.91.*

Walking into this neighborhood wine bar is like stepping into someone's French country living room. Comfortable, cozy, friendly, and an ideal refuge from the crowds near the Tour Eiffel. Perfect for a light lunch, with good omelets, salads, and dessert tarts. The wine? Sancerre, from the Loire Valley, of course.

44. AU BON ACCUEIL *(traditional/inexpensive)*, *14 rue de Monttessuy (7th, M:École Militaire). Tel. 01.47.05.46.11.*

After fighting the crowds at the Tour Eiffel, you will welcome this friendly, family-owned restaurant with open arms. It is the perfect place to savor a lovely lunch or intimate dinner, and to gather your wits over a *pot* of Beaujolais or Côtes du Rhône. This tiny restaurant sees relatively few tourists and offers discerning locals healthy portions of reasonably priced and well-prepared meals.

Dishes include endive salad topped with chunks of heady Roquefort cheese, tangy *oeufs en meurette*, magnificent fresh vegetable soups, rabbit fricasée, boudin with roasted apples, roast breast of pigeon, and sinfully rich tiramisu for dessert. Game season brings out the best of the talented young chef. One of our favorite small restaurants.

RIGHT BANK
Near the Champs-Élysées
8th & 16th Arrondissements

45. LA BUTTE CHAILLOT (*haute cuisine/moderate*), *110bis avenue Kléber (16th, M:Boissiäre). Tel. 01.47.27.88.88.*

This lively "baby bistro" belongs to master chef Guy Savoy, whose primary restaurant is located not far from the Chaillot and bears his very marketable name. The contemporary decor, with sienna painted stucco walls, hardwood floors, and turquoise seating that matches the wait staff's shirts, would look right at home in Seattle or Santa Fe. Savoy's signature inventive menu features dishes such as red mullet and sardines marinated in a basil vinaigrette; medallions of lamb with roasted rounds of goat cheese; ravioli with snails and fresh parsley; and a cassis-flavored duck breast. On the down side: the wine list is skimpy and the staff stretched too thin. Americans are often seated in the same corner, a practice that drives us nuts.

46. L'AVENUE (*French-Italian/moderate*), *41 avenue Montaigne (8th, M:Pont de l'Alma). Tel. 01.40.70.14.91.*

A trendy contemporary restaurant set on an upper crust avenue. The chic crowd is either affluent or just knows how to dress well. The food, with everything from snails to monkfish to pasta, blends French and Italian. A strange mix of genres, though it seems in general to work. The wine list is adequate, but doesn't go back much further than 1988, thus missing many of the best years of the 1980s. Truth be told: this is one of the most overrated spots in town.

47. L'ECLUSE *(traditional/moderate), 64 rue François-Ier (8th, M:George V). Tel. 01.47.20.77.09.*

This is one of a handful of comfortable wine bars by this name scattered around town. The one across from the Madeleine is our favorite (see number 56 below), but the menu is the same at each (simple, with salads and light meat dishes) and, if you like wine, you'll enjoy any of them.

48. GUY SAVOY *(haute cuisine/very expensive), 18 rue Troyon (17th, M:Charles-de-Gaulle). Tel. 01.43.80.40.61. Closed Sunday.*

First class. Newly redecorated in beige fabrics and with modern paintings and African sculptures, this contemporary classic is one of the city's most elegant restaurants. The food is equally stylish and creative, offering such dishes as marinated tuna with caviar, veal kidneys with a mousse of artichokes and mustard, roast veal chops with wild mushrooms, a cream of lentil soup with fresh parsley and langoustines, and chicken breast with spinach and morrel mushrooms in a light cream sauce.

The lengthy wine list is spectacular, with pages of Meursaults and Montrachets, Graves and Pommards, even Champagnes. Ask for the special hand-written list of vintages reaching back to the early 1900s. You'll talk about the food (and the price) for years to come.

49. LE BISTRO DE L'ÉTOILE *(traditional/moderate), 13 rue Troyon (17th, M:Charles-de-Gaulle). Tel. 01.42.67.25.95.*

L'Étoile in the name refers to the Charles-de-Gaulle traffic circle just a block south. But it might just as well have been named for the owner, Guy Savoy. He is one of the acknowledged superstars of Parisian cuisine and this tiny spot, just across the street from his two-star restaurant, was the first of several bistros he has opened since 1988.

L'Étoile offers the casual comfort and reasonable prices that are foreign to Savoy's flagship. That was the point. When he converted this former insurance company office, he just wanted a modest retreat near his restaurant where he could meet chums for a simple plate of food and a glass of *vin ordinaire*. But shortly after opening, L'Étoile was "discovered" and became quickly popular.

It is tiny, with just 25 seats, and the decor is minimalist (mirrors and blond wood), but the food is top-notch. The menu, made of cardboard, offers a handful of starters and main courses, most of which are tradi-

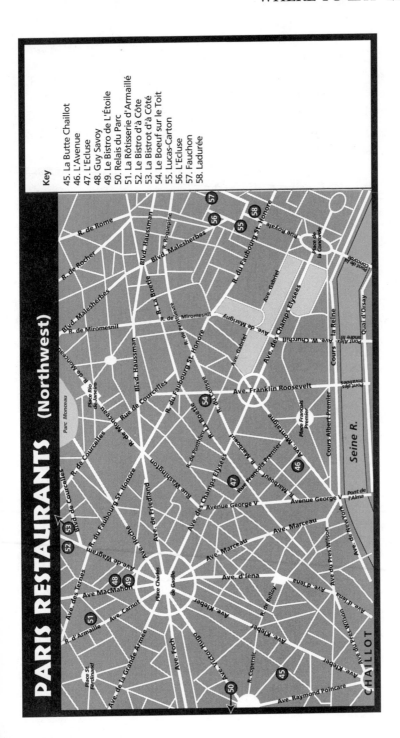

PARIS RESTAURANTS (Northwest)

Key

45. La Butte Chaillot
46. L'Avenue
47. L'Ecluse
48. Guy Savoy
49. Le Bistro de L'Étoile
50. Relais du Parc
51. La Rôtisserie d'Armaillé
52. Le Bistro d'à Côté
53. La Bistrot d'à Côté
54. Le Boeuf sur le Toit
55. Lucas-Carton
56. L'Ecluse
57. Fauchon
58. Ladurée

tional dishes that have been dressed up a bit, either through the preparation or presentation.

Dishes: a terrine of leeks and chicken livers, finely sliced cod marinated in a citrus vinaigrette, a batch of mussels and scallops pan-fried with saffron, back of rabbit stuffed with spinach, a *fricassée* of farm-raised chicken, a small veal roast with a preserve of onions, leeks and coriander, *sole meunière*, a coffee parfait with spoonfuls of chocolate mousse.

50. RELAIS DU PARC *(haute/expensive), 55 avenue Raymond Poincaré (16th, M:Victor Hugo). Tel. 01.44.05.66.10.*

Some say Alain Ducasse, associate of Jöel Robuchon, is the most accomplished chef in all of France (some have even said the world). If you can afford 900FF per person without wine (which would cost another 500FF or so per person), then you should make it a point to dine in his exquisite Michelin three-star restaurant at 59 avenue Raymond Poincaré, a few blocks southwest of the Arc de Triomphe. But if you want a taste of Ducasse at a more reasonable price and in a lovely setting, he is a hands-on consultant to the Relais du Parc next door to his restaurant.

Owned and run by Le Parc Hotel, the Relais is an absolute delight during warmer weather when you can enjoy the enormous but tranquil cobbled courtyard through a small passageway off the street. Canvas umbrellas the size of sails protect the wrought-iron tables, which are themselves covered in linen with table settings worthy of most any elegant restaurant. The interior is a bit more woody and masculine with a bit of the feel of a chic hunting lodge.

These dishes are not the works of art found in Ducasse's proper restaurant. Still, they are inventive and use the best possible ingredients: tangy caviar of eggplant, cold cream of cucumber soup, pan-fried John Dory with mashed potatoes made mostly of butter, lobster with basil, blood sausage with baked apple, pigeon baked in a pastry with broad beans and bacon, roast duckling.

51. LA RÔTISSERIE D'ARMAILLÉ *(nouvelle and traditional/moderate), 6 rue d'Armaillé (17th,, M:Charles-de-Gaulle). Tel. 01.42.27.19.20.*

Jacques Cagna, one of the several grand chefs of Paris, owns three "baby bistros," each of which is run by a chef who chooses his own menu (with Cagna's approval). This is the best of the three for a variety of reasons: for one, the *prix fixe* is quite reasonable, especially given the portions large enough to sate the biggest appetite. Second, the Armaillé, with its generous use of blond wood and its splashes of soft pink and green fabrics, is welcoming and comfortable. The bistro caters to a largely neighborhood clientele, so the waiters won't rush you out to make way for more tourists. And finally, the cuisine is more distinctive. It's inventive within reason and prides itself on fresh ingredients.

A sampling of dishes: lobster salad with massive chuck of lobster, a gathering of green and white asparagus with a light cream sauce, green lentils with mushrooms, saddle of rabbit with caramelized baby onions, veal chops with a tangy orange sauce, range chicken with black pasta, roast salmon, and Guinea fowl served with a *mélange* of eggplant and onion in a pastry shell tied and baked like a pretty package.

52. LE BISTRO D'À CÔTE (*traditional/moderate*), *10 rue Gustave-Flaubert (17th, M:Pereire). Tel. 01.42.67.05.81.*

Master chef Michel Rostang's first "baby bistro" — meaning a bistro owned by one of the top chefs recognized by the Michelin guide empire. But not only was this Rostang's first when he christened it in 1987, it was the first of its kind in all of Paris. Rostang's buddy, Guy Savoy, opened one the next year and several have since followed. Rostang, chatting with us in his two-star restaurant next door to the bistro, explained that not only does the bistro give his clients a much more affordable alternative to his two-star, but he makes money off the deal as well. While he has 30 employees on the payroll in the main restaurant, he has only 7 in the bistro.

Like all five of Rostang's bistros, this first is warm and inviting and decorated with one of his collections of *bibelots*, which he purchases from the massive flea markets on the edge of town. The walls here are lined with his collection of ceramic mugs and pitchers from the late 1800s, all depicting fops and dandies and questionable looking ladies.

Best of all, of course, is that the food here is first-rate. Rostang hires an outside chef, but keeps a close eye on the kitchen. The dishes are traditional, but with a bit of genius thrown in. (And you're likely to make a new friend here — the manager's tiny poodle, Ulysses, who wanders through periodically to check on your progress.)

Dishes: a starter of lobster and basil raviolis, a terrine of rabbit in aspic, cold pistachio and langoustine soup, roast quail with raviolis, lamb saddle grilled with shallots, thin sliced duckling with cassis, roast cod with lemon and fennel, flamed raspberry crêpes.

53. LA BISTROT D'À CÔTÉ (*traditional/moderate*), *16 avenue de Villiers (17th,, M: Villiers). Tel. 01.47.63.25.61.*

A truly wonderful homey restaurant in a pleasant and largely residential area, this was the second "baby bistro" opened by two-star chef Michel Rostang. The formula here is pretty much the same as in his first, which is located right next door (as you might guess by the bistro's name) to Rostang's chic flagship on rue Gustave-Flaubert. The setting is welcoming, the decor authentic, and the food first-rate. Dishes often follow traditional formulas, but are improved with a bit of imaginative seasoning or special presentations. The wine list is also typical of Rostang's smart approach, offering a limited list but one that is seeded with some real finds at reasonable prices. Highly recommended.

54. LE BOEUF SUR LE TOIT (*traditional/moderate*), *34 rue du Colisée (8th, M:Franklin-Roosevelt). Tel. 01.53.93.65.55.*

An Art Deco showplace that was remodeled in the mid-1980s, it once drew the likes of Picasso and Coco Chanel. Today, it still attracts an energetic crowd of snappy dressers, hot young professionals, and eager tourists. Try to convince the maitre d' to seat you in the first room, where much of the best people-watching is staged. Just outside you will pass the oyster shuckers who prepare the huge plates of shellfish placed on stands in the middle of so many people's tables. The staff is attentive but often harried.

55. LUCAS-CARTON, *9 place de la Madeleine (8th, M:Madeleine). Tel. 01.42.65.22.90. Closed Saturday and Sunday.*

This is genuinely elegant dining, set immediately across the avenue from the inspiring Madeleine church. The Belle Epoque decor, especially the remarkable carved wood partitions and paneling, is exquisite. The service, even down to the doorman, is refined and formal and attentive. The wine list is magnificent and the presentations of lamb, pigeon, pheasant, lobster, and various fish are wonderfully imaginative and artistic (desserts are visual masterpieces). On the menu, Chef Alain Senderens notes the perfect wine with each dish, and serves it by the glass so that you can profit from his wisdom. On the downside: the individual wines chosen are not always as good as they should be (inevitable because of the cost of the best wines), and with the money you spend on a single dinner, you could stay in a good hotel, savor a nice dinner somewhere else, and still have money left over for some modest shopping.

56. L'ECLUSE *(traditional/moderate), 15 place de la Madeleine (8th, M:Madeleine). Tel. 01.42.65.34.69.*

Our favorite of the wine bars that go by this name, and an ideal place for lunch — or, for that matter, for dinner. The ambiance is comfortable and stylish, especially the garden room in the back. The food is limited but satisfying, with carpaccio, smoked salmon, steaks, sausage, foie gras, and potato and watercress salad. And, of course, there is the wine, almost all of which is from the Bordeaux region and much of which is available by the glass, so you can experiment without risking several hundred francs at a throw. Look for the wines that are listed as the "second" wine of one of the premier châteaux. They are often memorable finds.

57. FAUCHON *(everything/moderate), 30 place de la Madeleine (8th, M:Madeleine). Tel. 01.42.66.92.63 for the brasserie and 01.47.42.56.58 for the restaurant.*

Fauchon is famous as a world-class grocery and take-out deli, with enormous selections of baked goods, fresh vegetables, booze, prepared dishes, candies, canned foods, and anything else you can consume. But the main store also has a brasserie downstairs and a more formal restaurant upstairs. The contemporary brasserie offers reasonable *prix fixe* lunches and dinners, while the predominantly peach-colored neo-classical restaurant serves a respectable range of traditional dishes with *haute cuisine* touches. You can order something as simple as *sole meunière* or filet of beef with Bordelaise sauce, or get a wee bit more complicated with something like filets of red mullet in basil butter with potato purée and olive oil. The grocery is a good place to find a gift for your hungry friends back home.

58. LADURÉE *(tea salon/moderate), 16 rue Royale (8th, M:Madeleine). Tel. 01.42.60.21.79.*

Founded in 1862, and probably one of the more adorable tea salons in town. Busy too, with locals and others who crowd into the tiny tables (often with their puppies by their sides or at their feet) and hold animated conversations over pots of tea, lunch salads, and buttery pastries. You'll have to arrive for an early lunch to find a seat in the downstairs section. Gift boxes available here, which you can stuff with pastry or chocolates.

Near The Louvre
1st & 2nd Arrondissements

59. CAFÉ DE LA PAIX *(traditional/moderate)*, *12 boulevard des Capucines (9th, M:Opéra). Tel. 01.40.07.30.20.*

Gloriously gaudy, this Belle Epoque café's main claim to fame is that it dates back to the opening of the Opéra Garnier, which is just across the street. Good for people watching over a cold beer on a hot day. Even better, sip wine in the evening and watch the smartly dressed crowd arriving at the opera house. Food is an afterthought.

60. LA RÔTISSERIE MONSIGNY *(combines nouvelle and traditional/ moderate)*, *1 rue Monsigny (2nd, M:4 Septembre). Tel. 01.42.96.16.61.*

This Rôtisserie is one of the three "baby bistros" owned in the city by master chef Jacques Cagna, whose primary Michelin two-star restaurant can be found at 14 rue Grands Augustins in the 6th *arrondissement*. Some of the grand chef owners of local baby bistros are dictatorial, demanding that the menus and preparations conform to the boss's will. Cagna takes a bit of a different angle, hiring first-rate chefs for his bistros and letting them do their own thing — within reason. Cagna drops into all three of his spots to taste the wares.

The Monsigny is comfortable and contemporary, as are all of Cagna's "babies." A palette of yellows and peaches and greens, with a forest of healthy plants, makes for a sort of soothing garden setting. The menu is promising, mixing standards with more experimental, almost nouvelle, fare. Roasted meats, as you might guess from the name, are the house specialty and, indeed, are among the best plates. Other dishes, frankly, seemed a bit flat in taste and might have sat on a shelf too long.

Dishes include: small cakes made of rabbit meat suspended in aspic, sole in a pastry, a *fricassée* of calamari, grilled river trout, veal with a sauce combining cream and sea urchins, saddle of rabbit roasted and served with gnocci, veal kidneys with shallots, farm-raised Guinea fowl with roasted breast meat and preserved leg meat, wild chicken with black pasta suffused with squid ink and an apple purée, *crème brulée* with a hint of bourbon-vanilla, an orange peel mousse.

61. HARRY'S NEW YORK BAR *(ambiance/moderate)*, *5 rue Daunou (2nd, M:Opéra). Tel. 01.42.61.71.14.*

If it looks like an American bar and smells like an American bar (sour and stale), then ... well, you know the rest. Harry's claim to fame is: one,

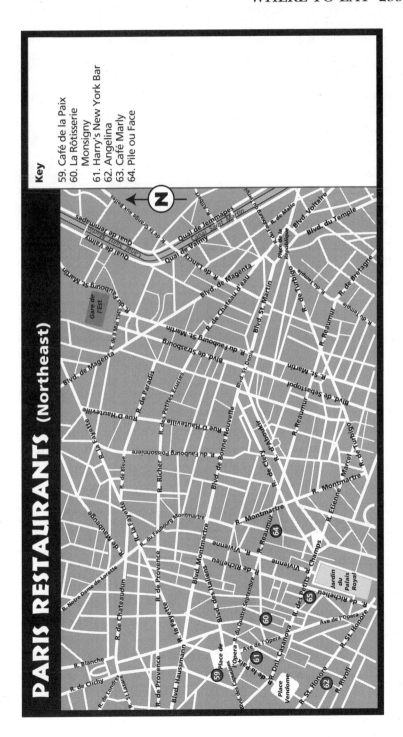

PARIS RESTAURANTS (Northeast)

Key

59. Café de la Paix
60. La Rôtisserie Monsigny
61. Harry's New York Bar
62. Angelina
63. Café Marly
64. Pile ou Face

that Hemingway drank here regularly; two, that the Bloody Mary was invented here; and three, that a bartender from The Plaza bought the place after World War I and gave it his name. The college pennants on the walls are faded, the hot dogs "served anytime" are not exactly ballpark grade, and the prices are absurd. Visit if you must.

62. ANGELINA *(tea salon/moderate), 226 rue de Rivoli (1st, M:Tuileries). Tel. 01.42.60.82.00. Open daily.*

Hot chocolate like you have never tasted before. So rich and heavy you need to ask for a small pot of steamed milk to thin out the marvelous mixture. This sinful and sumptuous tea salon is decked out in turn-of-the-century marble-topped tables and Empire knock-off chairs and is a civilized retreat from the chaos of the rue de Rivoli. Angelina offers salads, fish dishes, and other light fare, but the real reason for stopping is for the pastries, tea, and coffee.

63. CAFÉ MARLY *(international/moderate), Cour Napoléon, Palais du Louvre (1st, M:Louvre). Tel. 01.49.26.06.60.*

When we first spotted this stunning café we passed it by, only because we assumed the prices would be outrageous. We were wrong, and what a waste that we didn't know sooner.

The Marly is the restaurant that you can see in the arcades of the new Richelieu Wing of the Louvre. Technically the address is 93 rue de Rivoli, but you reach the restaurant from the interior of the Louvre courtyard near the glass pyramid. It is a must see. Comfortable tables are stretched the length of the arcades and give you the sense of eating outdoors, even though you are completely protected. And while you eat, you have a full view of the pyramid, the fountains and the crowds.

The Marly also has an interior section upstairs, with one room overlooking the pyramid and the other peering through generous windows into the new sculpture atrium of the Richelieu Wing. Fabulous! The decor is inspiring as well, with rich blue walls, light panels recessed in the walls and lots of hardwood. The food is solid, with all sorts of international standards such as gazpacho, melon with Parma ham, penne pasta with tomato confit and basil, tuna steak with corriander, a mixed grill, cheeseburgers, club sandwiches, thick salmon filets, luscious wedges of Camembert cheese, poached haddock, chocolate tarte, cheesecake and sorbets.

64. PILE OU FACE *(traditional-haute/moderate), 52bis rue Notre-Dame-des-Victoires (2nd, M:Bourse). Tel. 01.42.33.64.33. Closed Saturday and Sunday.*

This tiny restaurant, whose name translates as "Heads or Tails," enjoys a well-earned reputation for its warm welcome and inventive menu. Smartly decorated with burgundy-colored fabric walls, Pile ou Face attracts a trendy crowd, some of whom you will no doubt meet because the space is intimate. Dishes are essentially traditional with clever flourishes, such as the roast quail with braised halves of endives and a sauce laced with foie gras. The white asparagus spears are enormous and the tuna, grilled on one side only and steeped in a tangy caper and olive oil purée, is especially tasty. Their honey-flavored *crême brulée* is rightly famous.

65. WILLI'S WINE BAR *(nouvelle/moderate), 13 rue des Petits-Champs (1st, M:Bourse). Tel. 01.42.61.05.09. Closed Sunday.*

More contemporary, more casual, and less French than we ever imagined. In fact, you'll hear very little French spoken, even by the staff, which, like owner Mark Williamson, is British. Still, the food is quite good, with items such as lobster tail salad, roast pigeon, and hake wrapped around a moist tapenade. The wine list, as you might guess, is a gem. Lots of Bordeaux, Burgundy, and Châteauneuf du Papes from the 1980s, during which there were several good years. A few selections go back to the '50s and '60s. Willi's serves about a dozen relatively recent vintages by the glass.

66. JOE ALLEN *(American/moderate), 30 rue Pierre-Lescot (1st, M:Marcel). Tel. 01.42.36.70.13.*

Cut in the mold of the Joe Allen restaurants in New York and London, with essentially the same red, white, and blue menu. We're talking burgers, meat loaf with mashed potatoes, a T-bone grilled medium rare, Southern fried chicken with corn bread, and apple pie for dessert. Some of the best American food around in a semi-casual brick setting decorated, like the two sister restaurants, with theater posters. Too bad the neighborhood is so seedy.

67. AU CHIEN QUI FUME *(traditional/moderate), 33 rue du Pont-Neuf (1st, M:Pont Neuf, Châtelet). Tel. 01.42.36.07.42.*

This is one of the few genuinely inviting bistros in the sometimes gloomy and forbidding neighborhood around Les Halles. The restaurant looks across the top of the modern cement and glass Les Halles mall where, long ago, Paris's largest open market once stood. The bistro is cheery, well-lit, and welcoming, with a satisfying menu of traditional staples.

True to its name (The Dog Who Smokes), the decor is dominated by paintings of dogs. Not precious portraits of well-coiffed pure-breds sitting on pillows. But stuffy, ponderous dogs in smoking jackets sitting in overstuffed chairs and sucking on pipes that would have made Sherlock Holmes blanch. And winsome female dogs lounging around in lingerie, and dogs in the traditional black jackets and white shirts of the Parisian waiter.

House specials include a variety of terrines, an occasionally overpowering fish soup, a salad of avocados and citrus fruit, veal medallions doused with cream and cèpes, fine grilled *sole meunière*, roast lamb chops, *confit de canard*, and steaks with either pepper or Bearnaise sauce. The profiteroles for dessert are enormous and come with their own tub of chocolate. Seafood platters with oysters, clams, and the like are another house specialty.

The Marais & Bastille
3rd, 4th & 11th Arrondissements

68. BENOÎT *(traditional/moderate-expensive), 20 rue Saint-Martin (4th, M:Hôtel de Ville). Tel. 01.42.72.25.76. Closed Saturday and Sunday. No credit cards.*

This classy bistro first opened its doors way back in 1912 just around the corner from the Tour Saint-Jacques. In fact, they have adopted the tower as a part of their logo. This is one of the most chic bistros in town, with a near-elegant decor of brass light fixtures, cut-glass partitions, and an antique paint treatment on the walls. You'll see an unusual number of coats and ties.

The menu is unusually dressy for a bistro as well, with dishes such as artichoke hearts with asparagus and green beans, smoked salmon sprinkled with salmon eggs, a lobster and asparagus salad, chicken in a crust with a ragout of artichokes, mullet and tapenade, sole in spinach leaves – all served on bright new plates with Benoît written on top in a delicate script. Only the wine list is uninspired. Prices are too steep and, remember, no credit cards taken here.

69. LA PERLA *(Mexican/inexpensive), 26 rue François Miron (4th, M:Saint-Paul). Tel. 01.42.77.59.40.*

A fun corner restaurant with about fifteen tables that are almost always jammed full at dinner time. Lunch is a bit less crowded. Decorated in a Sante Fe prairie pink, La Perla has struck a chord with the youngish crowd, which can be found yammering at a million miles an hour, sipping beers, and digging into spicy chili and beans, quesadillas with shrimp, onions, cheese and *crème fraîche*, or burritos with chêvre, spinach, tomato, corn, pineapple and guacamole. For dessert try the brownies or cheese cake. The portions are not the mountains of food you'd find in Lubbock, but the quality makes up the difference.

70. JO GOLDENBERG *(deli/moderate), 7 rue des Rosiers (4th, M:Saint-Paul). Tel. 01.48.87.20.16.*

A classic Jewish deli that rivals even those in New York. With a jam-packed takeout case up front and often equally jammed restaurant in back, Jo's serves up Hungarian beef goulash, chopped meat balls "grand-mother style," cabbage leaves stuffed with meat and rice, borscht, marinated herring, moussaka, and other wonderfully filling dishes. Photos of Goldenberg with every conceivable local celeb decorate the walls inside and out. A tragic sidenote: Six patrons were killed in the summer of 1982 when anti-Semitic terrorists bombed the restaurant.

71. LE BISTRO DE BOFINGER *(traditional/inexpensive), 6 rue de la Bastille (4th, M:Bastille). Tel. 01.42.72.05.23.*

"The little pleasures of a good bistrot": That's the motto of this newly opened offspring of Bofinger, the Art Nouveau masterpiece of a restaurant directly across the street. Wood paneling, lots of mirrors, red leather banquettes, and a colorful tile floor give this baby bistro a warm and welcoming neighborhood feel to it. The prices are impressively reasonable and, though the menu and wine list are limited, the food is fresh and flavorful. Look for the house steak tartare, grilled andouilette, herring filets and potato salad, chicken fricasée, and clafloutie for dessert.

72. BOFINGER *(traditional-seafood/moderate), 5 rue de la Bastille (4th, M:Bastille). Tel. 01.42.72.87.82.*

Bofinger claims to be one of the oldest brasseries in town. It is also immaculate and the bursting flower arrangements in the ornate majolica vases give the place a youthful, spring-is-in-the-air atmosphere. Prices for standards such as the steak tartare and escargots are a bit higher than at the Bofinger bistro across the street, though there is a reasonable *prix fixe* menu that includes wine. Meat and choucroute are available here, but the house specialties tend toward fresh shellfish and other seafood.

73. CAFÉ DE L'INDUSTRIE *(light meals/inexpensive), 16 rue Saint-Sabin (11th, M:Bastille). Tel. 01.47.00.13.53.*

A hip neighborhood hangout that would be at home in the San Francisco Tenderloin – hardwood floors, Oriental rugs, paintings by the locals on the walls, young waitresses in black jeans, and a motorcycle or two out on the sidewalk. A great place to nurse a beer, drink too much coffee, or shovel in the house chili.

74. CHEZ PAUL *(traditional/moderate), 13 rue de Charonne (11th, M:Bastille). Tel. 01.47.00.34.57.*

Very popular bistro in a neighborhood that has come alive since the completion of the Bastille Opera House in 1989. A bit like a Left Bank restaurant, only more intense as locals cram into every nook until the wee hours, devouring such carefully prepared basics as legs of rabbit with chévre and mint, *steak au poivre* flamed in cognac, the house steak tartare, filet of trout, and *crème brulée*. The bistro's motto: "One drinks, one eats ..." What else is there?

75. CHARDENOUX *(traditional/moderate), 1 rue Jules-Vallés (11th, M:Charonne). Tel. 01.43.71.49.52.*

A delightful old-fashioned neighborhood bistro in a still peaceful corner of the 11th *arrondissement*. This is the way bistros must have been decades ago, with frosted glass partitions, black and white photos on the walls, slightly worn trim (especially on the doors into the kitchen), a bunch of regulars, a neighborly staff, and dishes that stick to your ribs. The *oeufs en meurette* (poached on small rounds of toast, accompanied by garlic and bacon in a tangy red wine sauce) are excellent, as are the foie gras and green bean salad, and the veal kidney with a mustard sauce.

Other dishes include endive with chunks of Roquefort, gazpacho, veal chops with morel mushrooms, roast saddle of lamb with thyme, chocolate mousse with orange, and vanilla ice cream blanketed with warm caramel. If you lived nearby, this is the kind of place where you'd eat all the time.

11. SEEING THE SIGHTS

MONUMENTS, MUSEUMS, & PARKS

Notre-Dame (4th), the **Tour Eiffel** (7th), and the **Arc de Triomphe** (8th) have become universally familiar symbols of Paris. But these are more than slabs of stone and webs of steel that have been pieced together cleverly. They demonstrate the strength of the French spirit and the genius of the nation's artisans and builders.

Smaller cases in point are scattered throughout the central section of the city. Taking a simple stroll you are likely to find yourself turning a corner and discovering a magnificent sculpture or an architectural tribute celebrating one of the many heroes or legends of French history.

Paris is equally famous for its museums, the best known of which is the **Louvre** (1st). No question, the Louvre is stunning in its scope and grandeur. Unfortunately, however, the crowds, especially with the opening in late 1993 of the new **Richelieu wing**, are often monstrously large.

In fact, if you are pressed for time, don't lose an entire day by trying to tame the Louvre. Save it for a longer visit, or spend a couple of hours touring just one or two of its galleries. The point is that there are other fine collections and museums in the city – some with more charm – and you don't want to have seen little more of Paris than the inside of a single museum, no matter how grand it is.

The **Musée D'Orsay** (7th), converted from a dingy railroad station and opened in 1986, is an absolutely beautiful setting for its 19th- and early 20th-century works. And the **Rodin** (7th) and **Picasso** (3rd) museums are must-sees. They are graceful, welcoming former homes and gardens that have been converted into museums. The Rodin especially is unlike any conventional museum you've seen.

In general, museums close one day a week, either Monday or Tuesday, so check in advance. Hours are roughly 10 a.m. to 5 p.m., and admission for adults runs from about 25 to 45FF, with half price for children and seniors. We have included prices for most museums and monuments, but admission fares have more than tripled in the last decade and they change constantly. Many museums will also have special exhibits, which almost always require an additional entrance fee.

A last bit of advice here: pace yourself. Museums are inspiring, but leave time for seeing the city and experiencing the people as well.

The parks, too, are a crucial element in the city's personality. There aren't many, and the city has less parkland than most cities its size. Still, there are several well-placed sanctuaries of green that give the city a bit of breathing room in some of its most crowded quarters.

These oases are often decorated with well manicured lawns and spectacularly colorful gardens. And the larger ones offer pony rides and puppet shows for children and tranquil trails where you can daydream in peace.

Touring By Neighborhood

As in chapters 9 and 10, *Where to Stay* and *Where to Eat*, this chapter is arranged by neighborhood. Grouping your sightseeing by neighborhood makes sense if you're pressed for time.

FARE CARDS SAVE MONEY

Save yourself time and money by purchasing a **pass** *valid for 1, 3, or 5 days (80FF, 160FF, and 240FF). The cards are good at almost all museums and monuments, and they allow you to skip the lines at the ticket booth and go directly to the exhibition spaces.*

You can find passes at most museums, monuments, Métro stations, and the **Paris Tourist Office** *at 127 Champs-Élysées (8th). Helpful phrase:* **Je voudrais une carte touristique pour les musées, s'il vous plaît.** *This means, "I would like a tourist card for the museums, please."*

THE ISLANDS
Îles de la Cité & Saint-Louis

1. PONT NEUF, *near the western end of the Île de la Cité, connecting the island with both banks (1st, M:Pont Neuf).*

Paris's oldest surviving bridge, begun in 1578 and completed in 1604. It was also the first major Parisian bridge without houses, allowing for a westward view of the city that today takes in the **Louvre** on the Right Bank and the apartment buildings and, if you stretch, the **Musée d'Orsay** on the Left Bank.

The **bronze of Henri IV** astride his steed is an early 19th-century copy of the version that was melted down during the Revolution.

2. MUSÉE DE LA CONCIERGERIE, *1 quai de l'Horloge (1st, M:Cité). Tel. 01.53.73.78.50. Open daily. Admission 32FF.*

A forbidding looking place, to say the least. This 14th-century prison was the last stop for Marie Antoinette and 2,600 others before their heads were lopped off in the name of the Revolution. In an upstairs chamber, you will find a list of 2,780 individuals who were officially condemned during the Revolution and subsequent Reign of Terror.

Just past the entrance hall is the enormous and impressive **Salle des Gens d'Armes** (Hall of the Men-at-Arms), and beside it a massive kitchen with four fireplaces where meals were prepared for as many as 3,000 at a time.

Also walk the **rue de Paris**, a small, depressing corridor leading to the cells and named after the state's chief executioner, not so fondly referred to as Monsieur de Paris. Further along you will find the **Salle de la Toilette** (where prisoners were prepared for death), a re-creation of Marie Antoinette's cell (she was executed October 16, 1793), and a small chapel now named after 22 Girondins (members of a liberal party that held power briefly in 1791). The Girondins said their last prayers here having been condemned by Danton, who was himself condemned shortly afterward.

3. SAINTE-CHAPELLE, *tucked inside the courtyard of the 19th-century Palais de Justice at 4 boulevard du Palais (1st, M:Cité). Tel. 01.53.73.78.51. Admission 40FF.*

Stained glass — lots of it. In fact, there is more stained glass here than in any other church in the world — 6,700 square feet of it, depicting 1,134

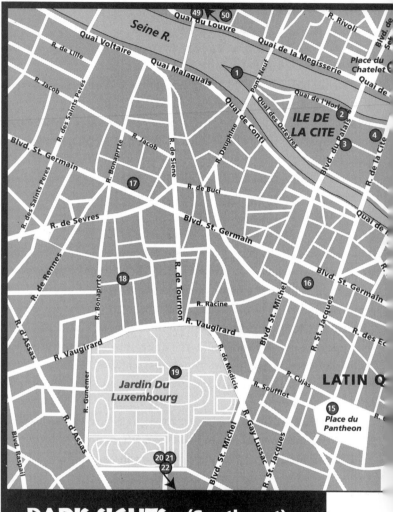

PARIS SIGHTS (Southeast)

1. Pont Neuf
2. Musée de la Conciergerie
3. Sainte-Chapelle
4. Place Louis-Lépine
5. Notre-Dame de Paris
6. Square de l'Ile de France
7. Memorial de la Déportation
8. Ile Saint-Louis
9. Bibliotheque Nationale
10. Jardin des Plantes
11. Institut du Monde Arabe
12. Arènes de Lutece
13. Manufacture des Gobelins
14. Mouffetard Marketplace

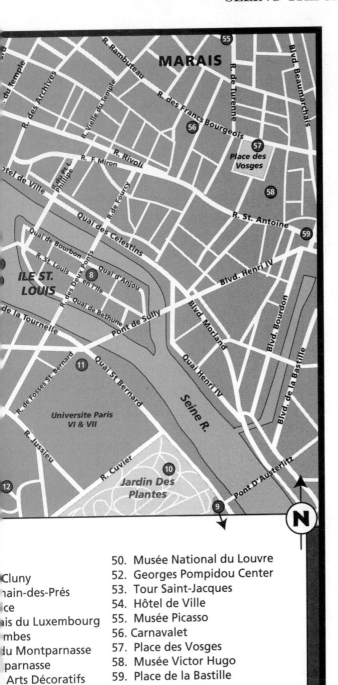

Biblical scenes. The scenes run chronologically, beginning with the story of Genesis just to the left inside the entrance. At the end ... well, it's The End – the Apocalypse.

On a brilliant day, with the sun backlighting the windows, the sight is breathtaking.

Sainte-Chapelle, completed in 1248 after just five years of labor, rises 67 feet into the air without the structural support of flying buttresses (a design considered revolutionary at the time). The cathedral was specifically intended to house various relics, including Christ's crown of thorns and a nail from the Cross. **Louis IX**, who was later canonized (Saint Louis), had purchased the relics for almost three times what it cost him to build Sainte-Chapelle to house them.

These relics are now found in Notre-Dame, and are shown on Good Friday.

Eugene-Emmanuel Viollet-le-Duc, a 19th-century architect who headed the restoration of Notre-Dame, also worked on Sainte-Chapelle, repairing damage done to the chapel after the Revolution, when the building was used as a warehouse for the courts.

4. PLACE LOUIS-LÉPINE, *on the north side of the island, just off of rue de la Cité, which cuts the island in half (4th).*

A lively flower market with an amazing variety of cut flowers and potted plants and trees. On Sundays, bird sellers take over the square, offering thousands of exotic birds, elaborate cages, and various supplies. A fabulous photo op.

5. NOTRE-DAME DE PARIS *(4th, M:Cité), at the eastern end of the Île de la Cité, Tel. 01.44.32.16.72. Admission to cathedral, free. Admission to the towers, 35FF.*

To stand in the Place du Parvis and to gaze at the western facade of this cathedral is to regain faith in humanity. Sometimes, you realize, the human race can subdue its petty squabbling long enough to fashion a miracle.

Begun in 1163, during the reign of **Louis VII**, Notre-Dame is the acknowledged masterpiece of French Gothic art and architecture. Built on a site where Romans worshiped a thousand years before, Notre-Dame took another 182 years and generations of craftsmen, stonecutters, architects, and glassworkers to complete. The two towers top off a perfectly balanced facade, and off the northern and southern sides of the cathedral you will find the remarkable flying buttresses that keep this stone marvel on its feet.

Also note the **"Gallery of Kings"** set above the three portals of the western facade, which are dedicated respectively to the Virgin Mary, the Last Judgment, and Sainte-Anne, the Virgin's mother. The gallery is a stunning array of sculptures depicting the 28 kings who are thought by the Catholic Church to be ancestors of Christ.

Understandably, Notre-Dame has frequently provided the backdrop for French history and literature. It was here where **Henri VI** of England, **Mary Stuart** (made Queen of France by her marriage to François II), and **Napoleon** were crowned. More recently, Requiem masses were held here for **Charles de Gaulle** and **Georges Pompidou**, both popular contemporary French presidents.

Supposedly pushed ahead in part by the huge public popularity of Victor Hugo's classic tale of *The Hunchback of Notre-Dame*, the cathedral received a major facelift in the mid-1800s, when an army of artisans marshaled together by architect Eugene-Emmanuel Viollet-le-Duc repaired the roof, reset the doors, and restored the stained-glass windows and small statues that adorn the facade.

For a view of the city and to appreciate the menacing gargoyles that line the western facade, climb the 255 steps leading up the north tower. At times you may think you'll never arrive, but the spiral trek is well worth the workout.

The **Square Jean XXIII**, a small park directly behind Notre-Dame, draws lots of visitors, in part because the tour buses for Notre-Dame park right behind it. Still, it is a pleasant place to stroll and gaze across the Seine to the apartments that line the Left Bank.

6. SQUARE DE L'ÎLE DE FRANCE, *also behind Notre-Dame at the easternmost tip of the Île de la Cité (4th, M:Cité). Admission free.*

A lovely little park with a dozen or so benches, where you can enjoy the sun, nibble on a sandwich, briefly escape the crush of tourists lined up outside their tour buses just a few yards behind you, and admire the apartments lining the bank of the Île Saint-Louis just off to your left.

FINDS & FAVORITES/SIGHTS

We simply never grow tired of these remarkable places.

5. NOTRE-DAME DE PARIS *(4th, M:Cité), at the eastern end of the Île de la Cité. Tel. 01.44.32.16.72*

14. MOUFFETARD MARKETPLACE, *rue Mouffetard, southeast of the Panthéon, parallel to the rue Monge in the heart of the Latin Quarter (5th, M:Censier-Daubenton)*

15. PANTHÉON, *rue Clotilde (5th, M:Cardinal Lemoine)*

19. JARDIN AND PALAIS DU LUXEMBOURG, *off of the boulevard Saint-Michel a few blocks south of the boulevard Saint-Germain (6th, M:Luxembourg). Tel. 01.42.34.25.95*

23. MUSÉE D'ORSAY, *1 rue Bellechasse (7th, M:Solférino). Tel. 01.40.49.48.14. or 01.40.49.48.84*

25. MUSÉE NATIONAL AUGUSTE RODIN, *77 rue de Varenne (7th, M:Varenne). Tel. 01.44.18.61.10*

44. OPÉRA GARNIER, *place de l'Opéra (9th, M:Opéra). Tel. 01.47.42.07.02*

55. MUSÉE PICASSO, *5 rue de Thorigny (3rd, M:Chemin Vert). Tel. 01.42.71.25.21*

57. PLACE DES VOSGES, *off of rue des Francs Bourgeois, just north of rue Saint Antoine in the Marais district (4th, M:Saint-Paul)*

SACRÉ-COEUR BASILICA, *35 rue du Chevalier-de-la-Barre (18th, M:Anvers). Tel. 01.53.41.89.00*

VINCENNES, *Parc Floral of the Bois de Vincennes (12th, M:Château de Vincennes)*

7. MÉMORIAL DE LA DÉPORTATION, *at the easternmost tip of the Île de la Cité in the Square de l'Île de France behind Notre-Dame (4th, M:Cité). Admission free.*

After the Nazi occupation of World War II, more than 30,000 Jewish citizens were rounded up, boarded onto boats at this very spot, and ferried away to death camps. Needless to say, this was not a distinguished moment in French history. Designed by **G.H. Pingusson** and finished in 1962, the small, below-ground memorial is somewhat like a tunnel, even though light filters in through narrow windows that open onto the river. All in all, it is quite disturbing, and, for that, also quite effective.

8. ÎLE SAINT-LOUIS *(4th, M:Pont Marie).*

Until the mid-1600s, there was no such thing as the Île Saint-Louis. Two smaller islands, the **Île aux Vaches** (the Island of the Cows) and the **Île Notre-Dame**, were fused together with landfill by real estate specula- tors, who then sold off lots for residential apartments — most of which are still standing.

In summertime, tourists flood **rue Saint-Louis-en-l'Île**, the small avenue that bisects the island from east to west. There are several fine small shops and galleries along this street, as well as a couple of decent restaurants and hotels.

For such a centrally located place, Saint-Louis's sidestreets and quais are surprisingly quaint and quiet — like an island in the city, you might say. Some of the apartments are quite grand, though many house artists and others who settle into the more reasonably priced apartments and never leave because rent controls keep the prices down.

Square Barye, at the eastern end of the island, is a haven of quiet and shade. But beneath its walls, the stone quai and walkway is one of Paris's better known "beaches," where young men and women bare virtually all on a sunny day.

LEFT BANK
The Latin Quarter
5th Arrondissement

9. BIBLIOTHEQUE NATIONALE DE FRANCE, *11 quai Francois Mauriac (13th, M:Quai de la Gare), Tel. 01.53.79.59.59. Parts are open daily. Admission to special exhibits are usually around 35FF.*

Some refer to this National Library as Mitterand's last revenge. It has been a common last rite for presidents to erect some signature structure before they leave office so that they will not soon be forgotten, and this was his. This library is far off the beaten path, but in some ways is well worth a look. It has four towers, one at each corner of a central low-lying structure, on top of which is a striking garden. The towers are meant to represent open books. An interesting intellectual concept, though it has had the predictable consequence of making it quite complicated for employees or researchers to get from one tower to the next. There are various readings and events, though very little in English. This would be a trip to admire the architecture, not the literature.

10. JARDIN DES PLANTES, *off of the Quai Saint Bernard, just east of the Jussieu campus of the University of Paris and just west of Gare d'Austerlitz (5th, M:Jussieu). Tel. 01.40.79.30.00. Open daily. Admission to galleries 15FF to 40FF; zoo, 30FF.*

This 350-year-old garden is one of Paris's most pleasant and least overrun stretches of green. Its long esplanade is planted with brilliant flowers of all kinds, including huge, fragrant roses and marigolds of every possible color. The **Herb Garden** that parallels the main esplanade is a cook's dream come true, the huge greenhouse is bursting with overripe exotica, and the modest zoo provides a pretty and pleasant diversion for the kids.

This is also home to the **Natural History Museum** *(36 rue Geoffroy St-Hilaire, near the Censier Daubenton Métro stop; Tel. 01.40.79.30.00).* This has all been renovated relatively recently, so it is very nicely done and highlights the French fascination for natural sciences. There is the Gallery of Evolution, as well as galleries for minerology, anatomy and paleontology. A great spot for the kids—what child doesn't like dinosaurs?

11. INSTITUT DU MONDE ARABE, *1 rue des Fosses-Saint-Bernard (5th, M:Jussieu). Tel. 01.40.51.38.38. Closed Monday. Admission to the museum, 25FF.*

On first glance, the **Arab World Institute**, which opened in 1987, resembles a lot of other modern buildings, and seeing modern buildings in a city as rich in history and architectural beauty as Paris always gives us an initial twinge of anxiety. But on closer examination, the award-winning Institute is fascinating – especially the windows.

The 240 windows on the southern facade incorporate what is described as traditional Arab geometry. Each square pane is backed by an ingenious metallic grid of different sized circles surrounding a central portal. When the windows are "closed," lens-like diaphragms fold over part or all of the circles, forming octagons and stars in the process. The guts of the windows, seen from inside the building, resemble the intricate workings of a clock. (The shop inside offers wristwatches patterned after the windows.)

The Institute is a treasure house of Arab culture and is meant to provide ways to further the West's appreciation of the Arab world. Inside is a massive library, an audio-visual center, a book shop selling jewelry, posters, CDs and, of course, books, and a museum that traces the evolution of Arab culture from a couple hundred years BC to the present. Particularly interesting pieces include a handwritten Koran circa 1400, a series of richly colored Syrian rugs from the 16th century, and hardwood chests with inlaid ivory.

The Institute also boasts a top-floor restaurant and a terrace overlooking the **Seine** at the Île Saint-Louis. If nothing else, plan a free visit to admire the windows and sip a quick coffee on the terrace.

12. ARÈNES DE LUTECE, *just off of the rue Monge at rue de Navarre (5th, M:Monge). Admission free.*

This Roman arena dating back to the first century once seated 15,000 people. It's a bit hard to imagine all those bodies crammed into this modestly sized stadium, but that's the number the officials quote. Today, the arena and small garden along **rue des Arènes** is more like a sanctuary. Even on a sunny day, there will rarely be more than 20 or 30 people, some of them children playing soccer, others adults sitting in the stone stands with a sack lunch or newspaper.

13. MANUFACTURE DES GOBELINS, *42 avenue des Gobelins (13th, M:Gobelins), Tel. 01.44.61.21.69. Guided tours Tuesday, Wednesday and Thursday. Admission 50FF.*

If you have visited many of the other historic museums in the city, and even many of the finer hotels and restaurants, you will already have seen some of the exquisite tapestries that were manufactured at Gobelins. They are among the most famous in the world—known for their brilliant colors, complex designs (often tableaux of historic moments or mythic tales), and durability. The tour will show you how these masterpieces were created.

14. MOUFFETARD MARKETPLACE, *rue Mouffetard, southeast of the Panthéon, parallel to the rue Monge in the heart of the Latin Quarter (5th, M:Censier-Daubenton).*

The cobbled **rue Mouffetard**, opened long, long ago as the Roman road to Lyon and beyond, stretches from the **Place de la Contrescarpe**, a picturesque square perfect for a leisurely coffee and a bit of people watching, to the **Place Médard** and the church by the same name. In the mid-1700s, the tiny innocent looking church was the site where young women routinely had themselves beaten into what was described as rapturous states of semi-consciousness beside a Jansenist grave that supposedly possessed miraculous powers. Such large and unruly crowds would gather that the local officials declared one day that there would be no more miracles performed there.

The marketplace near the bottom of Mouffetard, maybe the finest in the city, is a culinary wonderland of cheese shops, vegetable stands,

OPEN MARKETS

Browsing through one of Paris's marketplaces is one of the city's great pleasures. The experience will also help explain why so much of the Parisian cuisine is so good–the ingredients are fresh off the farm. Vegetables, fruits, cheeses, meats, pastries, mushrooms, olives, fish you've never seen before, fowl you've never seen in your local supermarket, game (we've seen whole wild boars propped up outside butcher shops), flowers. Really just about everything you'd ever hope to eat. And the people watching is exceptional as well. One tip: the market streets close up shop for a very long lunch, and the roving markets are open only during the morning.

RUE MONTORGUEIL, (1st, M:Les Halles). Tuesday through noon Sunday.

RUE MOUFFETARD (5th, M:Censier-Daubenton). Tuesday through noon Sunday.

PLACE MONGE (5th, M:Monge). Wednesday, Friday, Sunday.

RUE DE BUCI (6th, M:Mabillon). Tuesday through noon Sunday.

RUE CLER (7th, M:École Militaire). Tuesday through noon Sunday.

SAXE-BRETEUIL (7th, M:Ségure). Thursday, Saturday.

MARCHÉ BASTILLE (11th, M:Bastille). Thursday, Sunday.

MARCHÉ D'ALIGRE (12th, M:Ledru-Rollin). Tuesday through noon Sunday.

COUR DE VINCENNES (12th, M:Nation). Wednesday, Saturday.

RUE DAGUERRE (14th, M:Denfert-Rochereau). Tuesday through noon Sunday.

BOULEVARD DE GRENELLE (15th, M:Grenelle). Wednesday, Sunday.

AVENUE PRÉSIDENT WILSON (16th, M:Alma-Monceau). Wednesday, Saturday.

RUE PONCELET (17th, M:Ternes). Tuesday through noon Sunday.

BOULEVARD DE LA CHAPELLE (18th, M:Barbes-Rochechouart). Wednesday, Saturday.

butcher shops, fish shops and bakeries. On weekends, the Mouffetard is transformed into a kind of carnival as theater troupes, dancers, jazz bands, and accordion players serenade the crowd of locals and tourists.

You must stop in the **Brasserie Mouffetard** at the corner of Mouffetard and rue de l'Arbalete. It is the quintessential student, intellectual hangout, where you're also likely to find a small cluster of elderly local men sipping wine early in the morning and complaining about young people or the government.

15. PANTHÉON, *place du Panthéon (5th, M:Cardinal Lemoine). Tel. 01.44.32.18.00. Open daily. Admission 35FF.*

Another favorite of ours. The Panthéon is a bit like the father figure of the Latin Quarter, sitting soberly atop the highest knoll and gazing down on its domain, almost daring the young residents of the student quarter to misbehave. More literally, this onetime church was ordered built on the "peak" of the Sainte-Geneviève slope in the mid-1700s by a gravely ill **Louis XV**. He had vowed to dedicate a magnificent temple to Sainte-Geneviève if he should survive the sickness. He did and up went the building.

After the Revolution, the Panthéon evolved into a profound burial vault for the heroes of France. **Voltaire**, **Rousseau**, **Émile Zola**, **Victor Hugo**, **Louis Braille** (as in the reading language for the blind) and others repose here. **Marie Curie's** remains were removed to the Panthéon in 1995 to honor her scientific breakthroughs on behalf of Mother France.

The view from the top is well worth the climb.

16. MUSÉE DE CLUNY (*Musée National du Moyen-Age*), *6 place Paul-Painleve (5th, M:Cluny). Tel. 01.53.73.78.00. Closed Tuesday. Admission 38FF.*

Even if you're not a medieval history buff, you'd probably be impressed with this museum. This was the site of an enormous Roman bathhouse in the 3rd century and a religious residence beginning in the late 1400s.

The building, which changed hands many times, became a museum in 1844 and now houses an inspiring range of medieval art. Probably the most famous are the tapestries of the *Lady and the Unicorn*, which represent allegories of the five senses.

But there are other tapestries that rival that series, including the Life at the Manor series in a bottom floor gallery that places you in the heart of a lovely embroidered garden filled with young lovers, dogs, birds, and blossoms of all description on a blue background. Upstairs, the *Departure of the Prodigal Son*, a huge tapestry from the early 16th century is equally colorful, depicting a young man on his steed with his family and a crowd of friends saying goodbye, and rolling hills in the background.

Downstairs, you will also find a gallery of fragments of statues that were ripped from the facade of Notre-Dame by the frenzied mob during the Revolution and only rediscovered in 1977. Stained glass, painted wood panels, wood chests, pages from illuminated books, jewelry, and sculpture round out the striking collection.

A personal favorite is in gallery 16: a solid gold rose from 1330, with delicate petals and young buds surrounding it. Truly stunning.

Saint-Germain & Montparnasse
6th & 14th Arrondissements

17. SAINT-GERMAIN-DES-PRÉS, *place Saint-Germain-des-Prés (6th, M:Saint-Germain). Tel. 01.43.25.41.71. Closed Monday mornings. Admission free.*

The 11th-century Saint-Germain-des-Prés, the oldest church in Paris, takes its name from **Saint Germanus**, the 6th-century Bishop of Paris, and from the open fields (or *prés*) where the original structure was built. In some ways, it is a shadow of its former self, having only one of its original three towers. The other two towers were victims of the Revolution and subsequent neglect. The church was, in fact, used as a saltpeter factory shortly after the Revolution.

That wasn't all the damage done during the Revolution. Dozens of priests and monks from the church were rounded up and slaughtered in the small square to the south in 1792.

Today, the church and the square in front are focal points for a trendy neighborhood anchored by the well-known **Deux Magots** café across the lane from the entrance to the church. On a nice day, street musicians and artists abound.

18. SAINT-SULPICE, *on the Place Saint-Sulpice between the Luxembourg Gardens and boulevard Saint-Germain (6th, M:Mabillon). Tel. 01.46.33.21.78. Open daily. Free.*

The often peaceful square outside features Visconti's handsome 19th-century fountain adorned with four devotees of the church who were highly regarded at the time, though they never quite made the grade of cardinal.

Work began on the church itself in the mid-1600s and was intended to serve the local peasants. Unfortunately, money, politics, indecision, and several switches in architectural plans delayed completion for more than 130 years. Even now, the church has a not-quite-finished charm (in fact, the tower on the right is incomplete).

Inside you will find one of the most valued organs in Europe, with 6,588 pipes, and, in the first chapel on the right, a series of heroic murals painted in the mid-1800s by Delacroix.

Set into the floor in the transept is a copper strip running north and south. During the winter solstice, sunlight peeps through a small hole in an upper window, strikes and follows the copper band, finally climbing an obelisk on the far wall. In mid-summer the sunlight strikes a copper plaque at the southern end of the copper strip.

19. JARDIN and **PALAIS DU LUXEMBOURG**, *off of the boulevard Saint-Michel a few blocks south of the boulevard Saint-Germain (6th, M:Luxembourg). Tel. 01.43.29.12.62. Open daily. Admission to gardens, free. Admission charge for Sundays-only tour of the palace.*

The **Luxembourg Gardens** are the most popular gardens in Paris. During season, the beds spill over with incredible mixes of blazing flowers. The lawns are always flawlessly trimmed. The central pool draws hundreds of people, who sit admiring the palace or watching children use long sticks to guide wooden sailboats over the water's surface.

If you want more action, you can reserve an hour on the row of tennis courts or take your children on a pony ride or thump your feet to the bands playing just inside the **Place E. Rostand** gates on the eastern side of the gardens.

And if you tire of the crowds, stroll over to the perimeter enclaves along the garden's south and west sides, where you will find remarkable statues, peaceful glades and lawns, and locals reading a good book while they soak up some sun.

The palace itself, much more easily admired from the outside than the inside, is currently heavily guarded because it is home to the **French Senate**. Its political legacy goes back to its beginnings in 1612, when Marie de Medici, wife of Henry IV, bought the Duke François de Luxembourg's mansion on the spot and ordered a palace built in a style reminiscent of the Tuscany palace where she was raised.

Her stay was a short one. She unwisely turned against Richelieu and was banished only five years after having moved in.

20. LES CATACOMBES, *1 place Denfert-Rochereau (14th, M:Denfert-Rochereau). Tel. 01.43.22.47.63. Open 2-4 p.m. Tuesday through Sunday, also 9-11 a.m. weekends. Admission 33FF.*

"Stop! This is the Empire of the Dead," warns a sign to the caves crammed with human remains.

Just as creepy as you would expect. The first trick is to find the entrance. It's the somewhat abused looking green building at the southern rim of the Denfert-Rochereau circle. The big bronze lion in the center of the circle looks right at it. Next, remember to wear old, comfortable shoes. Many passages in the catacombs are slippery and uneven. And take a flashlight, both to see your footing and to better examine "the sights."

The first thing you do on this unguided tour is descend a spiral stone staircase 65 feet straight down. In the first couple of chambers you will learn that in the late 1700s, Parisian cemeteries were bursting at the seams. Local officials decided it was time to do something.

What they did was create the catacombs in old stone quarries and, beginning in 1785, bring in the remains of millions of late residents from cemeteries all over the city. Once you reach the ossuary, about a three block walk underground (not a tour for tall people or claustrophobics), various markers will tell you what cemetery the different mounds of bones once occupied. Part of the French underground used the catacombs as a headquarters during World War II.

Note that the makers of these piles of bones had an artistic flair, creating patterns such as crosses using skulls fitted into walls of leg and arm bones. Charming.

21. CIMETIÈRE DU MONTPARNASSE, *entrances along boulevard Edgar Quinet and rue Froidevaux (14th, M:Edgar Quinet), just off the boulevard Raspail. Admission free.*

Providing a bit of tranquillity near the Tour Montparnasse and the bustling boulevard Montparnasse, this cemetery serves as the final resting place of **Jean-Paul Sartre** and, naturally, his long-time companion and an intellectual great herself, **Simone de Beauvoir**. **Beaudelaire**, the master poet, and playwright **Samuel Beckett** are also tucked away among the hundreds of sculpted tombs here.

22. TOUR MONTPARNASSE, *33 avenue du Maine (15th, M:Montparnasse). Tel. 01.45.38.52.56. Open daily. Admission charge to observation decks, 38FF and 46FF.*

Until the late 1960s, Paris had refused to even consider erecting the kind of gigantic towers of steel and glass that were sprouting up in other world capitals. Why, citizens had said for decades, would we undo the great avenues and open vistas brought to us by Baron Haussmann in the mid-1800s.

Why indeed? Nonetheless, from 1968 to 1970 a massive 688-foot high black glass tower and two clunky black glass wings rose into the sky from a once cozy Left Bank neighborhood near such cultural landmarks as the Select, the Coupole, and the Dôme restaurants. The tower, besides which is the **Gare Montparnasse**, can be seen from anywhere in the city and dominates everything around it.

Though many highrises were built during the presidency of Gaullist Georges Pompidou (1969-1974), public outrage and political reality put a stop to the construction of any more towers like Montparnasse in the center of the city. (Instead, the monoliths were pushed to the perimeter of the city – especially La Défense to the west, which has an amazing diversity of modern skyscrapers.)

The two tourist draws of the tower are its loftily perched restaurant and the observation deck on the 56th floor, from which you can see literally for miles in all directions.

Near the Eiffel Tower
7th Arrondissement

23. MUSÉE D'ORSAY, *1 rue de la Légion d'Honneur (7th, M:Solférino). Tel. 01.40.49.48.14. or 01.40.49.48.84. Closed Monday. Admission 40FF.*

Our favorite large museum in Paris. The museum is a wonder not only for the fine collection of 19th-century and early 20th-century works it houses, but also for its near perfection as an urban renovation project.

This beautiful museum, which opened only in 1986 and was slated to be torn to the ground and replaced with a massive hotel complex, is a recaptured and beautifully refurbished *Belle Epoque* train station. On the outside, it still looks a bit like a train station. But inside, once past the lines and the ticket booths, you step into the interior under the magnificent barrel dome and look out on a central hall that is as light and lovely as an outdoor courtyard and that is magnificently decked out with sculptures by **Barye**, **Rude**, and others. Overhead, above the entrance, is the incredible massive gold clock that was painstakingly restored at monstrous expense.

The permanent collection of Impressionist paintings by **Manet**, **Degas**, **Renoir**, **Sisley**, **Pissarro**, **Van Gogh**, etc., etc., is largely culled from the works that once hung in the Jeu de Paume at the end of the Tuileries gardens. There is a great deal of fine sculpture from the 1800s, photography by **Stieglitz** and others who worked at the turn of the century, and a gathering of American works by **James MacNeil Whistler** (yes, a portrait of his mother), **Winslow Homer**, **John Singer Sargent**, and others. Special exhibits are usually quite good and very popular.

The lovely and not horribly pricey museum restaurant is worth a visit for lunch, though arrive early because tables quickly grow scarce. Concerts are also regularly held at the museum. The down side: lines grow very long in summertime and some people complain that the smaller exhibit rooms off the side of the main hall are a bit dark or that specific works are sometimes a bit hard to find. Special exhibits, often upstairs, wander from one small space to another and, on occasion, from one floor to another so that you feel a bit like a rat in a maze.

24. ASSEMBLÉE NATIONAL, *33 quai d'Orsay (7th, M:Invalides). Tel. 01.40.63.60.00. Closed Sunday.*

Built in 1722 as a home for the **Duchess of Bourbon**, this grand edifice on the opposite side of the **Seine** from the **Place de la Concorde** now hosts the 577 members of the lower house of the French parliament. Visits are limited to the sessions from the beginning of April to July and from the beginning of October to the week before Christmas. Visits are also limited by space. Some suggest that you write ahead and reserve a spot in the gallery; write to: *Affaires Administrative General, 126 rue de l'Université, 75007 Paris.*

PARIS SIGHTS (Southwest)

Key

24. Assemblée National
25. Musée National Auguste Rodin
26. Hôtel des Invalides/Musée de l'Armée
27. École Militaire
28. Tour Eiffel
29. Maison de Balzac
30. Trocadéro/Palais de Chaillot
31. Musée d'Art Moderne de la Ville de Paris

25. MUSÉE NATIONAL AUGUSTE RODIN, *77 rue de Varenne (7th, M:Varenne). Tel. 01.44.18.61.10. Closed Monday. Admission 28FF; park only, 5FF.*

A precious jewel of a museum that blends master works with a setting that would be vibrant and welcoming even without the art. Why aren't there more museums like this one?

Rodin himself did not move into this former manse until about 80 years after it was built in 1730. And he wasn't alone. The mansion had been subdivided into sections, with other tenants over the years including the likes of **Isadora Duncan, Henri Matisse**, and **Jean Cocteau**.

Today, the home and large garden surrounding the house belong to Rodin's magnificent work. The garden, aside from being a lovely place to listen to one's own dim muse, provides the setting for masterpieces like *The Thinker*, the troubling *Burghers of Calais*, and the even more disturbing *Gates of Hell*.

Inside, some of the smaller, lifelike white marble pieces take on added glow when the sun streams through the windows. Drawings are also on display. And Rodin's famous studies of **Balzac** can be found upstairs. Those powerful works leave one with a sense that Balzac was in total command of all he surveyed.

26. HÔTEL DES INVALIDES and **MUSÉE DE L'ARMÉE,** *avenue de Tourville (7th, M:Invalides). Tel. 01.44.42.37.72. Open daily. Admission 38FF.*

The magnificent golden dome and 350-foot spire of Invalides is visible from just about anywhere in the 7th *arrondissement*, as well as from the Right Bank around the Palais de la Découverte and the end of the Jardin des Tuileries.

Most famous now as the resting place of **Napoleon's tomb**, Invalides was begun by **Louis XIV** as a tribute and home to soldiers wounded during the many wars he sponsored. The original structures were completed after just a few years in 1676. The **Dome Church**, probably the finest specimen of religious architecture from its time, was begun the following year and not finished until 1735.

The vast green esplanade stretching from Invalides's north entrance to the river was also added in the early 1700s. Today, it serves as a green beach for sun worshippers, soccer players, kite flyers, and young lovers.

Inside Invalides you will find the **Army Museum**, with its enormous collection of swords, muskets, and other weapons dating from the 1700s through World War II. One hall contains flags and standards from various French armies, as well as some captured from their opponents. The large, cobbled interior courtyard is lined with cannon adorned with fire-breathing lions.

But the main historical attraction is Napoleon's huge red stone sarcophagus, sunk into a circular crypt directly below the gilded frame and epic murals of the golden dome. Set into the floor around the sarcophagus is a brilliant green garland of laurels and on the walls are frescos paying tribute to French culture, education, and industry.

Napoleon actually died on Saint Helena, where he was finally exiled. But his remains were brought to Paris, fulfilling his wish that he rest near "the banks of the Seine among the French people who I truly loved."

Other French heroes are likewise entombed at Invalides. One of the most impressive is the tribute to **Marshal Foch**. The bronze sculpture is composed of eight rank-and-file soldiers from *The War to End All Wars*, with their late leader lying on a bed of laurels resting on their shoulders.

27. ÉCOLE MILITAIRE, *avenue de La Motte-Picquet (7th, M:École Militaire), at the southern end of the Champ-de-Mars esplanade behind the Tour Eiffel. Visits by appointment only. Write to: General Direction, 1 place Joffre, 75007.*

Though it was completed in 1772 as a military school and barracks, the school has the architecturally refined and affluent look of a château from the Loire Valley. **Napoleon**, of course, attended, and the school is still active. Around the back of the school, you can see various soldiers taking their handsome steeds through their paces.

28. TOUR EIFFEL, *Champ-de-Mars (7th, M:Bir-Hakeim), near the Seine in the northwest corner of the 7th arrondissement, across from the Trocadéro and Chaillot Palace on the Right Bank. Tel. 01.44.11.23.23. Open daily. Admission charge of 15FF to 60FF, depending how high in the tower you wish to venture.*

A monstrosity. Well, that's what most people thought way back in 1889 when the tower was topped off. Why on earth, they asked, would the world care to see the guts of a modern building without the grace of its clothes?

Interestingly, this was the same objection made in the 1970s when the Georges Pompidou Center opened on the Right Bank sporting all the unsightly ductwork and plumbing on the exterior of that contemporary art museum.

Also, like the Pompidou Center, which is now the most-visited museum in the city, the Tour Eiffel muffled its critics by quickly becoming the city's most popular attraction.

Built for a world's exposition, the tower is 1,051 feet high (that includes the various transmission towers). The antennae are, in fact, a critical part of the tower's history. In 1909, the tower was almost ordered pulled down. But French radio, which relied on the fabulous reception and broadcasting powers of the tower, came to the rescue.

Despite its estimated weight of 7,000 tons of pig iron, the tower's design is so efficient that it presses no more dead weight to the earth per square inch than an average sized man sitting in a chair.

Elevators take visitors seeking a breathtaking panoramic view to any of three levels — 190 feet, 380 feet, or 900 feet. Or, if you're looking for a good workout, take the stairs — all 1,652 of them.

If you get tired of the crowds around the tower, stroll down the handsome **Champ-de-Mars** esplanade stretching out southward toward **École Militaire**.

RIGHT BANK
Near the Champs-Élysées
8th & 16th Arrondissements

29. MAISON DE BALZAC, *47 rue Raynouard (16th, M:Passy), Tel. 01.55.74.41.80. Closed Monday. Admission 30FF.*

If you are a devotee of the author of the *Human Comedy*, you can tour the master's well-preserved home. Guided tours are also available.

30. TROCADÉRO and **PALAIS DE CHAILLOT**, *place du Trocadéro (16th, M:Trocadéro).*

The **Trocadéro** is a fascinating blend of history, art, architecture, and gardens directly across the river from the Tour Eiffel. The name, taken from a French victory over Spain in the early 1800s (the conquered Spanish fort was named Trocadéro), refers to the neighborhood and not the gigantic palace, as so many visitors think.

The **Palais de Chaillot** is composed primarily of two magnificent wings that span out parallel to the Seine and bracket lovely gardens and a huge pool fed by more than 60 fountains and decorated with several neoclassic and modern sculptures. The palace was built just 57 years ago and replaced a building erected there for the 1878 world fair.

Though Chaillot is home to four museums, its primary draw is as a place to gaze down across the fountains and the river to the **Tour Eiffel**, **École Militaire**, the **Hôtel des Invalides**, and much of the rest of the western half of the Left Bank. The spray of the fountains is captivating and the gardens on either side of the long rectangular pool have several peaceful sanctuaries if you want to escape the crowds.

The small roads sloping down on either side of the pool are also gathering places on sunny days for daredevils on rollerskates who wow the crowd with their slaloms and jumps.

One sad note: several low walls are blemished with graffiti, a city-wide problem. The local government has recently increased the penalties to hundreds of thousands of francs, but we'll have to see if the get-tough stance makes a difference.

The four museums housed in Chaillot are:
- **Musée des Monuments Français**, *Tel. 01.44.05.39.10. Closed Tuesday. Admission 35FF.* Striking reproductions and models of famous French monuments and cathedrals.
- **Musée de la Marine**, *Tel. 01.53.65.69.69. Closed Tuesday. Admission 38FF.* A must for naval buffs, this museum chronicles the history of the French navy from the 17th century on, with detailed models of galleons that stand five to twelve feet high.
- **Musée de l'Homme**, *Tel. 01.44.05.72.72. Closed Tuesday. Admission 30FF.* An anthropology museum whose permanent collection examines early life in the Americas.

31. MUSÉE D'ART MODERNE DE LA VILLE DE PARIS, *Palais de Tokyo, 11 avenue du Président Wilson (16th, M:Iena). Tel. 01.53.67.40.00. Closed Monday. Admission 50FF.*

This is the city's own personal art collection and, sad to say, it's a bit strange. Significant special exhibits of Impressionist work are hosted here, but the permanent collection has mostly minor works. There is a great deal of **Raoul Dufy** (including the striking *La Vie en Rose*), a couple of fine portraits by **Amedeo Modigliani**, and a smattering of **Braques**, **Derains**, and others.

The best of the contemporary works are **Bernard Rancillac's** 1974 portrait of Diana Ross and **Yan Pei Ming's** 1990 portrait of Mao. Beyond that, there are some pretty silly "artworks" warehoused in these cavernous display rooms.

32. AVENUE DES CHAMPS-ÉLYSÉES, *running east to west from the Place de la Concorde to the Arc de Triomphe (8th).*

At the Place de la Concorde, get out your camera and focus down the length of the **Champs-Élysées** as the sun is setting behind the Arc de Triomphe. What a picture! The other direction, from atop the Arc de Triomphe looking toward the Louvre, is equally awe-inspiring.

But frankly, in between is a largely forgettable commercial strip clogged with traffic. And there is seemingly constant construction, in large part to create underground parking lots that will allow even more people to flood onto a street that simply does not have a Parisian character anymore.

Fast food, overpriced clothes, mini-malls, car dealers, banks, and huge movie houses showing American films in English dominate the avenue. This is one of the few very public places in the city where we watch our wallets.

Bright spots are the **Lido cabaret** and the **Virgin Megastore**, where you can buy just about any CD ever made or happily sip beers in the hip upper-floor café and watch the masses mill around below.

Bottom line: take the awestruck photos and explore more interesting neighborhoods.

33. ARC DE TRIOMPHE, *place Charles-de-Gaulle/Etoile (8th, M:Charles-de-Gaulle), at the head of the Champs-Élysées, Tel. 01.55.37.73.77. Open daily. Admission 35FF.*

The arch is a focal point not just of the famed **Champs-Élysées**, but also of French history. Built to memorialize Napoleon's triumphs, it wasn't until 1836 that the arch was finished and 1840 that the emperor's remains were taken by chariot through the arch.

Baron Haussmann, the brilliant city planner under **Napoleon III**, made the circle one of his most important projects. An even dozen avenues spill into the circle (don't try driving around it). **Victor Hugo's** body lay in state beneath the arch in 1885, and victory parades commemorating Allied triumphs in both world wars were staged at the arch.

The arch is also the site of the nation's **Unknown Soldier**.

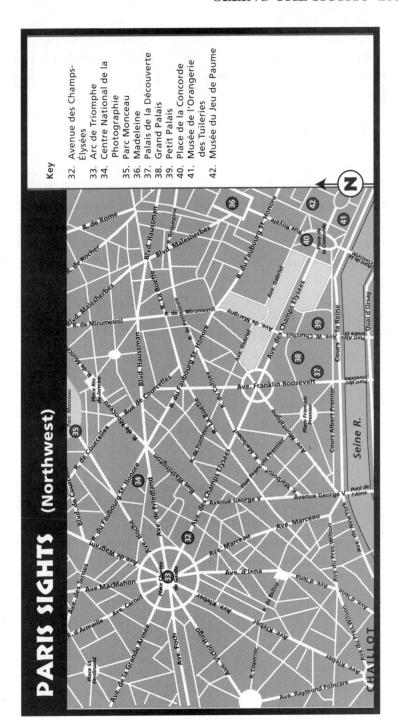

PARIS SIGHTS (Northwest)

Key

32. Avenue des Champs-Élysées
33. Arc de Triomphe
34. Centre National de la Photographie
35. Parc Monceau
36. Madeleine
37. Palais de la Découverte
38. Grand Palais
39. Petit Palais
40. Place de la Concorde
41. Musée de l'Orangerie des Tuileries
42. Musée du Jeu de Paume

From pedestrian tunnels beneath the traffic circle, you come up under the arch and can ascend to the top platform 164 feet up for a magnificent view of the **Champs-Élysées** and the **Louvre** to the east and of **La Défense** in the distance to the west.

34. CENTRE NATIONAL DE LA PHOTOGRAPHIE, *11 rue Berryer (8th, M:George V). Tel. 01.53.76.12.32. Closed Tuesday. Admission 30FF.*

The photo center in recent years moved into the **Hôtel Salomon de Rothschild**, a fabulous one-time mansion on a quiet street in a neighborhood just north of the **Arc de Triomphe**. They'll stay while their wing of the **Palais de Tokyo** is being refitted. Members of the center complain that they have less space, and it's true that the gift shop is inadequate and the exhibition rooms don't follow a nice neat pattern, so you have to double back at times. Still, the shows are usually comprehensive and well lit in handsome rooms.

As with painting, the French were pioneers in the art of photograph and it is quite common to see some extraordinary works here by the likes of André Kertész, Philippe Halsman, Robert Dousneau and Henri Cartier-Bresson.The building itself is also very striking, and there is a charming garden in the back where you can critique photographic techniques or just enjoy the afternoon.

35. PARC MONCEAU, *bordered on the north by the boulevard de Courcelles and a few blocks northeast on avenue Hoche from the Arc de Triomphe (8th, M:Monceau). Admission free.*

Not too many folks make it this far off the beaten path – aside from the residents of this very pleasant and affluent neighborhood. And it's probably true that the park offers little of huge historical significance, but it's still one of the prettiest parks in the city and is a delightful place to rest your feet.

Tucked away here and there you'll find odd architectural tributes to the pyramid, the windmill, Roman temples, etc. These little pleasantries were part of the original plan designed by the painter **Carmontel** in 1778 for the gardens' owner, the **Duke of Orléans**. The rotunda at the main entrance was once a tollhouse for farmers bringing their wares into the then-walled city of Paris.

36. MADELEINE, *place de Madeleine (8th, M:Madeleine). Tel. 01.42.65.52.17. Open daily. Free.*

Not long ago, a friend's young girl passed by the Madeleine and was horrified to find that the immense curtain painted with a church had been taken down and that a huge building stood in its place. "What happened to the painting?" she asked with some disappointment.

The **Saint-Mary Magdalen church**, known as **The Madeleine**, was covered seemingly forever while restorers did their jobs inside and out. Finally, the magnificent windowless church with its fifty-two 66-foot Corinthian columns and exquisite rose marble and gilded interior is open to the public.

Up the rue Royal from the Place de la Concorde, the church was begun in 1764. But that and the subsequent structures were torn down before they were finished. The current structure resembling a Greek temple was finally completed in 1842. It remains a church, though over the years it was almost transformed into a railway station and a stock exchange.

Josephine Baker's funeral was held here with great pomp and ceremony in 1975.

Concerts are periodically conducted in the Madeleine. We've attended a performance of Mozart's *Requiem*. Unbelievable! Tickets are available from FNAC, *Tel. 40.41.40.00*, and the Virgin Megastore.

37. PALAIS DE LA DÉCOUVERTE, *avenue Franklin D. Roosevelt a block and a half down from the Champs-Élysées (8th, M:Champs-Élysées). Tel. 01.56.43.20.21. Closed Monday. Admission 30FF.*

This museum is the all-time high school science fair housed in a building connected to and directly behind the **Palais des Beaux Arts**. It's ideal for the kids. Though the exhibits seem a bit out of place set in and off the magnificent turn-of-the-century rotunda, they are a whole lot of fun. There are glass cages with live bugs of all kinds. There are charts and models and interactive displays of the solar system. There are pulleys and fulcrums and light shows, and a Planetarium with shows every day.

38. GRAND PALAIS, *3 avenue du Général Eisenhower (8th, M:Champs-Élysées). Tel. 01.44.13.17.17. Closed Tuesday. Admission varies by exhibition..*

Sad to say, the Grand Palais, built for the **1900 World Exhibition**, is showing its age. The facade still boasts two magnificent equestrian statues at either end of the roof line, but the main facade and interior have been undergoing repairs for some time.

Inside, you used to be able to see all the way to the massive domed ceiling, but much of the interior has been converted into an enclosed maze of exhibition spaces that never gives you even a peek at the once grand skylights of the ceiling.

Still, the building, which once hosted massive commercial expos of various kinds, is now devoted to art exhibitions — some of them significant shows, highlighting, among other things, Sweden's long relationship with France and the beginnings of Impressionism.

39. PETIT PALAIS, *avenue Winston-Churchill, just across the street from the Palais des Beaux Arts (8th, M:Champs-Élysées). Tel. 01.42.65.12.73. Closed Monday. Admission 27FF.*

Like the Palais des Beaux Arts, this building was constructed in 1900 as part of the **World Exhibition**. Today, it is home to a very respectable permanent exhibit of 19th-century sculpture and painting (including some massive oils with scenes from the Revolution). Two barrel-shaped wings extend off the main rotunda and look across the street at Beaux Arts. It's beautifully ornate, but the interior is looking somewhat run-down.

A highlight is the semi-circular garden in back, surrounded by an arcade with a wonderful mural on the arched ceiling depicting a trellis blanketed with colorful vines and populated by a host of lovers and images of Night, Day, and Fertility.

40. PLACE DE LA CONCORDE, *directly across the Seine from the National Assembly, and between the Jardin des Tuileries and the Champs-Élysées (8th, M:Concorde).*

Chaos. That's one of the first impressions because of the insane traffic swirling around what is probably the most elegant and historic traffic circle in the world.

Covering 21 acres, this square came into being in the late 1700s and quickly became soaked with the blood of the bourgeoisie and the innocents who were guillotined in the years just following the Revolution of 1789. **King Louis XVI**, **Marie Antoinette**, and **Robespierre** were just three of thousands who lost their lives here (the location of the guillotine is marked near the statue dedicated to the city of Brest in the northwest part of the square).

At the center stands the **Obelisk of Luxor**, a 220-ton Egyptian obelisk (column) dating back to the 13th century BC and blanketed with hiero-glyphics. Found in the ruins of the temple at Luxor, it was given to the French in 1833. Flanking the obelisk are two marvelous statues of horses, the **Chevaux de Marly** and the **Chevaux Ailes**, and surrounding it are eight statues dedicated to prominent French cities.

For a bit of contemporary glitz, step into the **Crillon**, a top-drawer hotel on the northwest side of the place. This is luxury at its very finest.

The **American Embassy**, on avenue Gabriel, is just across rue Boissy d'Anglais to the west of the Crillon.

Near the Louvre
1st & 2nd Arrondissements

41. MUSÉE DE L'ORANGERIE DES TUILERIES, *at the western end of the Jardin des Tuileries on the Place de la Concorde (1st, M:Concorde). Tel. 01.42.97.48.16. Closed Tuesday. Admission 49FF.*

A rather homely museum from the outside, this former 19th-century greenhouse nonetheless possesses a treasure of Impressionist art. The collection gathered over past decades by Jean Walter and Paul Guillaume includes key works by **Monet, Cézanne, Picasso**, and **Renoir**. Many of Monet's *Les Nympheas*, water lily murals, are here.

The lilies downstairs are divided into two immense oval rooms, the walls of which are almost totally covered with four canvases each of Monet's water lilies. It's as if you're floating in the heart of his pond. He donated the works "*comme un bouquet de fleurs*" (like a bouquet of flowers) to France on Armistice Day after World War I, though the works were not accessible to the public until after his death in 1927.

Upstairs the collection is dominated by minor works of major artists — though there are many gems. Personal favorites: *Odalisque à la Culotte Rouge* by Matisse, 1924; *Le Jeune Apprenti* by Modigliani, 1917; and *La Grande Baigneuse* by Picasso, 1921.

The Orangerie is on the small side and will only take an hour or so, but there are many lovely works and is well worth your time.

42. GALERIE NATIONALE DU JEU DE PAUME, *place de la Concorde at the rue du Rivoli (1st, M:Concorde). Tel. 01.42.60.69.69. Closed Monday. Admission 38FF.*

Though this museum (once a royal indoor tennis court) lost most of its best work to the Musée d'Orsay, it now serves as a very effective showplace for temporary exhibits of major modern artists. Check your *Pariscope* for a description of the current show.

43. PLACE VENDÔME, *between the Opéra Garnier and the Jardin des Tuileries (1st, M:Tuileries).*

This place was first planned in 1680 as a grand square honoring **Louis XIV**, whose statue was to stand proudly in the center of property purchased from a convent and from the **Duke of Vendôme**. However, the equestrian monument erected in 1699 was leveled during the Revolution and replaced during Napoleon's time by a 144-foot column honoring the Little Emperor's triumphs in Germany. In fact, much of the bronze that is wrapped around the stone core of the column was melted down from captured enemy cannon.

Gustav Courbet, the painter, disliked the column so much that he was party to a conspiracy in May 1871 to topple the memorial. He was discovered and ordered to restore the monument at his own expense, which was considerable. The Place itself is quietly elegant, almost a bit stuffy. The magnificent **Ritz Hotel** is located here, as are offices for the **Ministry of Justice**. More importantly, if you are in the market for fine pearls, jewelry, perfume and haute couture, or you just like to drool over luxuries displayed in opulent store windows, you've come to the right place.

44. OPÉRA GARNIER, *place de l'Opéra (9th, M:Opéra). Tel. 01.47.42.07.02. Open daily. Admission 30FF.*

This grander-than-grand opera house went under the knife in 1995 and 1996 and is more magnificent than ever.

"Opera house," however, is a bit misleading these days. Since the opening of the Opéra Bastille in 1989, the Garnier has been dedicated largely to dance (with only occasional operas). Despite the huge stage complex at Garnier, which can in theory accommodate up to 450 artists at a time, it was felt that its 2,200 seats were grossly insufficient for grand (and profitable) opera.

It's really a shame. The exterior of this magnificently ornate art house from the 1870s is just a foreshadowing of what you find inside. Mouths hang wide open at the marble staircases, the ornate gilded reception rooms, the six-ton chandelier, the (seemingly out-of-place) Chagall mural on the interior ceiling, and the rows of red velvet-lined boxes hovering over and around the stage.

Charles Garnier, the state architect who designed this chef d'oeuvre, pulled every imaginable excess out of his hat for this beauty. And really

PARIS SIGHTS (Northeast)

Key

43. Place Vendôme
44. Opéra Garnier
45. Bourse des Valeurs
46. Baccarat Museum
47. Palais-Royal
48. Jardin des Tuileries
51. Grevin Wax Museum

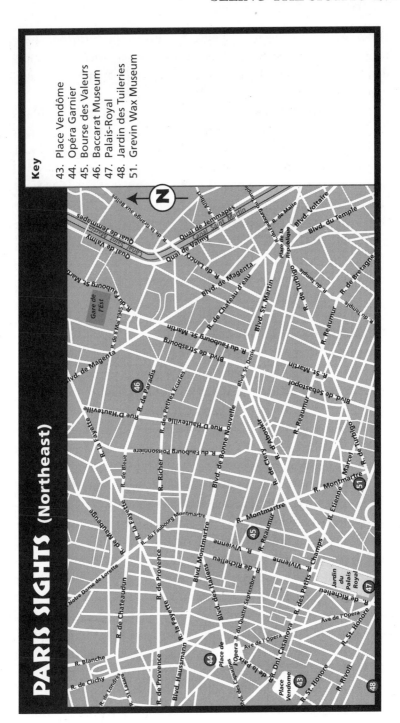

the best way to see this opera house, as with any performance space, is during a performance. Seats, if the theater is open when you come, can be had in the nosebleed section for very reasonable rates — though we suggest you buy a box for the experience.

45. BOURSE DES VALEURS, *4 place de la Bourse (2nd, M:Bourse). Tel. 01.42.33.98.83. Closed Saturday and Sunday. Admission 30FF.*

Welcome to the Paris stock exchange. French capitalism in all its chaotic glory can be watched from the spectators gallery of this Romanesque temple built at Napoleon's order in the early 1800s. It's a spectator sport of a different kind.

46. BACCARAT MUSEUM, *30bis rue du Paradis (10th, M:Chateau d'Eau), Tel. 01.47.70.64.30. Closed Sunday. Admission 15FF.*

A collection of hundreds of historic and contemporary works by the famed maker of fine crystal. Some truly dazzling pieces if you are a fan

47. PALAIS ROYAL, *place Palais-Royal, just north of the Louvre (1st, M:Palais-Royal).*

Though the interior is now closed to the public because it belongs to the very wary **Council of State**, the building and interior gardens are worth a quick visit. The main building was constructed in 1632 for then **First Minister Richelieu,** who willed it to the royal family — thus the name change from the Cardinal's Palace to the Royal Palace.

The buildings surrounding the garden went up in the late 1700s, and now house businesses as well as an arcade of pricey art galleries (**Raymonde Duval** has lovely watercolors) and shops offering haute couture, perfume, rare stamps, and miniature soldiers. Poet **Jean Cocteau** and author **Colette** once lived in the apartments above those shops.

The main garden is really a large esplanade surrounding a central fountain and two gardens brimming over with blooms of all kinds. It's a tranquil place to catch your breath.

And you can't miss, even if you want to, the **Court d'Honneur,** a square just behind the main building in which you will find a grid of black-striped stone columns of heights varying from a few inches to about six feet. This "sculpture" by **Daniel Buren** went up in 1986, causing a stink between the conservatives, who hated the project and fought it in court, and the liberals, who happened at that point to have a stronger than usual voice in government and defended it. (Try to land a coin atop the one column that is set in a below-surface-level niche near the northwest corner of the square. It's not as easy as it looks.)

48. JARDIN DES TUILERIES, *the huge garden to the west of the Louvre, stretching up to the Place de la Concorde (1st, M:Tuileries).*

Named after the tile *(tuil* in French) factories that once occupied this property and first laid out in the mid-1600s, the Tuileries is a remarkable example of how the French reign in their passionate and sometimes disorganized nature when it comes to gardening. The Tuileries is a picture postcard of meticulous lawns, hedges, trees, and flower beds — a lovely place to stroll, or sit and feed the birds.

This site was also once the home of a palace ordered built by Catherine de Médicis. Louis XVI and Napoleon lived in the castle as well. However, the palace was destroyed during the revolution in 1871 and never rebuilt.

These gardens, which survived the test of various revolutions, were originally laid out by Le Nôtre, the genius who also planned the gardens at Versailles for Louis XIV, the Sun King.

49. MUSÉE DES ARTS DÉCORATIFS, *107 rue de Rivoli (1st, M:Palais-Royal). Tel. 01.44.55.57.50. Closed Monday and Tuesday. Admission 35FF.*

This museum is pretty much what it sounds like — paintings, furniture, tapestries, table settings and other decorative flourishes from way, way back to new works by the likes of **Philippe Starck**. The museum is very popular, and offers special exhibits on such subjects as the history of fine Delft china.

Though real fans of decorative touches will enjoy this museum immensely, its holdings are generally less spectacular than can be found elsewhere. Of particular note: the Nouveau bed and armoire in the 20th-century gallery, which were made by Hector Guimard for the Nozal family in 1902; the remarkably detailed porcelain bibelots of the 18th-century gallery; the stunning silver urns and goblets of the 1st Empire, and the gold and wood *Berceau du duc de Bordeaux*, a crib dating back to 1820 and featuring a soaring golden angel emerging from one end of the crib and offering a gold wood-inlaid horn of plenty.

50. MUSÉE NATIONAL DU LOUVRE, *rue de Rivoli (1st, M:Palais-Royal). Tel. 01.40.20.51.51 or 01.40.20.53.17. Closed Tuesday. Admission 45FF.*

The **Louvre** is considered the mother of all museums. When the first small fortress known as the Louvre was built in 1200 to keep invaders out of the city, King Philippe-Auguste could not possibly have imagined it would evolve into the largest palace in Europe and later into probably the best known art museum in the world. And he certainly never would have pictured **I.M. Pei's glass pyramid** that now stands at the heart of the inner courtyard and serves as the main entrance. Another seven rooms opened in the Richelieu wing recently, showing a collection of 19th century porcelain, furniture and crystal. In the Denon wing, another 41 rooms have been refurbished to show off such works as Greek and Roman antiquities, and Italian and Spanish paintings from the Renaissance.

The Louvre won universal praise when it opened a completely refurbished **Richelieu wing** in November 1993, on the 200th anniversary of the museum. The new wing, which doubled the exhibition space of the Louvre, is roomy, well lit, well organized and maybe the best part of the whole museum.

Also, the new shops and cafés of the underground **Carousel area**, which features an upside-down version of Pei's glass pyramid at its center, is spacious and inviting. There is a particularly great print shop, where you might find a fabulous gift or memento of your trip.

Overall, the addition was a masterstroke. It not only allowed the showing of much more of the Louvre's vast collection, it also improved the image of a museum that was beginning to be perceived by some as a bit grim, stuffy, and confused. (In fact, it's still hard to find some pieces.)

The permanent collection is fat with classics that are household names, such as the *Venus de Milo* and the *Mona Lisa*, and such artists as **Titian**, **Raphael**, **Botticelli**, **Hieronymus Bosch**, **Breugel** and **Vermeer**. The list goes on and on. There are epic sculptures, whole chunks of ancient palaces, Egyptian, Roman, and Greek antiquities, paintings reaching back six centuries, graphic arts, and furniture.

Still, we recommend that if you are coming to Paris for the first time and only have a few days, don't dedicate too much time to the Louvre. The Louvre is awesome, as is the crowd. And as fabulous as the museum is, it would be a mistake to spend all your time in Paris fighting this crowd and not seeing the Paris that is humming with life all around you.

51. GREVIN WAX MUSEUM, *10 boulevard Montmartre (1st, M:Grands Boulevards), Tel. 0147.70.87.99. Open daily. Admission 58FF.*

A bit eerie, but kids especially seem to like this sort of thing. Well over 400 wax figures trace the history of the Revolution, Napoléon's reign, the two world wars and modern culture, including some stars you'll recognize instantly.

The Marais & Bastille
3rd, 4th, & 11th Arrondissements

52. GEORGES POMPIDOU CENTER, *rue Rambuteau at the corner of rue Saint-Merri (4th, M:Châtelet). Tel. 01.44.78.12.33. Closed Tuesday. Varying admission charges to expositions.*

Hailed by some as a work of architectural genius and damned by others who consider it an overcrowded monstrosity, this tribute to the late **Georges Pompidou**, a Gaullist who served as president of France from 1969 to 1974, is The Most Visited Monument in all of Paris.

In a sense the Pompidou is a contemporary version of the Tour Eiffel. Its inside-out architectural plan, in which ductwork and plumbing are visible and escalators ride up the exterior of the building in large glass tubes, was reviled by neighborhood residents when it was unveiled in 1977 (as was the Tour Eiffel at the turn of the century). But it was also instantly accepted, especially by the young crowd that was drawn to its extensive library and research facilities.

The building is a remarkable resource for the study of modern arts and other intellectual endeavors. It houses the fine **Musée National d'Art Moderne**, with many important 20th-century works, it hosts significant shows examining modern architecture, it has a video library and regularly screens European film masterpieces, it has a heavily used regular library, and it hosts concerts of all kinds.

A practical note: the interior can be a bit intimidating at first. If you are interested in exhibits or concerts, drop by the large information desk for a map of the floorplan. And all tickets are purchased at the multi-windowed cashier's offices in the northeast corner of the bottom floor.

If nothing else, ride the escalators to the top floor, where you can enjoy a panoramic view of the city. An outdoor seating area for the top floor café is a perfect place to enjoy the sun.

You should also stop by the fountain on place Stravinsky just to the south of the Pompidou. You've probably seen pictures of this before — the red pouty lips, the playful elephant, the multi-colored coiled snake, and other mechanical gizmos spinning around and spewing water.

53. TOUR SAINT-JACQUES, *off the rue de Rivoli at the boulevard de Sebastopol (4th, M:Châtelet).*

Turning a corner on the hectic rue de Rivoli or emerging from the Métro, it's a bit startling to see this 171-foot, 16th-century tower standing solo in the middle of a square. What's missing is the medieval **Saint-Jacques-la-Boucherie church**, which was one of the beginning points for pilgrims who set off regularly to the shrine of Santiago de Compostella in northwestern Spain.

The church was brought down in 1802, but the tower was saved and used in the manufacture of lead pellets for muskets. Today, the Gothic tower serves as part landmark and part weather station.

54. HÔTEL DE VILLE, *rue de Rivoli at the Place de l'Hôtel de Ville (4th, M:Hôtel de Ville). Tel. 01.42.76.40.40. Guided tours only.*

Home to the city government, the Hôtel de Ville (or City Hall) was first built here in the early 17th century, but was largely destroyed in 1871 when the **Paris Commune** took power after Napoleon III's miserable failure in the Franco-Prussian War.

What you see now was rebuilt from the ruins and completed in 1882. Its intricate facade, heavily adorned with statues of national heroes, blends Renaissance elements with the *Belle Epoque*.

Ask about tours of the interior state hall and reception rooms at the information office at 29 rue de Rivoli, where small, free exhibits are held honoring the city's remarkable past.

55. MUSÉE PICASSO, *5 rue de Thorigny (3rd, M:Chemin Vert). Tel. 01.42.71.25.21. Closed Tuesday. Admission 30FF.*

Another gem of a museum.

Less than twenty years old, this tribute to **Picasso** is set in a fabulous renovated mansion built in the 17th century. The collection of paintings, drawings, collages, and sculpture walks you chronologically through Picasso's awesome career. There may not be many of the familiar masterpieces, but the collective impact of the exhibit is quite powerful and instructive.

What makes the collection even better is that these pieces came from the master's own collection, donated in part by heirs who couldn't afford the huge inheritance tax slapped on the collection after Picasso's death in 1973.

You will also find assorted memorabilia and some works of **Cézanne**, **Braque**, and others who Picasso admired and whose works he collected.

The mansion itself, the **Hôtel Salé** (salt), is named in tribute to the wealth the original owner acquired in the mid-1600s by collecting taxes on salt for the crown.

56. CARNAVALET, *(Musée de l'histoire de Paris), 23 rue de Sévigné (3d, M:Saint-Paul). Tel. 01.42.72.21.13. Closed Mondays. Admission 30FF.*

This museum, which focuses on the history of the city, was a delightful suprise. We anticipated an arid display of charts and books and all of the dullest tools one associates with history. Instead, this museum, which is only blocks from the stunning Place des Voges, recounts the history of Paris largely through paintings and sculpture.

Though galleries do touch on the very early eras of local cultural activity, reaching back to Gallo-Roman days, the lion's share of the displays cover the 18th century through the early 1900s. There are some absolutely stunning *Belle Epoque* furnishings.

Learn also what the heros and villains of the past look like. There are particularlly good portraits of the figures who dominated the Revolutionary period, such as Danton, **Louis XVI**, and **Marie Antoinette**. A recent special exhibition focused on late 19th-century Montmartre, home of the best of the cabarets (the Moulin Rouge, the Boîte à Fursy, the Glu, and the Chat Noir, among others) and artists such as **Toulouse-Lautrec**. Hundred-year-old posters advertising the shows have miraculously retained their brilliant colors.

57. PLACE DES VOSGES, *off of rue des Francs Bourgeois, just north of rue Saint Antoine in the Marais district (4th, M:Saint-Paul).*

The epitome of elegance. Dating back to the very early 1600s, this is the oldest surviving square in Paris. The square is surrounded by 36 houses of red brick and stone, all perfectly balanced and in architectural synch with one another. The large **King's Pavilion** occupies the southern side, while the Queen's is located at the north.

Along the arcade are a couple of very pleasant bistros and several respected art galleries.

In the center of the square is an equally geometric park, with plenty of shaded spots to catch up on your reading, as well as plenty of open space which is often quickly filled by playing children.

It's hard to picture the decay that came to the square in the 1700s and 1800s. In fact, it was saved finally only in the 1960s, when it was declared an historic district and was painstakingly restored.

58. MAISON DE VICTOR HUGO, *6 place des Vosges (4th, M:Saint-Paul). Tel. 01.42.72.10.16. Closed Monday. Admission 27FF.*

In the southeastern corner of the elegant **Place des Vosges**, this was home to the literary giant from 1833 to 1848 and claims to have the largest collection anywhere of Hugo memorabilia, including clothes, furnishings, and his sometimes bizarre drawings and doodles.

59. PLACE DE LA BASTILLE, *at the eastern end of rue Saint-Antoine (4th, M:Bastille).*

A dozen roads converge on this monster of a traffic circle, where the striking 171-foot **July Column** has replaced the dreaded Bastille prison that was torn down 200 years ago. The original layout of the prison is outlined in the paving stones of the circle.

The prison, of course, was a focal point of the Revolution. In truth, the 400-year-old prison had outlived its usefulness and, a few years before the Revolution arrived, the local government had agreed in principle to demolish the structure. Ultimately the mobs beat them to it, freeing in the process the mere handful of prisoners still held there. Nonetheless, the "storming" was a symbolic victory for the masses, who quickly razed the aged structure.

The area received a very welcome boost on the 200th anniversary of the Revolution, when the 3,000-seat **Bastille Opera House** was opened. The neighborhood in the blocks just east of the opera house has since blossomed with trendy restaurants and clubs.

OUTSIDE THE CITY CENTER

The sights listed below are not located in the heart of Paris, but they are all within easy reach by Métro. They are listed in geographic order, beginning north and moving clockwise to the east, south, and then west.

Montmartre
18th Arrondissement

Generally speaking, this area is best known for the striking Sacré-Coeur Basilica, the view of all of Paris below, and the artists who have called this butte home for decades.

SACRÉ-COEUR BASILICA, *35 rue du Chevalier-de-la-Barre (18th, M:Anvers). Tel. 01.53.41.89.00. Open daily. Admission charge to church dome with panoramic view, 15FF.*

The marvelous white elongated onion domes of Sacré-Coeur can be seen throughout the city, a stunning monument to a stunning French defeat in Napoleon III's ill-advised Franco-Prussian War of 1870.

The basilica, completed in 1910 after 34 years work, is a Catholic tribute to the 58,000 soldiers who fell in the war, which was a rout. Prayers have been said non-stop for the fallen since the church was consecrated in 1919.

The grounds are as inspiring as the church itself, with seemingly countless steps leading down a steep esplanade to the **Square Willette**. The view of the city is magnificent, the slopes below will be peppered with children feeding the birds, and at the foot of the butte you'll likely run into all manner of artists and musicians, including an ever-present South American group playing haunting melodies on wooden flutes.

For those who'd just as soon ride as walk the 250 steps of the adjacent and much photographed rue Foyatier (see below), there is a small funicular pumping up and down the steep slopes for the price of a Métro ticket.

RUE FOYATIER, *just to the west of the slope leading up to Sacré-Coeur (18th, M:Abbesses).*

You'll recognize this street the instant you see it. Steps. Steep steps. Well over 200 steep steps, with an occasional traditional Paris lamppost. Get out your camera.

ESPACES MONTMARTRE-SALVADOR DALI, *9 rue Poulbot-place du Tertre (18th, M:Anvers). Tel. 01.42.64.40.10. Open daily. Admission 40FF.*

Just a few years old, this modernish museum doesn't quite fit the character of the neighborhood. Nevertheless, if you're a Dali fan, this is a must-see. There are many familiar and minor prints and reproductions, and quite a few sculptures, like the girl with the neck of a giraffe and various clocks melting over tree limbs. The shop at the end of your tour is first-rate, with Dali postcards, prints, sculptures, puzzles, neckties, watches (you can guess what these look like), T-shirts, and other odds and ends.

PLACE DU TERTRE, *just a block or two east of Sacré-Coeur (18th, M:Abbesses).*

How did such an adorable little square in a neighborhood where the likes of Van Gogh and Modigliani toiled become such a silly place? The square itself is a swarm of street artists just dying to paint your portrait (some are much better than others). An outdoor café occupies the central core of the plaza, and cafés surround the square so that people can watch tourists have their likenesses immortalized in their choice of oil, pastel, or watercolor. The neighborhood here and at the base of the steps to Sacré-Coeur still hosts a few decent art galleries, but much of the shop space has been taken up by vendors hawking T-shirts and trinkets.

MONTMARTRE VINEYARD, *at the corner of rue Saint-Vincent and rue des Saules (18th, M:Lamarck-Caulaincourt).*

That's right, a vineyard. Well, it's not exactly going to put Château Margaux out of business, but it does have the distinction of being the last remaining producing vineyard in Paris proper. You can buy wine from this bucolic little plot in the back of the city hall for the 18th *arrondissement* (each *arrondissement* has one), just off the place Jules Joffrin.

RUE DU MONT-CENIS, *just a block or two behind Sacré-Coeur (18th, M:Lamarck-Caulaincourt, Jules Joffrin).*

There's not much in the way of famous museums or galleries on this street. It's just a pretty walk that extends from the **Saint-Pierre de Montmartre** (the city's oldest church, at the top of the butte) down to the **place Jules Joffrin** and the market street of rue du Poteau. The southern half of the street is mostly a series of steps, scores of them, climbing the northern slope of the butte. It may be a bit of work, but the view is pretty, as are many of the apartment buildings lining Mont-Cenis.

CIMETIÈRE DE MONTMARTRE, *with the entrance off rue Caulaincourt, just above the boulevard de Clichy (18th, M:Place de Clichy).*

This maze of tombs and markers lined cheek-by-jowl up and down the slopes is a refuge from the unsightly porn houses of nearby Clichy and is home to the remains of a few French giants. **Degas** is here, as is **Stendhal** and **Alexandre Dumas**, author of the highly popular and romantic tale of vengeance, *The Count of Monte Cristo*. You're likely to run across a few dozen cats here as well — French cemeteries are very popular with cats, and you can easily guess why.

PLACE PIGALLE, *near the eastern end of the boulevard de Clichy (18th, M:Pigalle).*

Clichy and Pigalle were made famous in part by **Henry Miller**. But as much as we admire Miller and think him one of the truly original American writers of the 20th century, the neighborhood today is a cultural cesspool, with barkers from the sex clubs literally grabbing you as you try to pass by. Remember that no matter what they say and no matter how convincingly they say it, they are lying. They want only one thing – to separate you from your hard-earned money.

Clignancourt Flea Market

Take the number 4 Métro line north to the Porte de Clignancourt stop at the very end. When you come up out of the subway, just follow the crowds (and there will be crowds) walking north, past the Périphérique beltway and into the suburban neighborhood of Saint-Ouen.

This is probably the most famous of the Parisian flea markets, known in these parts as **Marchés aux Puces** (now you know the French word for "fleas"). At first you're probably going to wonder why the market is so popular. In the two or three blocks it takes to get to the actual market you will walk a gauntlet of vendors hawking crummy T-shirts, used CDs, firecrackers, "American" jeans, and other assorted trash. This is not the flea market you're looking for.

You want the traditional antique dealers wedged in the 'V' formed by avenue Michelet and rue des Rosiers. Here you'll find gilded mirrors and marble-topped tables, shiny sets of silver, ancient armoires, coins, tins, combs and dolls, spurs, stamps, prints, and buttons, turn-of-the-century tabloids ... well, you get the drift.

Yellow markers on the paths, or *allées*, help you remember where you are and where you saw some special item you've finally decided to go back to buy.

Prices surprised us. They are not too bad. But never, never pay full price or we'll never speak to you again. Bargain. It's the tradition.

In the heart of this little commercial corner is **Chez Louisette's**, a funky brasserie with edible food, reasonable prices, and often a woman who looks like she just walked in off the streets singing her heart out.

Before you bail out, cross Rosiers to the **Marché Dauphine**, which is another set of small antique alleys. In fact, the very best and priciest furnishings are found here. If you like Deco or Empire, you'll spot some truly beautiful pieces.

Saint-Denis Basilique

Located at the end of the number 13 Métro line, at 22 rue Gabriel Péri. Tel. 01.42.43.05.10. Closed Tuesday. Admission 20FF.

The burial place of kings (literally a couple of dozen), Saint-Denis takes its name from the first bishop of Paris. **Saint Denis** was decapitated in the 3rd century by a jealous regional king who thought Denis was becoming too influential. But, legend has it, Denis retrieved his severed head and marched from Montmartre north to the suburb of Saint-Denis, where he was buried by a peasant woman.

Don't be put off by the seedy shopping mall you see when you step out into the village of Saint-Denis. And don't be put off by the exterior of the church, which is just around the corner and is cathedral-like in its majesty, but just a bit sad because it lost one of its towers and is dark with soot.

Don't be put off, especially if you are a history buff, because the tombs of the basilica are astounding. The building has a fascinating history as well, beginning as a Gallo-Roman cemetery, then being reborn in 475 as a small church built at the order of Sainte-Geneviève. Its heyday was under **Abbott Suger** in the 1100s, who decided a grand edifice was in order and set the plans in motion. Still, the cathedral was not completed until the 13th century, and bits and pieces were added, destroyed, rebuilt, and destroyed again over the centuries. (Display cases inside give a very good history of the building and the people who shaped it.)

But again, the *raison d'être* for this visit is the tombs and the crypt. The oldest tomb found so far dates back to about 565 and contains the remains of **Aregarde**, wife of Clotaire I, King of Paris. Magnificent tombs in the main hall honor **Henri II** and **Catherine de Medicis**, **François I** and his wife **Claude de France**, **Dagobert I**, and **Louis XII** and his wife **Anne de Bretagne**.

The remains of **Marie Antoinette** and **Louis XVI** lay beneath elegant black marble slabs in the crypt, and a beautiful marble sculpture off the ambulatory honors their violent deaths. A small sideroom in the crypt lists the burials here of 18 kings dating from Dagobert I in 638 to Henri III in 1589, as well as dozens more queens and various and sundry relatives.

In terms of history, Saint-Denis rivals Notre-Dame.

Cité Des Sciences et de l'Industrie

Located at Parc de la Villette, 30 avenue Corentin-Cariou (19th, M:Porte de la Villette). Tel. 01.40.05.80.00. Closed Monday. Admission 50FF for the basic pass, more if you want to see the Cité and the Géode.

Kids, young or old, who are infatuated with science will find hours of entertainment in this high-IQ theme park in the northeast corner of Paris. Displays bring the science of space exploration and theories of time and matter down to earth for the rest of us. Lots of interactive exhibits — many of which you'll find engulfed by swarms of youngsters.

Also visit the **planetarium**, the **aquarium**, and, most certainly, the **Argonaute submarine**, which you'll find just a few yards from the gleaming spherical **Géode**. Inside the Géode, watch science films on the kind of high-tech screen that sits you down in the center of the action.

Cimetière Père-Lachaise

The main entrance is off the boulevard de Menilmontant (20th, M:Père-Lachaise).

Paris's largest cemetery pitches and rolls over hundreds of acres and is probably best known to Americans as **Jim Morrison's** final resting place, although some local pols are currently trying to give him the boot. The graffiti besotted tomb of the lead figure of The Doors still draws small crowds of restless neo-hippies, most of whom hadn't been born when the rock band toured in the late '60s. Other "residents" here who are far more deserving of admiration include **Oscar Wilde**, **Marcel Proust**, **Balzac**, **Modigliani**, **Chopin**, **Georges Bizet** and **Colette**. Vandals recently desecrated more than 100 graves, and, once again, the city has promised, but so far failed, to get to the bottom of things.

Vincennes, The Château, & Bois

Go to the eastern edge of the city, just outside the city proper, at the end of the number 1 Métro line (12th, M:Château de Vincennes). Tel. 01.48.08.31.20. Admission 22FF and 32FF, depending on the tour.

Step out of the Métro, pivot, and there it is: the gate tower of a medieval castle completed in 1370. Pretty impressive stuff for this modest suburb.

The castle is complete with moat all around (though it is dry now). Through the gate and into the courtyard, you will find an archaelogical dig where workers with small trowels and brooms are gently bringing to light long forgotten foundations of the earliest castle structures.

Further inside is the towering **Donjon** and the striking **Chapelle Royale**, which was modeled after Sainte-Chapelle and dates back to the 14th century. There are guided tours of the 170-foot-tall Donjon, though, unfortunately, the Chapel is closed to the public.

Beyond the castle, the **Bois** (meaning woods) is enormous and has what is considered to be Paris's finest zoo, two lakes with islands where you can rent rowboats, and several sports fields. But in our view, the highlight here is the **Parc Floral de Paris**.

The Parc Floral (10FF admission) is probably the prettiest, most instructive garden in all of Paris. Depending on the season you visit, you will find brilliant tulips springing out of the ground everywhere, a small lake in the center bordered by beds of marigolds, petunias, impatiens and other flowers, and a lily pond populated by ducks and dozens of turtles, who climb the banks on a hot day to sun themselves.

But this isn't just a picture of beauty and tranquillity. There are separate gardens carefully seeded around the grounds that contain medicinal plants, aromatic flowers, bonsai, hothouse ferns, bamboo forests, and other manner of flora, all clearly labeled so you can tell your *Syringa micrphylis superba* from your *Poncirus trifoliata*.

What's more, you'll be walking along admiring the plants, turn a corner, and there will be a dazzlingly blue and green peacock standing in your path giving you the once-over. A nice restaurant and a crèperie are tucked into unobtrusive corners.

Saint-Cloud

Go to the western end of the number 10 Métro line, getting off at Boulogne/ Pont de Saint-Cloud. Then cross the bridge over the Seine and look left for a sign that says "Piètons, Parc Saint-Cloud." Tel. 01.46.02.67.18.

This massive park of 1,100 acres was once the sight of a magnificent château that was Napoleon's favorite residence. This is where he married his second wife, Marie-Louise, after having dumped Josephine. This is also where Henri III was assassinated in 1589 by a young Jacobin monk. You can glean a bit more history from the **Musée Historique** near the *Grille d'Honneur* (main gate).

But today, Saint-Cloud's attraction is the tranquillity of its verdant parkland and the majesty of its fountains. The **Grande Cascade** a couple hundred yards from the entrance is famous for its multi-terraced fountain, with water spewing from the mouths of stone frogs, gargoyles, lions, dogs and other fearsome beasts. The **Grand Jet** just a few yards more to the south shoots water 140 feet into the air. Notice the carp darting around in the waters below. The fountains are turned on only from May through September, on late Sunday afternoons.

The terrace which begins above the Grande Cascade was the site of the château (a marble map shows you exactly where it stood) and is now an immaculate lane of greenery and splashy floral beds leading up to the impressive **Rond Point** with its 24 fountains and cozy café.

The **Jardin du Trocadéro**, just up the slope to the north of the terrace where the château stood, is particularly tranquil and inspiring, mixing colorful trees and flowers of all kinds. With a pond at the center, it's a bit like Wonderland. There is a panoramic view of Paris from the southeast corner of this garden.

If you want total privacy, just wander into the forests east of the terrace. Even though there is not much in the way of monuments left here, Saint-Cloud is a very pretty stop.

Musée Marmottan-Claude Monet

2 rue Louis Boilly (16th, M:Muette). Tel. 01.42.24.07.02. Closed Monday. Admission 40FF.

Facing the quiet Jardin du Ranelagh along the western edge of the 16th *arrondissement*, the **Marmottan** houses a collection of 65 Monets painted throughout his career and donated to the museum by the painter's son Michel in 1971. Most of the Monets, including well known studies of water lilies, a Japanese bridge, and train stations, line the walls of a basement level gallery that contains a few works by Renoir, Pissarro, and other followers of the **Impressionist school**.

Monet's *Impression–Sunrise*, one of his most influential pieces, is on view, having been donated to the museum in 1950. It is credited by some with having given the Impressionist movement its name.

The museum was opened in 1934 at the bequest of Paul Marmottan, an art historian who donated his beautiful home as well as his collection of furnishings largely from the Empire and Consular periods.

After visiting the museum, stroll east through the park and up the sloping road to **Dominique Geffroy**, *8bis rue de la Muette*, a lovely tea salon.

Bois de Boulogne

Located along the western edge of the 16th arrondissement (16th, M:Porte Maillot, Porte Dauphine, or Porte d'Auteuil).

While the French generally prefer to reign in nature, composing meticulously ordered gardens and parks with crisp lawns, obedient hedges, and sharply delineated beds of flowers arranged by color, the Bois de Boulogne is a virtual wilderness.

The woods themselves, favorites of local dog owners, are ragged and woolly, with paths that meander through the underbrush. In fact, way back in the 1300s, this was a favorite hunting ground, and later it became a trusty hideaway for bad guys who prayed on the rich, then hid in the bushes.

Aside from providing a place of relief for local dog owners and a refuge for young lovers, the 2,200-acre Bois is also home to a great deal of organized activity. To the south end is the famous **Roland Garros** tennis stadium where the **French Open** is played every spring, as well as the **Hippodrome d'Auteuil**, where millions of francs are won and lost daily on the horses (when in season). An even more famous Hippodrome is the **Longchamp**, in the southwestern corner of the park, where the **Paris Grand Prix** is held in June.

At the northern end of the bois is the **Jardin d'Acclimatation**, with its many amusements for children (see Chapter 13, *Child's Play*), and the **Musée National des Arts et Traditions Populaires**, with exhibits on agriculture and folklore.

But the biggest draw of the Bois de Boulogne are the two lakes in the center, the Inferieur and Superieur lakes, where you can hire a canoe and float around for hours. You can also catch a tiny ferry across to the islands, where you can have a bit of lunch at the café or soak up the sun on the grassy knolls.

The more familiar formal French garden of the **Bagatelle**, where Charles X designed and built a house in three months on a bet with Marie Antoinette, is also worth a peek if you've got time.

La Défense & The Grande Arche

West of the city at the end of the number 1 Métro line (M:Grande Arche de la Défense). Tel. 01.49.07.27.57. Open daily. Admission 43FF to the observation deck.

To best appreciate this enormous experiment in urban planning and contemporary architecture (with more than 30 office towers), get off at the Esplanade Métro stop and walk the last few hundred yards of the **La Défense** quarter to the **Grande Arche** at the western end. At the eastern base of the esplanade is a large pool with tall masts topped with different colored lights, an artistic theme repeated at the other end, on the other side of the Arche.

The esplanade (no cars allowed) is a brilliantly conceived walkway adorned with gardens, potted plants, sculptures of various kinds, and some "sidewalk" style cafés. On either side, you will gawk up at some truly imaginative office towers (whose indexes read like a Who's Who of international business). It's not exactly a warm and cuddly human space, but students of architecture will be spellbound.

Baron Haussmann himself, the 19th-century designer of the grand avenues of Paris, might even approve of the esplanade, which spills at the foot of the Arche into an enormous plaza ringed by department stores. **Quatre Temps**, **FNAC**, **Habitat**, all the big French stores have an outlet here. You'll no doubt also run into the rollerskaters who seem to be all over the city these days, slaloming between pink pontoons or leaping off ramps.

And finally you will climb the 54 white marble steps that bring you to the underbelly of the Grande Arche, which is quickly becoming another of the universally recognizable Paris sights — this one a monument to the contemporary corporate world. The Arche, designed by architect Johan Otto von Spreckelsen, is referred to as *A Window on the World, A Symbol of Hope for the Future.*

Glass-bubble elevators take you up underneath the arch to the observation platform on top, where you will marvel at the panoramic view. What you see in the distance is the classic Paris. What you see around you is the future.

ROOFTOP VISTAS

Because the center of Paris has none of the high rise office buildings we associate with most cities, the views are blissfully unobstructed. Great views are yours from the top of:

NOTRE-DAME DE PARIS *(4th, M:Cité), at the eastern end of the Île de la Cité.*

INSTITUT DU MONDE ARABE, *1 rue des Fosses-Saint-Bernard (5th, M:Jussieu).*

PANTHÉON, *rue Clotilde (5th, M:Cardinal Lemoine).*

TOUR MONTPARNASSE, *33 avenue du Maine (15th, M:Montparnasse).*

TOUR EIFFEL, *Champ-de-Mars (7th, M:Bir-Hakeim).*

ARC DE TRIOMPHE, *place Charles-de-Gaulle (8th, M:Charles-de-Gaulle).*

SAMARITAINE, *19 rue de la Monnaie (1st, M:Pont Neuf). This department store's observation deck also has a small café.*

GEORGES POMPIDOU CENTER, *rue Rambuteau at the corner of rue Saint-Merri (4th, M:Châtelet).*

SACRÉ-COEUR BASILICA, *35 rue du Chevalier-de-la-Barre (18th, M:Anvers).*

LA GRANDE ARCHE, *1 parvis de la Défense, at the end of Métro Line 1.*

12. CULTURE

Long-hairs complain that French culture is going through a bit of a slump. They demand to know who's going to replace the Robbe-Grillets of literature, the Genets of theater, and the Truffauts of film.

While it may be true that giants are in short supply (and not just in France), there is no shortage of French talent on any cultural front. Local theater is very much alive, as is French film, and internationally renowned performers of all stripes include Paris in their itinerary.

And what better way to appreciate such remarkable settings as the **Opéra Garnier** (9th *arrondissement*) than by attending one of the opera or dance performances there. The **Bastille Opera House** (12th *arrondissement*) should also be on your short list of places where you can enjoy a performance and sightsee from the comfort of your reserved seat.

The **Madeleine** (8th *arrondissement*), recently reopened after a total facelift, hosts choral and chamber works regularly. There's nothing quite so moving as a piece like Mozart's *Requiem* in such a magnificent setting.

If you are interested in contemporary works — film, theater, dance — pick up a schedule of events from the **Pompidou Center** (4th *arrondissement*).

DANCE

Though dance holds a beloved place in the French arts and the finest companies in the world routinely schedule stops in Paris, there is not a great deal to see at any given moment. However, Paris is home to one of the most magnificent dance performance halls in the world in the **Opéra Garnier** (see Chapter 11, *Seeing the Sights*), opened originally in 1875. It has been devoted primarily to dance since the opening in 1989 of the **Bastille Opera House** across town.

Seating just over 2,000, the Garnier is a masterwork of opulent decor, with massive staircases, ornate reception halls, gilt all around, a six-ton chandelier and, oddly, a Chagall mural on the ceiling.

Prices at various theaters are reasonable by dance standards, often beginning at 40 or 50FF, depending on the company performing.

The Opéra Garnier is located at the place de l'Opéra (9th, M:Opéra), Tel. 40.01.17.89.

Other halls where dance is performed include:

- **CENTRE MANDAPA**, *6 rue Wurtz (13th, M:Glacière). Tel. 01.45.89.01.60*
- **CHÂTELET THÉÂTRE MUSICAL DE PARIS**, *1 place du Châtelet (1st, M:Châtelet). Tel. 40.28.28.40.* Primarily an opera house, but some dance.
- **GEORGES POMPIDOU CENTER**, *19 rue Beaubourg (4th, M:Châtelet). Tel. 01.44.78.13.15.* Mostly contemporary.
- **THÉÂTRE DES CHAMPS-ÉLYSÉES**, *15 avenue Montaigne (8th, M:Franklin-Roosevelt). Tel. 01.44.52.50.50*
- **THÉÂTRE DE LA BASTILLE**, *76 rue de la Roquette (11th, M:Bastille). Tel. 01.43.57.42.14*
- **THÉÂTRE DE LA VILLE**, *2 place du Châtelet (4th, M:Châtelet). Tel. 01.42.74.22.77.* Mostly contemporary works.

FILM

Parisians are obsessed with film, which is not surprising because France has spawned such giants as Truffaut, Rohmer, Godard, Malle and many others.

There are more than 100 cinema houses in Paris proper and more than 250 houses in the metropolitan area, most of which have several screens. About 300 different films are screened each week in Paris.

In fact, one cinema house, **Le Grand Pavois**, *364 rue Lecourbe, in the 15th at the Balard Métro stop, Tel. 01.45.54.46.85*, shows more than 40 different films a week. The Pavois screens everything from first run hits to cult classics like *Blade Runner* — some in French, some in English.

Parisians are so nuts about movies that it is easier in Paris to see American classics on the big screen than it is in almost any American city. On rue des Écoles (5th *arrondissement*) in the Latin Quarter there are three houses (the **Action Écoles**, **Le Champo**, and **Grand Action**, each with multiple screens) where you can watch Hitchcock's best, Audrey Hepburn festivals, musicals like *Guys and Dolls*, and even Westerns.

Where Are the Movies?

How do you find them? Simple. Once again, you can't go wrong with *Pariscope*, *L'Officiel*, or the Wednesday supplement in the *Figaro* newspaper. They list every film, with times, prices, and descriptions. The films are even cross-referenced so that if you're in the mood for sci-fi, just look under the sci-fi heading to see what's in town.

Though American films often arrive in Paris weeks, sometimes even months, after they have been released in the US, there's always a bunch of first-runs to choose from. They are clustered in three primary spots: along the Champs-Élysées (8th *arrondissement*), the boulevard Saint-Germain (6th *arrondissement*), and avenue Montparnasse (on the border of the 6th and 14th *arrondissements*).

Listings also note whether the film is being shown 'VF' or 'VO,' meaning the French Version or the Original Version. English films shown VF have been dubbed, and there won't be any English subtitles to help.

Like so many Parisian pleasures, movies are a bit pricey. New releases will run you anywhere from 35FF to 50FF. There are student and senior discounts, and just about any ID seems acceptable as long as it's presented with confidence. Repertory houses are also somewhat cheaper, with specials running about 25FF.

Helpful phrase: *"Deux places pour (name of movie), s'il vous plaît,"* means "Two tickets for (name of movie), please."

OPERA

The enormous new opera house at **Bastille** dominates the local opera scene. The 3,000-seat main hall, which opened in 1989, hosts all the major production companies, not the least of which are French companies performing such French classics as Georges Bizet's *Carmen*. The modern complex is worth a visit even if you don't stay for a performance, but combine the two experiences if you can. Prices in the nosebleed section are down to earth at about 60FF.

The Bastille Opera House is located on the place de la Bastille (12th, M:Bastille), Tel. 01.44.73.13.00, or recorded information at Tel. 01.43.43.96.96.

Other venues that host opera:

- **OPÉRA GARNIER,** *place de l'Opéra (9th, M:Opéra). Tel. 01.44.73.13.00 and 08.36.69.78.68*
- **CHÂTELET, THÉÂTRE MUSICAL DE PARIS,** *1 place du Châtelet (1st, M:Châtelet). Tel. 01.40.28.28.40.* Also a major house, attempting such difficult works as Wagner's Ring cycle.
- **OPÉRA COMIQUE,** *5 rue Favart (9th, M:Richelieu-Drouot). Tel. 01.42.86.88.83*
- **PENICHE-OPÉRA,** *across from 200 quai de Jemmapes (20th, M:Jaures). Tel. 01.43.49.08.15*
- **THÉÂTRE DES CHAMPS-ÉLYSÉES,** *15 avenue Montaigne (8th, M:Franklin-Roosevelt). Tel. 01.49.52.50.50*

SYMPHONY

Classical music can be heard all over town all the time. Literally ten to twenty performances are scheduled every day, with solo artists, choral groups, chamber pieces and full orchestras playing the work of Bach, Mozart, Scarlatti, Schumann, Rossini, Bizet and countless other masters.

Full formal symphonies of world-class orchestras can be heard at the **Ópera Bastille.** But the most fun (and economical) performances are those held in one of the great churches (see the **Madeleine, Sainte-Chapelle,** and **Saint-Germain-des-Prés** in Chapter 11, *Seeing the Sights*). The better conductors make the most of the haunting acoustics, and the combination of eloquent music and grand surroundings can be quite moving.

For a long list of times and places, check your *Pariscope* guide. Also, when you visit museums and churches, odds are that you will find flyers near the entrance announcing a performance or two that week.

Formal symphony houses include:

- **THÉÂTRE MUSICAL DE PARIS,** *1 place du Châtelet (1st, M:Châtelet). Tel. 01.40.28.28.40*
- **SALLE PLEYEL,** *252 rue du Faubourg Saint-Honoré (8th, M:Ternes). Tel. 01.45.61.53.00*
- **SALLE GAVEAU,** *45 rue La Boétie (8th, M:Miromesnil). Tel. 01.49.53.05.07*
- **CITÉ DE LA MUSIQUE,** *221 avenue Jean-Jaurès (19th, M:Porte de Pantin). Tel. 01.44.84.44.84*

THEATER

The Paris theater scene is hugely active with more than 100 productions onstage every single week. Anglophones will spot all sorts of familiar names, from Shakespeare and Oscar Wilde to Harold Pinter and Woody Allen. A special stop on the local theater circuit is the **Odéon Théatre de l'Europe** in the 6th arrondissement just above the Luxembourg Gardens *(Tel. 01.44.41.36.36)*. Its renovation has brought out the best of this architectural beauty. It is also a key stop in some of the more accomplished ensembles as well as many avant-garde troups from all over Europe.

The down side is that there is very little available in English, and unless your French is very, very good, you'd have a rough time trying to keep up with a French production.

Still, if you're hungry for the stage, scan the *Pariscope* theater listings for the **On Stage Theatre Company**, **Dear Conjunction**, and **Gare Saint-Lazare Players**, all of which stage English-language productions.

WHERE TO FIND TICKETS

All theaters and concert halls sell their own tickets, but they are scattered all over town and not always convenient. Some box offices will also annoy you to no end with odd hours and long lunch breaks. Three central clearing houses for tickets to most events can ease your troubles:

• FNAC, 1 rue Pierre Lescot, third level down in the Forum des Halles (1st, M:Châtelet), 40.41.40.00.

• KIOSQUE THÉÂTRE, across from 15 place de la Madeleine (9th, M:Madeleine).

• VIRGIN MEGASTORE, 52 avenue des Champs-Élysées (8th, M:Franklin-Roosevelt), 40.74.06.48. A second, small Virgin outlet is located at the Carrousel du Louvre (1st, M:Palais Royal), 49.53.52.90.

Houses that sometimes host English productions include:
• **THÉÂTRE DE LA MAIN D'OR BELLE DE MAI**, *15 passage de la Main d'Or (11th, M:Ledru-Rollin). Tel. 01.48.05.67.89*
• **THÉÂTRE MARIE STUART**, *4 rue Marie Stuart (2nd, M:Étienne-Marcel). Tel. 01.45.08.17.80*

- **THÉÂTRE DE NESLE,** *8 rue de Nesle (6th, M:Odéon). Tel. 01.46.34.61.04*
- **THÉÂTRE DU TOURTOUR,** *20 rue Quincampoix (4th, M:Rambuteau). Tel. 01.48.87.82.48*
- **TREMPLIN THÉÂTRE DES TROIS FRÈRES,** *39 rue des Trois Frères (18th, M:Abbesses). Tel. 01.42.54.91.00*

13. NIGHTLIFE

As you might expect, there is no shortage of nightlife in Paris. Clubs, discos, and cabarets are scattered all over town.

There are three things you should keep in mind before you set out on your nocturnal quest. One, and this is sounding like a broken record: clubs are very expensive. Don't be surprised if you drop a couple hundred francs in the first hour (if not in the first few minutes).

Two, bands won't strike the first note until about ten or eleven, and discos and other hip and groovy nightspots often don't begin to fill up until midnight or later (though many will sizzle until the sun pushes up into the early morning haze).

Three, the Métro shuts down just after midnight, and cabs are increasingly difficult to find in the wee hours of the morning (except at a few major cab stands, such as the boulevard Saint-Michel). So figure out beforehand how you're going to get home.

CABARETS & EXTRAVAGANZAS

There are cabarets and then there are cabarets. The cabaret of yesteryear, which is a kind of old fashioned variety show of singers, dancers, and comedians in a homey theater with too many chairs in too little space, has enjoyed a revival of late. In fact, they abound and are a blast. But they are in French and even when you speak the language well, it's not always so easy to get the punchline.

Then there are the big cabarets, the Extravaganzas, which are mostly for tourists, including French tourists from the countryside. They are high-tech, often lavish variety shows with a cast of beautiful dancers, elaborate stages, live orchestras, suave crooners, amazing jugglers, even more amazing magicians, agile acrobats, and the odd elephant or horse threatening to prance right into the audience.

The big cabarets are expensive — 150 to as much as 1,000FF, depending on the show and whether you include dinner. The food at these places is a bit pedestrian, so our advice is to have a nice dinner somewhere else and enjoy a nightcap at the cabaret for dessert.

These shows have an unfair reputation for peddling pure T&A. The better shows are actually good clean fun. Our most straight-laced friends have taken their young daughters to the Lido, and the kids described the show as an elaborate circus — which, in fact, is exactly what it is.

Old-Style Cabarets

L'ANE ROUGE, *3 rue Laugier (17th, M:Ternes). Tel. 01.47.64.45.77.*

Mostly comedy and a fair amount of gags that draw the audience in. All in French at this typically cozy traditional cabaret.

AU LAPIN AGILE, *22 rue des Saules (18th, M:Lamarck). Tel. 01.46.06.85.87.*

Lots of singing, comedy, and even poetry. Poetry? Hey, why not.

CHEZ MICHOU, *80 rue des Martyrs (18th, M:Pigalle). Tel. 01.46.06.16.04.*

A parody of the big shows, in drag.

LA BELLE EPOQUE, *36 rue des Petits-Champs (2nd, M:Pyramides), Tel. 01.42.96.33.33. Open nightly. Prices vary; sometimes they have special rates.*

Traditional cancan, plus after the show you can dance to the orchestra.

L'ELEPHANT BLEU, *49 rue de Ponthieu (8th, M:Franklin D. Roosevelt), Tle. 01.47.64.45.65. Open nightly. Admission 300 to 600FF.*

Around for many years, this cabaret usually has a bit of an Asian flavor to it. This is another club where you can dance to the band after the show is over.

Extravaganzas

CRAZY HORSE SALOON, *12 avenue George V (8th, M:George V). Tel. 47.23.32.32. Open nightly. Admission for revue starts at 290FF.*

The classy and cozy (by comparison to the bigger theaters such as the Lido) Crazy Horse set in a safe and upscale neighborhood selects a very particular look in its army of dancers, then enhances the physical similarity by dressing the women (with names like City Nebula and Funky Coconut) in identical wigs and costumes. Stage numbers make the most of contemporary light shows, and the magicians are wild.

LIDO DE PARIS, *116bis avenue des Champs-Élysées (8th, M:George V). Tel. 01.40.76.56.10, Fax 01.45.61.19.41. Open nightly. Admission prices begin at 460FF.*

Wow! Probably the biggest and brightest of the big bright shows, with a stunning cast of dozens of men and women who clearly get more than adequate exercise. Elaborate shows feature a frenzy of lights, a live orchestra, jugglers doing the impossible, some truly wacky skits, and fountains, ice rinks, and a submarine that emerges from the floor. How do they do that?

MOULIN-ROUGE, *82 boulevard de Clichy (9th, M:Blanche). Tel. 01.52.09.82.82. Open nightly. Admission begins at 500FF.*

Named for the red windmill, this is supposedly where the can-can was kicked off. They still perform it with style. But there's a lot more to this show, which boasts 100 performers, 1,000 costumes (with headdresses towering to the ceiling), and a pool of crocodiles.

PARADIS LATIN, *28 rue du Cardinal Lemoine (5th, M:Cardinal Lemoine). Tel. 01.43.25.28.28. Open nightly. Admission for renue only 465FF.*

Though tucked away on a quiet street in the Latin Quarter (thus its name), this production is lavish and loud and a great deal of fun. The high-tech extravaganzas feature acrobats, a legion of lovely dancers, accomplished crooners, and comics.

LIVE MUSIC

If you're in the mood for a trashy garage band, no problem. If you want some funk, you got it. Or if you're feeling cool and would like to sit in a corner booth and soak in some jazz, Paris has that in abundance. Jazz is still particularly popular here, and there seem always to be a few big names in town. The Madonnas pass through regularly as well, playing to thousands in the newish Bercy sports palace on the Right Bank a few blocks east of the Gare de Lyon.

For the big concerts and popular clubs, stop by the **Virgin Megastore** or **FNAC** (see Chapter 14, *Shopping*), check out the posted listings, and buy your tickets there. For more intimate settings, buy *Pariscope* or pick up a free copy of *FUSAC, Paris Voice, Paris City Magazine* or the *Time Out Guide*, all of which are distributed widely and have current music listings.

Once again, be prepared to spend. Even at the smaller clubs there is likely to be a cover charge, or you will be charged a premium rate for your first (and mandatory) drink. Play it safe and reserve ahead.

A few live music clubs:

BATACLAN, *50 boulevard Voltaire (11th, M:Oberkampf). Tel. 01.43.14.35.35*

A jazz club that pulls in lots of visiting artists and the occasional big name.

BILBOQUET, *13 rue Saint-Benoît (6th, M:Saint-Germain-des-Prés). Tel. 45.48.81.84.*

Jazz nightly, with mostly local talent in a real party neighborhood.

LA COUPOLE, *102 boulevard du Montparnasse (14th, M:Vavin). Tel. 01.43.20.14.20.*

Have a hearty meal upstairs, then head downstairs for a mambo combo or two.

DUC DES LOMBARDS, *42 rue des Lombards (1st, M:Châtelet). Tel. 01.42.33.22.88.*

Local and imported jazz talents.

FRONT PAGE, *56 rue Saint-Denis (1st, M:Etienne-Marcel). Tel. 01.40.26.26.56.*

A rocking spot for traditional blues, jamming, even an occasional Hendrix tribute. Funky neighborhood at night, with lots of streetwalkers. Not for everyone.

HOT BRASS, *Parc de la Villette, 211 avenue Jean-Jaures (19th, M:Porte de Pantin). Tel. 01.42.00.14.14.*

A bit of Latin with a dash of jazz. Talents like Les McCann and Abbey Lincoln grace this club.

MERIDIEN, THE LIONEL HAMPTON JAZZ CLUB, *81 boulevard Gouvion-Saint-Cyr (17th, M:Porte Maillot). Tel. 01.40.68.30.42.*

Lots of solid and often young talent. Mostly imported to this very classy house that Lionel, the jazz giant, built.

NEW MORNING, *7 rue des Petites-Écuries (10th, M:Château-d'Eau). Tel. 01.45.23.51.41.*

Contemplative jazz the likes of Cedar Walton.

IRISH PUBS

Feeling a bit o' that Irish yearning, are ye? Need a nice warm Guinness to pick up your spirits? Maybe want to toss a dart or two with a few good fellas? Well, you're not in sweet Dublin, but put your mind and body at ease. The Irish are everywhere.

CARR'S, *1 rue du Mont Thabor (1st, M:Concorde), 01.42.60.60.26*

CONNOLLY'S CORNER, *12 rue de Mirbel (5th, M:Censier-Daubenton), Tel. 01.43.31.94.22. A personal favorite.*

AU GOBELET D'ARGENT, *11 rue du Cygne (1st, M:Étienne-Marcel), Tel. 01.42.33.29.82*

THE JAMES JOYCE, *71 boulevard Gouvion-Saint-Cyr (17th, M:Porte Maillot), Tel. 01.44.09.70.32*

KITTY O'SHEA'S, *10 rue des Capucines (2nd, M:Opéra), Tel. 01.40.15.00.30*

MOLLY MALONE'S, *21 rue Godot-de-Mauroy (9th, M:Madeleine), Tel. 01.47.42.07.77*

THE QUIET MAN, *5 rue des Haudriettes (3rd, M:Rambuteau), Tel. Tel. 01.48.04.02.77*

FLANN O'BRIEN'S, *6 rue Bailleiul (1st, M:Louvre), Tel. 01.42.60.13.58*

FINNEGAN'S WAKE, *9 rue des Boulangers (5th, M:Jussieu), Tel. 01.46.34.23.65.*

FROG & ROSBIF, *116 rue St-Denis (2nd, M:Etienne-Marcel), Tel. 01.42.36.34.73. Really British but we'll give it a pass.*

CAFÉ OZ, *184 rue St-Jacques (5th, M:Luxembourg), Tel. 01.43.54.30.48; and 18 rue St-Denis (1st, M:Chatelet), Tel. 01.40.39.00.18. Really Australian, but one of the few places where we were actually given a freebie. Besides, everyone loves the Aussies.*

PETIT JOURNAL MONTPARNASSE, *13 rue du Commandant Mouchotte (14th, M:Montparnasse-Bienvenue). Tel. 01.43.21.56.70.*

A fun mix of local jazz and cabaret style music.

LA VILLA, *29 rue Jacob (6th, M:Saint-Germain-des-Prés). Tel. 01.43.26.60.00.*

Lots of quality mid-range jazz talents playing interpretations of classics in a basement *boite*.

NIGHTCLUBS & DISCOS

After the spring and fall fashion shows, the models inevitably cruise uptown to **Les Bains** for a party with likewise beautiful people. Though it is certainly one of the most popular clubs, it can be frustrating too. Doors open around midnight and the bouncers will give you a good looking over before they let you in. The bouncers aren't quite as fussy as local lore would have you believe, but it can still be a bit unnerving to be given the once-over. Fortunately there are lots of other options.

Check the *Pariscope* listings for one-nighters that feature the hot DJs. They will also draw the most interesting crowds — and they can get pretty interesting if you like loud costume parties.

Women often get in free (gee, why is that?). And things get going late. Real late.

Some nightclubs for you to try:

LES BAINS, 7 *rue du Bourg-l'Abbe (3rd, M:Étienne-Marcel). Tel. 01.48.87.01.80.*

So named because this building once housed Turkish baths. The dance floor is elbow to pretty elbow; you can find some calm at the upstairs bar.

LA LOCOMOTIVE, 90 *boulevard de Clichy (18th, M:Blanche). Tel. 01.53.41.88.88.*

Monster disco club where the crowds rock out into the wee hours.

QUEEN, 102 *avenue des Champs-Élysées (8th, M:George V). Tel. 01.53.89.08.90.*

Big new night spot. Very popular with the gay crowd, but everyone is invited. Entertainment ranges from disco to drag shows.

PLANET ROCK, 8 *rue des Bernardins (5th, M:Maubert-Mutualité), Tel. 01.43.36.21.66.*

One of the city's only indie nights, with DJs cranking out every kind of dance music there is.

L'ÉTOILE, 12 *rue de Presbourg (16th, M:Charles de Gaulle), Tel. 01.45.00.78.70.*

The former Club d'Arc has been cleaned up. Features lengthy bar, small summer garden when the weather cooperates and a dance floor that can be a bit too confining.

ÉLYSÉE MONTMARTRE, *72 boulevard Rochechouart (18th, M:Anvers). Tel. 01.55.07.06.00.*

A mixed menu, from hard rock to country in another popular party neighborhood.

LE REX CLUB, *5 boulevard Poissonière (2nd, M:Bonne Nouvelle). Tel. 01.42.36.28.81.*

Theme nights range from reggae to rock, sometimes with DJ's and sometimes with live bands.

ZED CLUB, *2 rue des Anglais (5th, M:Maubert-Mutualité), Tel. 01.43.54.93.78.*

Lots of rock and roll standards mean this may not be the hippest spot but, in our view, it's got some of the best of the dance classics going for it.

ABSOLUTELY ADULT

Paris has a reputation for being the free love capital of the world. The French are not nearly as promiscuous as Americans would like to believe and, as we've said so many times by now, virtually nothing is free.

Still, there are plenty of opportunities to satisfy carnal interests in bookstores concentrated around the **Place Pigalle** (9th) and **rue Saint-Denis** (1st) on the Right Bank, and along **rue de la Gaîté** (14th), just below the boulevard du Montparnasse on the Left Bank. The area around Place Pigalle also has oodles of strip joints eager to serve you crummy drinks and separate you from as much money as they can — probably without showing you a thing. Live sex shows, or *Spectacles Érotiques*, are sprinkled around town. Some are listed in *Pariscope*. Costs range from 200 to 400FF. Clubs known as American Bars, also listed in Pariscope and elsewhere, thrive on bad champagne and hostesses looking for a "date."

Keep these thoughts in mind: One, streetwalking is legal in France (the rue Saint-Denis is lined with perfectly legal but largely unattractive ladies of the evening), but pimping and prostitution initiated in clubs are not. And two, France has a frighteningly high AIDS rate and only a knucklehead would tempt such an awful fate. **Helpful phrase**: *"Je voudrais des préservatifs, s'il vous plaît."* Translation: "I'd like some condoms, please."

14. SHOPPING

To shop or not to shop? ... Are you kidding? You go, girl!

As irresistible as the shops are here, there is one hitch—the matter of money. This is not exactly bargain shopping.

No matter where in North America you live, you're bound to come to the same conclusion. We came to France from fifteen years in New York and Washington, DC — two of America's most expensive cities — and with ample warnings about the prices, and we were still stunned.

So what's a dedicated shopper on a limited budget to do? Give up? Never! Instead, strategize!

You can have more fun window shopping in Paris than spending real money in most places. Paris has some of the most lushly appointed shop windows (*vitrines*) in the world. You can soak up enough fashion to flesh out a million fantasies. And don't be shy about stepping inside to admire the *bibelots* (knick-knacks) and other *objets* even if you have no intention of opening your wallet. Why deprive yourself?

If you plan to return home with gifts, look around before you buy. On past trips, we'd browse for a few days, then set aside some time on the last day to return to the places with the best values.

THE TAX MAN

Every time you feel your taxes are too high in the States, come to France. Their combination of income, social security, and property taxes equal more than 50 percent of the average worker's earnings (though to be fair, their social safety and health care net is unbelievable).

That won't concern you, of course. But the **VAT** will. VAT (the French acronym is **TVA**) stands for value-added tax — a whopping 19.6 percent sales tax that is already included in the price you see on the tag.

The bad news is that you have to pay that tax on virtually everything you buy. The relative good news is that if you buy more than 2,000FF worth of merchandise in any one store and you're taking it all back to the States, you can arrange to be reimbursed for the tax.

The refund is called a *détaxe*. All reputable store owners and managers will have the proper paperwork. If they don't volunteer it, speak up.

All you need is your passport. You'll be asked whether you want the refund mailed to you in a French-franc check (it's a hassle) or have it credited to one of your credit cards (it's fast, easy, and the money is in dollars).

When you leave France, give the *détaxe* paperwork to the Customs officials for stamping. Do this before you hand over your bags or go through customs or passport control. When you get home, mail the documents to the store, and *Voilà!* It's a done deal.

Don't forget your own Tax Man. As we write this, each person can bring back $400 worth of merchandise purchased overseas duty free. After that, there will be a 10 percent tax on the next $1,000 worth of items. Beyond $1,400, each item is assessed an individual duty and the rates vary wildly according to the type of item you purchase.

SHOPPING TIPS
Hours
Many small shops close for one or two hours at lunch and all day Sunday and Monday. Most stores close at 7 p.m. The department stores stay open later one night a week, though each store stays open a different evening. Exceptions include T-shirt, post card, and similar stores in the most touristy neighborhoods.

Sales
Although there are almost always some sales racks in department stores, smaller retailers have sales (*soldes*) twice a year. Period. Winter merchandise goes on sale in January (sales sometimes extend into early February), and summer merchandise is available at reduced prices in July and sometimes August.

The sales are not always much to boast about. We've seen signs announcing all of "10 percent off." We've also seen signs that say "one for 50FF, two for 100FF." Go figure.

Cashiers

When you are ready to pay, look around for a sign that reads *Caisse,* meaning cashier. Sometimes, you will be asked to leave the item you are purchasing with the sales clerk while you go to the *caisse* and pay. You then return to the sale clerk to show your receipt and retrieve your purchase.

Courtesy

It's customary in small shops for the sales person to greet the customer with a *"Bonjour Madame/Monsieur,"* and for the customer to respond in kind. When you leave, regardless of whether you've made a purchase, saying *"Merci, Au revoir,"* is also customary.

Dressing Rooms

These are called *cabines.*

Credit Cards

Virtually all stores take major credit cards. In fact, using them may make more economic sense than you realize. For one, you won't have to carry as much cash or as many travelers checks. Second, credit card companies give you the exchange rate that's valid the day the purchase goes through — and with no fee for conversion.

Returns

Not in this lifetime. Except for the high end shops, be sure, be sorry, or be prepared to do battle before you'll be allowed to return something.

SIZES

To paraphrase the alleged exchange between Fitzgerald and Hemingway (this is Paris, after all), French women's bodies are different from yours and mine. They have no hips.

Be prepared to take several sizes into the fitting room. Beware of buying clothes as gifts. Even two items marked with the same size aren't always really the same.

DEPARTMENT STORES

The *grands magasins* are huge, and hugely popular, department stores — not at all unlike the big city counterparts in the States. The *grand magasin*

CLOTHING SIZES

Women's Suits & Dresses

American	6	8	10	12	14	16	18	20
French	36	38	38	40	42	44	46	48

Women's Stockings

American	8	9	9	10	10
French	1	2	3	4	5

Women's Shoes

American	4	4	5	5	6	7	8	9	9	10
French	35	36	36	37	37	38	39	40	41	41

Men's Suits

American	35	36	37	38	39	40	42
French	36	38	40	42	44	46	48

Men's Shirts

American	14	14	15	15	16	16	17	17	18
French	36	37	38	39	40	41	42	43	45

Men's Shoes

American	6	7	7	8	9	9	10	11
French	39	40	41	42	43	44	44	45

with something completely different is **La Samaritaine**, *75 rue de Rivoli (1st, M:Pont-Neuf), Tel. 01.45.08.33.33 or 01.40.41.20.20,* because its rooftop is an observation deck (and restaurant) with a view that should not be missed.

BAZAR DE L'HÔTEL DE VILLE, *52-64 rue de Rivoli, (4th, M: Hôtel-de-Ville). Tel. 01.42.74.90.00.*

Known mostly by its initials, BHV, this mammoth store has a basement hardware department that would make any do-it-yourselfer think he or she had died and gone to heaven. But it also has clothing, perfumes, books, furnishings and just about anything else a general interest department store should carry.

LE BON MARCHÉ, *22 rue de Sèvres (7th, M:Sèvres-Babylone). Tel. 01.44.39.80.00.*

One of the translations of *bon marché* is 'bargain.' That doesn't seem to apply here. In fact, most Parisians will tell you that Bon Marché is the most expensive of the *grands magasins*. It does, however, have a huge supermarket (yes, food), and the enormous prepared food section carries dozens of delicacies and can be fun to stroll through. This store, too, has clothing, furnishings, housewares, etc., etc.

CARROUSEL DU LOUVRE, *99 rue de Rivolli (1st, M:Louvre), Tel. 01.43.16.47.46.*

This is not really a department store, but a mall. And you're likely to discover it even if you're not looking because it is on the underground level of the museum, right where you buy your tickets. It is worth a look around. There are some chic clothing stores, a Lalique shop, a large shop with antique and reproduction prints, groovy glasses—really quite a variety. And the food court beats anything you're likely to have back home.

GALERIES LAFAYETTE, *40 boulevard Haussmann (9th, M:Chausée d'Antin). Tel. 01.42.82.34.56.*

This prestigious store, built in 1912, hosts fashion shows every Wednesday, also Fridays from April through October, in the Salon Opera (*for reservations, call 48.74.02.30*). The store has grown so large that it has been divided into various sections, such as *Galfa*, where you will find mostly menswear. Floorplans can be found near the escalators, but you should also find that the sales clerks are quite helpful in guiding you to the department you're seeking.

MARKS & SPENCER, *35 boulevard Haussmann (9th, M:Chausée d'Antin). Tel. 01.47.42.42.90.*

The big British chain comes to Paris. The place to shop for your favorite British-made products if you didn't include London on your itinerary.

LE PRINTEMPS, *64 boulevard Haussmann (9th, M:Chausée d'Antin). Tel. 01.42.85.22.22 or 01.42.82.50.00*

As you can tell by the address, this massive store is next door to the Galeries Lafayette. Like its competitor, Printemps has divided itself into various departments, such as **Brummell**, the related men's store, which is actually in an adjacent building and which we found to have one of the best selections and among the best values in town.

LES TROIS QUARTIERS, *17 boulevard de la Madeleine (1st, M: Madeleine). Tel. 01.42.60.39.30 or 01.42.97.80.12.*

Many call this mall, located near the magnificent Madeleine church, the chicest in all of Paris. It doesn't have the scale of a Printemps, but it does dazzle with its select shops.

HIGH FASHION

The big names in fashion, whether you want to buy or just gawk:

- **CÉLINE**, *26 rue Cambon (1st, M:Concorde), Tel. 01.42.61.34.45; 58 rue de Rennes (6th, M:Saint-Sulpice), Tel. 01.45.48.58.55; in Au Bon Marché department store, 38 rue de Sèvres (7th, M:Sèvres-Babylone); 24 rue François-1er (8th, M:George V), Tel. 01.47.20.14.33; men only, 38 avenue Montaigne (8th, M:Franklin-Roosevelt), Tel. 01.49.52.08.79; 3 avenue Victor-Hugo (16th, M:Victor-Hugo), Tel. 01.45.01.80.01*

- **CERRUTI.** For women: *15 place de la Madeleine (8th, M:Madeleine), Tel. 01.47.42.10.78; 42 rue de Grenelle (7th, M:Sèvres-Babylone), Tel. 01.42.22.92.28; 17 avenue Victor-Hugo (16th, M:Victor-Hugo), Tel. 01.45.01.66.12.* For men: *27 rue Royale (8th, M:Madeleine), Tel. 42.65.68.72; 48 rue Pierre Charron (8th, M:Franklin-Roosevelt), Tel. 01.40.70.18.81*

- **CHANEL**, *29 rue Cambon (1st, M:Concorde), Tel. 01.42.86.28.00*

- **CHRISTIAN DIOR**, *11 rue François-Ier (8th, M:Franklin-Roosevelt), Tel. 01.40.73.54.44; 30 avenue Montaigne (8th, M:Franklin-Roosevelt), Tel. 01.40.73.54.44; 16 rue de l'Abbaye (6th, M:St. Germian-des-Prés), Tel. 01.56.24.90.53*

- **CHRISTIAN LACROIX,** *26 avenue Montaigne (8th, M:Franklin-Roosevelt), Tel. 01.47.20.64.92; 73 due du Faubourg Saint-Honoré (8th, M:Miromesnil), Tel. 01.42.68.79.00.*

- **COURRÈGES**, *40 rue François-1er (8th, M:Franklin-Roosevelt), Tel. 01.47.20.70.44; 46 rue du Faubourg Saint-Honoré (8th, M:Madeleine), Tel. 01.42.65.37.75*

- **EMANUEL UNGARO**, *2 avenue Montaigne (8th, M:Franklin-Roosevelt), Tel. 01.53.57.00.00*

- **GIANI VERSACE**, *62 rue du Faubourg Saint-Honoré (8th, M:Madeleine), Tel. 01.47.42.88.02; 41 rue François-1er (8th, M; Franklin-Roosevelt), Tel. 01.47.23.88.30*

- **GIVENCHY**, *3 avenue George V (8th, M: George V), Tel. 01.44.31.50.06;* for women: *8 avenue George V (8th, M:George V), Tel. 01.47.20.81.31; 28 rue du Faubourg Saint-Honoré (8th, M:Madeleine), Tel. 01.42.65.54.54;* for men: *56 rue François-Ier (8th, M:Madeleine), Tel. 01.40.76.00.21*

- **GUCCI**, *2 rue du Faubourg Saint-Honoré (8th, M:Madeleine), Tel. 01.53.05.11.11*

- **HERMÉS**, *24 rue du Faubourg Saint-Honoré (8th, M:Madeleine), Tel. 01.40.17.47.17; 42 avenue George V (8th, M:George V), Tel. 01.47.20.48.51*
- **KENZO**, *60 rue de Rennes (6th, M:Saint Sulpice), Tel. 01.45.44.27.88*
- **LANVIN**. For women: *22 rue du Faubourg Saint-Honoré (8th, M:Madeleine), Tel. 01.44.71.33.33.* For men: *15 rue du Faubourg Saint-Honoré (8th, M:Madeleine), Tel. 01.44.71.33.33*
- **MAX MARA**, *31 avenue Montaigne (8th, M:Sevres-Babylone), Tel. 01.45.49.22.03*
- **NINA RICCI**, *17 rue François-1er (8th, M:Franklin-Roosevelt), Tel. 01.49.52.56.00*
- **PACO RABANNE**, *for men, 7 rue de Cherche Midi (6th, M:Saint-Sulpice), Tel. 01.42.22.87.80*
- **PRADA**, *10 avenue Montaigne (8th, M:Sevres-Babylone), Tel. 01.45.48.63.12*
- **YVES SAINT LAURENT**. For women: *6 place Saint-Sulpice (6th, M:Saint-Sulpice), Tel. 01.43.29.43.00; 38 rue du Faubourg Saint-Honoré (8th, M:Madeleine), Tel. 01.42.65.74.59; 12 Rond-Point Champs-Élysées (8th, M:Champs-Élysées), Tel. 01.45.62.00.23; 19 avenue Victor-Hugo (16th, M:Victor-Hugo), Tel. 01.45.00.64.64.* For men: *12 place Saint-Sulpice (6th, M:Saint-Sulpice), Tel. 01.43.26.84.40*

WINE

L'AMOUR DU VIN, *48 avenue de la Bourdonnais (7th, M:École Militaire). Tel. 01.45.55.68.63. Also, 94 rue Saint-Dominique (7th, M:École Militaire). Tel. 01.45.56.12.94.*

Very good wines at shockingly good prices chosen by owner Patrick Dussert-Gerber, author of *Le Guide Dussert-Gerber des Vins de France.*

CCA, *128 rue Vieille du Temple (3rd, M:Saint-Sébastien). Tel. 01.48.87.55.67; 37 boulevard Malesherbes (8th, M:Saint-Augustin); 51 avenue La Motte Picquet (15th, M:La Motte Picquet). Tel. 01.43.06.26.65.*

A small chain that offers a variety of smart recent vintage wines at reasonable prices. Look for several of the "second" wines produced by the major Bordeaux châteaux.

CAVE JEAN-BAPTISTE BESSE, *48 rue de la Montagne Sainte-Geneviève (5th, M:Maubert-Mutualité). Tel. 01.43.25.35.80.*

A trusty neighborhood wine shop for more than sixty years.

CAVES ESTÈVE, *10 rue de la Cerisaie (4th, M:Bastille).* *Tel.* *01.42.72.33.05; 292 rue Saint-Jacques (5th, M:Port Royal). Tel. 01.46.34.69.78;* *32 avenue Félix Faure (15th, M:Lourmel). Tel. 01.44.26.33.05).*

A very good small chain that offers regular tastings and stocks lots of reasonably priced, carefully selected alternatives to the obvious Grand Crus. Popular with the locals.

LES CAVES TAILLEVENT, *199 rue du Faubourg Saint-Honoré (8th, M:Saint-Philippe-du-Roule). Tel. 01.45.61.14.09.*

Though only open since 1987, this shop profits from its association with the famous restaurant by the same name.

NICOLAS. A large chain with shops everywhere. Popular, though we've never been terribly impressed with their selection.

AU VERGER DE LA MADELEINE, *4 boulevard Malesherbes (8th, M:Madeleine). Tel. 01.42.65.51.99.*

Family-run since 1937, with a large selection of rare wines.

LES CAVES AUGÉ, *116 boulevard Haussmann (8th, M:St-Augustin), Tel. 01.45.22.16.97.*

Literary giant Marcel Proust was said to frequent this, the oldest wine shop in Paris.

CAVES DU MARAIS, *64 rue Francois-Miron (4th, M:St-Paul), Tel. 01.42.78.54.64.*

Owner Jean-Jacques Bailly is often on hand and has sampled all his wares, so knows exactly what the best buys are.

LEGRAND FILLES ET FILS, *1 rue de la Banque (1st, M:Bourse), Tel. 01.42.60.07.12.*

Family nurtured variety.

TCHIN TCHIN, *9 rue Montorgueil (1st, M:Les Halles), Tel. 01.42.33.07.77.*

In this newish shop, owner Antoine Bénariac breaks the rule by including wines from places other than France.

ANTIQUES

Rather than list individual shops, we note several antique shopping districts and centers housing hundreds of dealers, scores of which are top-notch.

CARRÉ D'OR, *46 avenue George V (8th, M:George V).*

Several shops dealing primarily in jewelry.

CARRÉ RIVE GAUCHE *(7th, M:Rue du Bac).*

An area of usually high quality independent dealers just east of the Musée d'Orsay, bounded on the river by the Quai Voltaire, on the east by rue des Saints-Pères, on the south by rue de l'Université, and on the west by rue du Bac.

COUR DES ANTIQUAIRES, *54 rue du Faubourg Saint-Honoré (8th, M:Concorde). Tel. 01.42.66.38.60.*

Twenty dealers mostly showing artworks.

LOUVRES DES ANTIQUAIRES, *2 place du Palais Royal (1st, M:Palais Royal). Tel. 01.42.97.27.00.*

More than 200 dealers in high-end antiques and art.

MARCHÉ AUX PUCES, *Porte de Clignancourt (18th, M:Porte de Clignancourt).*

Open Saturday through Monday. Paris's largest flea market with very good sections and very bad sections.

PUCES DE VANVES, *avenue Georges-Lafenestre (14th, M:Malakoff).* Open-air flea market on weekends only.

SAINT-PAUL *(4th, M:Saint-Paul).*

An area of often quirky dealers in an area between the rue Charlemagne and the quai des Célestins.

VILLAGE SUISSE, *78 avenue de Suffren (15th, M:La Motte Picquet).* Well over 100 high end dealers. Open Thursdays through Sundays.

GLASS & CRYSTAL

• **BACCARAT**, *11 place de la Madeleine (8th, M:Madeleine). Tel. 01.42.65.36.26*

• **LALIQUE**, *Galerie Carrousel du Louvre (1st, M:Louvre). Tel. 01.42.86.01.51; and 11 rue Royale (8th, M:Concorde). Tel. 01.42.66.52.40*

ENGLISH-LANGUAGE BOOK STORES

In case you've run out of things to read on the plane going home:

ABBEY BOOKSHOP, *29 rue Parcheminerie (5th, M:Saint-Michel). Tel. 01.46.33.16.24.*

This small shop specializes in the works of Canadian authors.

BRENTANO'S, *37 avenue de l'Opéra (2nd, M:Pyramides). Tel. 01.42.61.52.50.*

This is the biggest and probably the best known of them all.

FNAC, *Forum des Halles (1st, M:Les Halles), Tel. 01.42.61.81.18; or 136 rue de Rennes (6th, M:Saint-Placide), Tel. 01.45.55.39.12; or 26 avenue de Wagram (8th, M:Wagram), Tel. 01.47.66.52.50.*

Not, strictly speaking, English-language bookstores, but they are enormous and have some English language books and magazines.

GALIGNANI, *224 rue de Rivoli (1st, M:Tuileries). Tel. 01.42.60.76.07.*

A distinguished shop with good variety and not so great prices. But it is centrally located.

SHAKESPEARE AND COMPANY, *37 rue de la Boucherie (5th, M:Saint-Michel). Tel. 01.43.26.96.50.*

Once the loving brainchild of Sylvia Beach, this is the most famous of all English-language bookstores in Paris. Though there are used paperbacks you can pick up just outside the shop's doors, the prices inside (even for used books) are a bit staggering. If you buy a book, the clerk will stamp the inside cover with the Shakespeare logo — as a sort of memento of your visit to the legendary shop.

W.H. SMITH & SON, *248 rue de Rivoli (1st, M:Tuileries). Tel. 01.42.60.37.97.*

Another distinguished and well located shop.

TEA AND TATTERED PAGES, *24 rue Mayet (6th, M:Duroc). Tel. 01.40.65.94.35.*

Mostly used books, good prices. Also a tea shop with American-style baked goods.

VILLAGE VOICE, *6 rue Princesse (6th, M:Mabillon). Tel. 01.46.33.36.47.*

SAN FRANCISCO BOOK CO., *17 rue Monsieur Le Prince (6th, M:Odéon). Tel. 01.43.29.15.70.*

OPEN MARKETS
Plants, Birds, Stamps, & Stuff

Generally speaking, most of the open markets (*marchés*) listed below are worth a visit just because they are so different from anything in the average American's shopping experience. They're informal, wide-open and there's absolutely no pressure to buy. The main open-air markets are:

PLANT AND PET MARKET, *quai de la Mégisserie (1st, M:Pont-Neuf). Daily, 9 a.m. to 6 p.m.*

Noisy and sometimes a bit smelly, but fun to see all the pups and more exotic animals.

MARCHÉ AUX FLEURS (flowers), *place Louis-Lépine, Île de la Cité (4th, M:Cité). Monday through Saturday, 8 a.m. to 4 p.m.*

Beautiful. And smells great!

MARCHÉ AUX OISEAUX (birds), *place Louis-Lépine, Île de la Cité (4th, M:Cité). Sunday only, 9 a.m. to 7 p.m.*

Interesting, even for those who prefer warm-blooded pets. A great place for taking photos.

MARCHÉ AUX TIMBRES (stamps), *Rond-Point des Champs-Élysées (8th, M:Champs-Élysées). Open Thursday, Saturday and Sunday, 10 a.m. to 7 p.m.*

Did you see the classic film *Charade*? The crucial scene takes place here. Echoes of Cary Grant and Audrey Hepburn can still be heard by film buffs.

MARCHÉ AUX PUCES (flea market), *by Porte de Clignancourt, (18th, M:Porte de Clignancourt). Open Saturday through Monday, 9:30 a.m. to 6:30 p.m.*

Allegedly the largest flea market in France. Don't be put off by the offerings of junk you will probably find as you approach the real market. Keep going and you will come to scores of tiny stalls filled with everything from vintage posters, silver thimbles, and glass doorknobs to dining tables and armoires that would have made William Randolph Hearst proud (see Chapter 11, *Seeing the Sights*).

SHOPPING NEIGHBORHOODS

If department stores aren't your style, there are several well-known retail neighborhoods where you can feast your eyes on products of all kinds.

LEFT BANK
Boulevard Saint-Germain
6th Arrondissement

Though **Saint-Germain** is a grand boulevard that cuts through the trendy 6th *arrondissement*, here we're really using the name as a point of departure. And what we're really talking about is the **Saint-Germain-des-Prés area** between the boulevard Saint-Germain and the Seine — a quarter that is defined by style, sidewalk cafés, and narrow twisting streets that are home to charming boutiques and restaurants galore.

Here, you'll find lots of the biggest names in chic French and international fashion and home furnishings, including Issey Miyake, Sonya Rykiel, Yves Saint Laurent, and Roche Bobois stores. There are also a number of smaller shops to explore.

Selected shops worth a visit:

DEBAUVE & GALLAIS (chocolate), *30 rue des Saints-Pères (6th, M:Saint-Germain-des-Prés). Tel. 01.45.48.54.67.*

A real find! If you love chocolate, these are the people for you. Founded in 1800, Debauve & Gallais bill themselves as the oldest chocolate store in Paris. It seems that Monsieur Debauve, while serving as the pharmacist to Louis XVI, discovered the curative powers of chocolate and capitalized on the idea. There are 40 types of bite-sized confections (*bouchées*) and bars (*tablettes*) to choose from. French chocolate is generally darker and less sweet than its Swiss and Belgian counterparts. Indeed, Debauve & Gallais sell a tablette that purports to be 99 percent cacao. Ask about the perfect replicas of golf balls. Great gifts for the folks back home.

ATELIER D'ANAIS (needlepoint), *23 rue Jacob (6th, M:Saint-Germain-des-Prés). Tel. 01.43.26.68.00.*

For those who do needlepoint or cross-stitch. Also a selection of tassles, as well as scissors and other tools of the art that are perfect as souvenirs or gifts.

LA MAISON IVRE (pottery), *38 rue Jacob (6th, M:Saint-Germain-des-Prés). Tel. 01.42.60.01.85.*

A find! You can bring sunshine into the darkest winter with the handmade pottery sold at this warm and welcoming shop. The bright colors that one associates with the South of France are here in abundance and the store's friendly staff is glad to pack it up so it won't break on your trip home. Although you could spend a fortune here, there are also plenty of small items such as egg cups, salt shakers, and candlesticks with prices that fit any budget.

DEMONS ET MERVEILLES (exotic gifts), *45 rue Jacob (6th, M:Saint-Germain-des-Prés). Tel. 01.42.96.26.11.*

Arts and crafts, costumes, jewelry, and furniture from Eastern Europe, Afghanistan, Tibet, and India. A treasure trove for people who enjoy mementos from off the beaten path.

L'ÎLE DU DEMON (exotic gifts), *13 rue Bonaparte (6th, M:Saint-Germain-des-Prés or Mabillion). Tel. 01.43.26.92.53.*

Similar to, but different from, Demons et Merveilles, this somewhat larger shop sells everything from jewelry (necklaces of African stones start at 50FF) to very large items such as the gilded sculpture of the Indian god Shiva-Bhiraba (a mere 200,000FF). Also dozens of different African masks and other pieces of tribal art.

PATRICK FREY (fabric), *2, rue de Furstemberg (6th, M:Saint-Germain-des-Prés or Mabillion). Tel. 01.46.33.73.00.*

Parisians love to decorate their walls with fabric and they adore to be comforted by fine linens.

AU FOND DE LA COUR (antiques), *49 rue de Seine (6th, M:Mabillion or Odéon). Tel. 01.43.25.81.89.*

What first drew us into the aptly-named Au Fond de la Cour was its setting at the back of a courtyard visible through open wooden doors from the sidewalk. The courtyard is set up as if a small garden party is about to take place. With the exception of some rattan furniture and a fine collection of elegant bird cages, this shop is dedicated to majolica, including an entire fireplace with beautiful white lilies tinged with lavender and flowing gracefully into long green stems.

GALERIE DOCUMENTS (posters), *53 rue de Seine (6th, M:Mabillion). Tel. 01.43.54.50.68.*

Magnificent authentic period posters from theaters, fairs, arts exhibitions, etc. They can take care of shipping, and the prices, though high, seem reasonable for such historic pieces.

Rue d'Alésia
14th Arrondissement

This street has many affordable shops.

If your closet is crammed with things from Filene's bargain basement or factory outlet stores, then you won't want to miss **rue d'Alésia** in the 14th *arrondissement*.

An avenue of average charm and grace, rue d'Alésia is lined on both sides by off-price retailers, factory outlets, and multi-maker close-out stores. The street is a bit out of the way and you won't find many tourists here, but there's absolutely no reason to fear you'll come into harm's way.

Take the No. 4 Métro line in the direction of Porte d'Orléans and get off at Alésia, the second to the last stop.

The bulk of the stores are concentrated between Stock and Sold (56 rue d'Alésia) and the Chevignon outlet (122 rue d'Alésia). In between you will find clothing styles to match virtually any taste. There's lots for men and kids to choose from, but the largest selection is in women's casual clothes.

It's possible at most of the stores to buy last year's styles for as much as 60 percent off their original price. And many stores have super discount racks with even greater savings. Offerings from the current season are readily available in the 20 percent off category.

Keep in mind that it usually takes a year or two for Paris styles to reach America's most fashion-conscious cities, so you can buy last year's merchandise at low, low prices and still be ahead of the style curve when you get back home.

Try to avoid shopping on Saturdays when the sharp Parisians with their even sharper elbows will be out in force. Although very little English is spoken along here, prices are clearly marked so there shouldn't be a problem. Take lots of cash if you are a serious shopper because not every place takes credit cards. And be sure to ask about the *détaxe* (see the beginning of this chapter) if you buy more than 2,000FF worth at any one store.

Below is a partial list of stores offering better-known brands. Not every store on the street is a discounter; the key words to look for are *Stock* or *Dégriffé*. The words *Solde* and *Promotion* mean additional markdowns. Hours tend to be 10 a.m. to 7 p.m. (although some of the smaller shops will close for one to two hours for lunch).

STOCK AND SOLD, *56 and 85 rue d'Alésia (14th, M:d'Alésia). Tel. 01.43.27.04.31.*

Two shops across the street from each other. Pierre Cardin and other brands. Women's clothing only. Good selection.

EVOLUTIF, *72 rue d'Alésia (14th, M:Alésia). Tel. 01.45.45.34.34.*

Mostly menswear. Brands include Kenzo, Yves Saint Laurent (YSL), Cerrutti.

DIAPOSITIVE, *74 rue d'Alésia (14th, M:Alésia). Tel. 01.45.39.97.27.*

Womenswear from this one maker. Good markdowns. One of the best bargain racks.

PRET-A-PORTER STOCK 2, *92 rue d'Alésia (14th, M:Alésia). Tel. 01.45.41.65.57.*

A real find! This Daniel Hechter outlet is the largest of all the stores we visited and, not surprisingly, offered the best range. You can find men's and women's clothes in casual and professional styles, as well as outerwear and kids' clothes. The large staff means there's always someone to help, but the ability to speak English doesn't seem to be a condition of employment. Discounts go as high as 40 percent.

STOCK SAINT CLAIR, *110-112 rue d'Alésia (14th, M:Alésia). Tel. 01.45.43.80.86.*

Forty percent off last season's clothes for men and women. Lots of outerwear. Great prices in men's sports jackets. Well-lit and spacious.

KOOKAI, *111bis rue d'Alésia (14th, M:Alésia). Tel. 01.45.42.33.66.*

An outlet for one of France's most ubiquitous brands of play clothes. Great for juniors.

COMPAGNIE SCANDINAVE DE FOURRURES, *113 rue d'Alésia (14th, M:Alésia). Tel. 01.40.44.94.44.*

Another find! Furs and leather goods at discount prices. In midwinter it seemed that every woman in Paris was wearing a mink. Now we know where many shopped. We're not experts, but we saw nice three-quarter length dark mink jackets for 7,900FF (roughly $1,400). If you take advantage of the *détaxe* that will bring the price down another $260. Not bad for being able to say for 20 years that you bought your mink in Paris. If your politics and your purse permit it, worth a stop.

CACHAREL STOCK, *114 rue d'Alésia (14th, M:Alésia). Tel. 01.45.42.53.04.*

Men's, women's, and children's clothes in casual and dressy styles from the well-known maker. Up to 50 percent off clothes from last year.

MAJESTIC S.A. CHEVIGNON, *122 rue d'Alésia (14th, M:Alésia). Tel. 01.45.43.40.25.*

Chevignon is one of the trendiest brands for the young in Paris and those in the know in the States. Other outlets for this brand are located at 82 rue du Commerce in the 15th and 42 rue de Levis in the 17th.

RIGHT BANK
Rue Saint-Honoré
1st & 8th Arrondissements

The richest, most glamorous people in the world shop here. Why shouldn't you? The primest of this prime real estate runs from **avenue Matignon** in the 8th *arrondissement* to **rue de Castiglione** in the 1st *arrondissement*.

The giants of the postwar international elegance industry include Yves Saint Laurent, Lanvin, Hermès, Valentino, Cartier, Givenchy, Armani, Chanel, Mikimoto, Gucci and many more. They're all here and easy to find just by strolling along.

Selected shops worth a visit:

HERMÈS (scarves and clothing), *24 rue du Faubourg Saint-Honoré (8th, M:Madeleine). Tel. 01.40.17.47.17.*

Many of the stores are on the small side and the sales people can seem intimidating, especially if you have no intention of buying. One notable exception is Hermès. It's more like a small department store, and the staff is enormous. Indeed, you can have your own personal escort who can converse in the language of your choice. Or you can walk around unbothered to check out the suede T-shirts ($1,000) and handmade shoes.

KENNETH JAY LANE (jewelry), *249 rue Saint-Honoré (1st, M:Concorde). Tel. 01.42.60.06.27; and 14 rue de Castiglione (1st, M:Tuileries). Tel. 01.42.60.69.56.*

If you're shopping for that special woman in your life, whether she's a girlfriend or your mother, you will want to know the name Kenneth Jay Lane. An American, he built his reputation back in the '60s on high quality reproductions of some of the world's most elegant jewelry. Another advantage to shopping at Kenneth Jay Lane's is that you can exchange a piece at one of his shops in the States.

SWANN'S (American-style drug store), *6 rue de Castiglione (1st, M:Tuileries). Tel. 01.42.60.72.96.*

If you forgot your prescription medicine at home, don't panic. Marylene Rocher, the *docteur en pharmacie*, speaks excellent English and is equipped to fill virtually any American prescription. Also, if you forget your over-the-counter American remedies (Sudafed, Maalox, Listerine, etc.), Swann's is one of the rare places in Paris that might have them.

PARFUMERIE CATHERINE (perfume), *6 rue de Castiglione (1st, M:Tuileries),*. *Tel. 01.47.44.02.15.*

Next door to Swann's, this tiny but well-stocked cosmetics and perfume boutique swears it takes all the taxes off the price of your purchases right at the register (even if the total is less than 2,000FF). A very friendly mother, father, and daughter team run the store.

The Golden Triangle
8th Arrondissement

The **rue Saint-Honoré** is hardly Paris's only elegant and expensive shopping playground. The quarter known by some as the **Golden Triangle** (bounded by the Champs-Élysées to the north, avenue George V to the west, and avenue Montaigne to the east) offers a stunning variety of luxury shopping experiences and out-of-this-world prices.

The avenue des Champs-Élysées may very well be one of most famous streets in the world, but, as we've said before, it's hardly the place where you'd want to do any serious shopping. Today, it's primarily movie theaters, fast food restaurants, airline ticket offices, and a construction project (underground parking) that many believe will never end.

If you can't resist shopping there, check out boutiques in the dozens of galleries that snake off the main thoroughfare. And don't say we didn't warn you if you pay too much for something you probably could have found at home.

Now, if you're looking for a memorable shopping experience, leave the Champs-Élysées behind and walk south a couple of blocks to rue François Ier or avenue Montaigne. Flanked by many of the world's most famous designers, these streets offer window shopping at its best.

Selected shops worth a visit:

CARTIER, *51 rue François 1 (8th, M:George V). Tel. 01.40.74.61.84*

CHRISTIAN DIOR, *30 avenue Montaigne (8th, M:Franklin-Roosevelt). Tel. 01.40.73.55.14*

HERMÈS, *42 avenue George V (8th, M:George V). Tel. 01.47.20.48.51*

INES DE LA FRESSANGE, *14 avenue Montaigne (8th, M:Champs-Élysées). Tel. 01.47.23.08.94*

LOUIS VUITTON, *54 avenue Montaigne, (8th, M:Champs-Élysées). Tel. 01.45.62.47.00*

VIRGIN MEGASTORE, *52 avenue des Champs-Élysées (8th, M: George V). Tel. 01.40.74.06.48.*

The prices for CDs and books are way too high, but, as the store's own PR promises, "from its creation in October 1988, the store has revealed itself to be a phenomenon of society." With 15,000 to 20,000 visitors a day, you know there's something going on. It's hip, it's cool, and it's open until midnight every day and on Sundays, which in France is about as radical as you can get.

15. CHILD'S PLAY

Just because children don't have a taste for fine wines and Empire period furnishings doesn't mean they can't have a good time in Paris.

There are circuses, pony rides, carousels, science museums and puppet shows galore to keep the kids entertained. Most organized activities are scheduled for weekends and Wednesdays, when Parisian children are off from school.

A word about food for kids: they are likely to be disappointed by the local hamburgers and hot dogs, and they are only marginally welcome in many of the better restaurants, where the local clientele wants to savor dinner without childish interruption. But children's eyes light up when they see all the pastries in bakery windows.

Some folks who might know about special events or might have useful general information: **The American Church**, *Tel. 01.47.05.07.99*, the **Boy and Girl Scouts office**, *Tel. 01.43.12.22.22*, and the **American School**, *Tel. 01.46.34.78.05*.

BABYSITTING SERVICES

EUROBABY, *Tel. 43.44.23.04*, a service "For Babies Who Like to Travel," rents prams, car seats, and other doodads necessary for taking care of small children.

Some of the top-rung hotels can arrange babysitting. An alternative is one of the city's many au pair services, some of which can provide a babysitter for a night or two, or refer you to a service that can.

Babysitting and au pair services include:

AU PAIR CONTACT INTERNATIONAL, *Tel. 01.43.54.40.82*.
INTER-SERVICE PARENTS, *Tel. 01.44.93.44.93*
A free advisory service for parents looking for help.

NANNIES INCORPORATED, *Tel. 01.45.74.62.74.*
KID SERVICES, *Tel. 01.42.61.90.00.*
BABY SITTING SERVICE, *Tel. 01.46.37.51.24.*
AMERICAN CHURCH, *Tel. 01.40.62.05.00.*

CIRCUSES, ZOOS, & ANIMAL PARKS
Circuses

The French—young and old—are absolutely fascinated by circuses. It seems as if there is one on television virtually every night. But there are plenty of real ones, especially during the warmer seasons, when outdoor circuses come to town. A quick check under the heading *Enfants* in a *Pariscope* will probably list at least a handful of circuses. There are often shows at the **Bois de Boulogne** or the **Bois de Vicennes,** each easily accessible by the Métro. Your concierge should be able to guide you to the location and even call ahead to arrange tickets.

Zoos

- **MÉNAGERIE DU JARDIN DES PLANTES,** *57 rue Cuvier (5th, M:Jussieu). Tel. 01.40.79.37.94. Admission 30FF for adults, 20FF for children.*
- **PARC ZOOLOGIQUE DE PARIS,** *Bois de Vincennes, 53 avenue de Saint-Maurice (12th, M:Porte Dorée). Tel. 01.44.75.20.10. Admission 40FF for adults, 30FF for children..*

Animal Parks

PARC ZOOLOGIQUE DE THOIRY, *For information in English: Tel. 01.34.87.45.90, or Fax 01.34.87.54.12. Admission 105FF for adults, 79FF for children.*

From the safety of your car or a touring trolley, watch elephants, giraffes, hippos, and 800 of their closest friends cavort freely in this beautiful wooded park. The park also features a 16th-century château, known as the Château du Soleil for the way its architectural layout is patterned after the path of the sun.

To reach the park, which is 25 miles west of Paris, take a SNCF train from Gare Montparnasse to the Montfort l'Amaury station. There, you can hop on a Thoiry shuttle bus the rest of the way. If you have a car, take the A13 autoroute to the A12 toward Versailles and Dreux, exiting at D11 to Thoiry.

SAINT-VRAIN, *For information: Tel. 01.64.56.10.80. Admission 75FF for adults, 65FF for children under 10.*

This re-creation of a prehistoric world also boasts wild animals and a boat safari ride. By car, take the A6 autoroute south to the Viry-Chatillon exit, toward Bretigny-sur-Orge, and look for signs reading Saint-Vrain.

CLASSES FOR KIDS

For drawing and painting lessons, at home or in your hotel room, call *01.45.24.58.27.*

LENNEN BILINGUAL SCHOOL OF THE AMERICAN CHURCH, *Tel. 01.47.05.66.55.*

Language lessons, arts and crafts, storytelling, and other activities.

LA PISCINE PONTOISE, *19 rue de Pontoise (5th, M:Maubert-Mutualité). Tel. 01.43.54.82.45.*

Swimming instruction for ages 3 and above.

THÉÂTRE MARIE STUART, *4 rue Marie-Stuart (2nd, M:Étienne-Marcel) Tel. 01.45.48.24.13 or 01.45.08.17.80.*

Theater workshop for ages 8 through 13.

PUPPET SHOWS

Puppets are another traditional passion of French children. Language could be a problem here, though many foreign children still enjoy the universal slapstick humor. Once again, *Pariscope* will help with times and prices, listing puppet shows under "Marionnettes." Shows in the major city parks are usually scheduled for about an hour in the mid-afternoon on Wednesdays, Saturdays, and Sundays. Prices range from 10 to 20FF.

- **MARIONNETTES DU CHAMP-DE-MARS**, *on Champ-de-Mars (7th, M:École Militaire). Tel. 01.48.56.01.44.*
- **MARIONNETTES DES CHAMPS-ÉLYSÉES**, *Rond point des Champs-Élysées (8th, M:Champs-Élysées). Tel. 01.42.45.38.30.*
- **MARIONNETTES DU LUXEMBOURG**, *in the Jardin du Luxembourg (6th, M:Vavin). Tel. 01.43.26.46.47.*
- **MARIONNETTES DE MONTMARTRE**, *Auditorium de la Halle Saint-Pierre, 2 rue Ronsard (18th, M:Anvers), Tel. 01.42.58.72.89.*

MISCELLANEOUS FUN STUFF

THE AMERICAN LIBRARY, *10 rue du General Camou (7th, M:École Militaire). Tel. 01.53.59.12.60. Admission free.*

There's a children's section with storytelling and other activities every Wednesday afternoon.

AQUABOULEVARD DE PARIS, *4 rue Louis-Armand (15th, M:Balard). Tel. 01.40.60.10.00. Admission varies from 49 to 55FF for kids, and 68 to 75FF for adults.*

A paradise for children (and adults), where they can swim, play tennis, bowl, putt their way around two miniature golf courses, or just fool around. Also located here is **Gymborée**, which offers a variety of exercises and games for parents and their infants and very small children.

PARC ASTERIX, *in the northern suburb of Plailly off the A1 autoroute at the Parc Asterix exit (or take the B line RER to Roissy Charles-de-Gaulle, where you can catch a shuttle bus the rest of the way). Tel. 01.44.62.31.31, 01.44.60.60.00 or 01.36.68.30.10. Admission, 150FF for adults and 105FF for children.*

A theme park that takes its name from the famous cartoon character and recreates the world of the Gauls.

DISNEYLAND PARIS. Did you really come all the way to France to see Mickey and Minnie? If you did (or even if you didn't but your kids insist anyway), see Chapter 17, *Excursions & Day Trips*, for more information.

JARDIN D'ACCLIMATATION, *in the northern section of the Bois de Boulogne (16th, M:Sablons). Admission charge depends on activities, but the total charge per child shouldn't be much more than 20FF.*

The Children's Amusement Park has a small zoo, an art museum where youngsters can experiment in a workshop, a miniature railroad, and a giant doll's house.

MUSÉE GREVIN, *10 boulevard Montmartre (9th, M:Rue Montmartre). Tel. 01.47.70.87.99. Admission 58FF for adults, 38FF for children.*

This is the century-old wax museum with more than 400 characters from history and films. Also demonstrations and "fantasy shows."

PALAIS DE LA DÉCOUVERTE, *avenue Franklin D. Roosevelt (8th, M:Franklin-Roosevelt). Tel. 01.40.74.81.82 or 01.40.74.80.00. Admission 27FF for adults, 17FF for children, free for children under 7.*

A paradise of hands-on science-fair projects that teach kids about everything from bugs to supernovas.

PONY RIDES, *available at the Luxembourg Gardens (5th, M:Luxembourg) and the Champ de Mars (7th, M:École Militaire), on weekends. Fees vary.*

In addition to pony rides, children can also rent small wooden sailboats for the huge pool just behind the Luxembourg palace.

16. SPORTS & RECREATION

Paris is not exactly swarming with joggers on a dewy morning, and Parisian athletic clubs often hype their in-house cafés as much as their Nautilus equipment. Still, health and fitness are of increasing concern to the French. Even smoking levels are down a bit — except for teenagers, who seem to do little else.

If walking several miles a day sightseeing isn't enough exercise, there are several pools and clubs in town that offer single day rates. As always, it's a good idea to call ahead (or, better yet, have the concierge of your hotel phone for you) to see what the rules and rates are. Some facilities, especially pools, are seasonal and won't be open at all.

AEROBICS & WEIGHTS
AQUABOULEVARD, *4 rue Louis-Armand (15th, M:Balard). Tel. 01.40.60.10.00.*

See also "Bowling" and "Swimming Pools" below.

BODY GYM, *157 rue Faubourg Saint-Antoine (11th, M:Faidherbe-Chaligny). Tel. 01.43.42.42.33.*

CLUB QUARTER LATIN (see Piscine Pontoise below).

ESPACE VIT'HALLES, *48 rue Rambuteau (3rd, M:Rambuteau). Tel. 01.42.77.21.71.*

Major fitness center with all the latest gizmos and dance steps.

GYM CLUB OPERA, *2 rue Scribe (9th, M:Opéra). Tel. 01.40.07.31.03.*

SPORTIVE DU PRINTEMPS, *28 rue Joubert (9th, M:Chausée-D'Antin). Tel. 01.48.74.56.42.*

GYMNASE CLUB, more than 20 locations around town:
- *147 bis rue Saint-Honoré (1st, M:Palais-Royal). Tel. 01.40.20.03.03*
- *26 rue de Berri (8th, M:Georges V). Tel. 01.43.59.04.58*

- *10 rue de la Victoire (9th, M:Le Pelletier). Tel. 01.48.74.58.49*
- *149 rue de Rennes (6th, M:Montparnasse), Tel. 01.45.44.24.35*
- *14 rue Vandrezanne (13th, M:Tolbiac), Tel. 01.45.80.34.16*
- *208 rue de Vaugirard (15th, Volontairs), Tel. 01.47.83.99.45*
- *28 avenue Général-Leclerc (14th, M:Denfert-Rochereau). Tel. 01.45.42.50.57*
- *24 rue de Chazelles (17th, M:Courcelles). Tel. 01.43.80.66.14.*

BOWLING

AQUABOULEVARD, *4 rue Louis-Armand (15th, M:Balard). Tel. 01.40.60.10.00.*

See "Aerobics and Weights" and "Swimming Pools" — get the idea of the scope of this place?

BOWLING CHAMPERRET, *2 rue Corporal-Peugeot (17th, M:Champerret). Tel. 01.43.80.24.64.*

BOWLING INTERNATIONAL STADIUM, *66 avenue d'Ivry (13th, M:Porte d'Ivry). Tel. 01.45.86.55.52.*

BOWLING MONTPARNASSE, *25 rue Commandant René Mouchotte (14th, M:Gaîté). Tel. 01.43.21.61.32.*

BOWLING MOUFFETARD, *73 rue Mouffetard, in back and underground (5th, M:Monge). Tel. 01.43.31.09.35.*

BOWLING DE PARIS, *Jardin d'Acclimatation in the Bois de Boulogne (16th, M:Porte Dauphine). Tel. 01.40.67.94.00.*

SWIMMING POOLS

AQUABOULEVARD, *4 rue Louis-Armand (15th, M:Balard). Tel. 01.40.60.10.00.*

The big daddy of them all, with huge indoor and outdoor pools, water slides, wave machines, tennis, everything.

PISCINE EMILE-ANTHOINE, *9 rue Jean-Rey (15th, M:Bir-Hakeim). Tel. 01.45.67.10.20.*

A pool and gym near the Tour Eiffel.

PISCINE HEBERT, *2 rue des Fillettes (18th, M:Marx-Dormoy). Tel. 01.46.07.60.01.*

Newly renovated.

PISCINE HENRY-DE-MONTHERLANT, *32 boulevard Lannes (16th, M:Porte-Dauphine). Tel. 01.45.03.03.28.*

Large new pool with an accompanying gym and tennis courts.

PISCINE DU MARCHÉ SAINT-GERMAIN, *7 rue Clément (6th, M:Mabillon). Tel. 01.43.29.08.15.*

An underground pool in an old covered market.

PISCINE PONTOISE, *19 rue de Pontoise (5th, M:Maubert-Mutualité). Tel. 01.43.54.82.45.*

Large below street-level pool with health club facilities upstairs.

PISCINE SUZANNE-BERLIOUX, *10 place de la Rotonde (1st, M:Châtelet). Tel. 01.42.36.98.44.*

Underground in the Forum des Halles complex. For the young and trendy.

TENNIS & SQUASH

ACTION TENNIS, *145 rue Vaugirard (15th, M:Falguière). Tel. 01.47.34.36.36.*

FOREST HILL, a chain with several locations for squash and tennis, though all are in the suburbs except the one at Aquaboulevard (see above).

LE PARISIEN TENNIS CLUB, *7 rue des Petites-Écuries (10th, M:Château-d'Eau). Tel. 01.48.24.16.96.*

SQUASH CLUB QUARTIER LATIN (see Piscine Pontoise above).

SQUASH MONTMARTRE, *14 rue Achille Martinet (18th, M:Lamarck). Tel. 01.42.55.38.30.*

SQUASH RENNES RASPAIL, *149 rue de Rennes (6th, M:Montparnasse). Tel. 01.45.44.24.35.*

STADIUM SQUASH CLUB, *66 avenue d'Ivry (13th, M:Porte d'Ivry). Tel. 01.45.85.39.06.*

17. EXCURSIONS & DAY TRIPS

Paris is surrounded by precious gems — majestic castles, sumptuous gardens, mysterious forests and villages steeped in color and history. If it's your first trip to Paris and you're spending a week or less, we suggest you stick to the city. But if you need a break from the big city or if you've visited Paris a couple times before and have an afternoon or two to spare, it's time to branch out.

We've chosen just a few of the more spectacular nearby sights, all of which are within an hour from Paris. Almost all of them can be reached by using the **RER commuter train service** that branches out of Paris in all directions, is reliable (except during strikes), and is reasonably priced.

If you want to cut the logistical strain of an out-of-town afternoon to a minimum, you might consider a tour bus. Companies such as **Paris Vision** visit every destination we've listed below, sometimes combining two or three sights in a single long day.

In a few instances, we've ignored our own warning against the hazards and hassles of renting a car. There are times that such a luxury allows you the flexibility to sightsee as long as you like and even, if you are transfixed by some charming village, to stay overnight in a local inn.

The list below is arranged geographically, beginning to the north of Paris and moving clockwise to the east, the south and, finally, the west.

EXCURSIONS FINDS & FAVORITES
· *Chantilly*
· *Vaux-le-Vicomte*

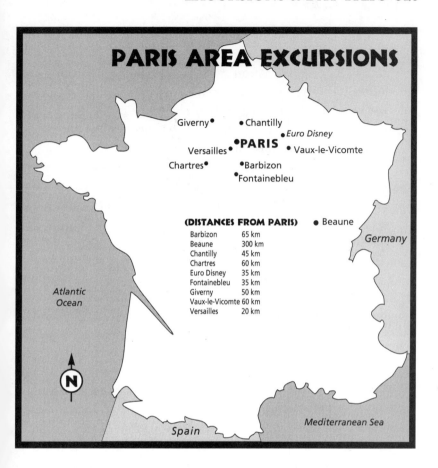

PARIS AREA EXCURSIONS

Giverny• • Chantilly
• Euro Disney
Versailles• •**PARIS** • Vaux-le-Vicomte
Chartres• •Barbizon
•Fontainebleu

(DISTANCES FROM PARIS) • Beaune

Barbizon	65 km
Beaune	300 km
Chantilly	45 km
Chartres	60 km
Euro Disney	35 km
Fontainebleu	35 km
Giverny	50 km
Vaux-le-Vicomte	60 km
Versailles	20 km

Germany

Atlantic
Ocean

N

Mediterranean Sea

Spain

CHANTILLY

Rolling green hills, dense forests rustling with birds of all kinds, a picturesque village, a magnificent racecourse, and a castle surrounded by a moat and expansive gardens lush with all manner of wild and tamed flowers. There's more: **Chantilly**, about 45 kilometers (27 miles) north of Paris, is far enough away from the city that most tourists forgo this masterpiece, allowing you plenty of room to wander at will and gawk at the castle and grounds.

What more could you ask?

The most famous legend associated with Chantilly goes back to 1671, when the owner, Louis de Bourbon, invited Louis XIV and several hundred of his court to dinner. Vatel, the most renowned chef of the era, was to do the culinary honors. Unhappily, the fish course was late and, overcome with humiliation, Vatel took his own life.

Much of the original château was dismantled by the mobs during the Revolution. What you see now can be credited largely to Henri d'Orléans, who was the duc d'Aumale and a Bourbon himself. The duke helped restore the castle in the 19th century and then bequeathed the château and grounds to the Institute of France.

The interior is now largely given to the **Conde Museum**, a rich collection of tapestries, portraits, miniature paintings, works in silver, books and other items. A favorite for us was the **Galerie des Cerfs**, a huge dining hall in the center of which stands a 30-foot-long table.

The dining hall is decorated with tapestries glorifying the hunt, the skins of two lions felled by a nobleman, stags' horns, and candlestick holders in the shape of men's arms protruding from the walls. Over one doorway there is also an unusually seductive painting of Diana of the hunt, lolling about in a forest clearing with a weary cherub and a stag by her side.

Two sections of the museum are open only to guided tours in groups of 10, which can be a bit annoying if you're mostly interested in the antique furnishings in those areas.

When you're ready for a break, there is a pleasant little café in the château cellar. Other nearby cafés can be found across from the stables. Or bring a picnic lunch and set yourself down on the racecourse grounds.

Horses never had it so good as with the **Grand Écuries** – the Chantilly stables, which are a couple of hundred yards from the château (this is a separate entrance fee). The massive, 610-foot-long structure with soaring interior arches once sheltered 240 horses and as many dogs.

Today, there are probably fewer than 20 horses and not a dog in sight. Still, you can meet (but not touch) Petit Blond, a playful Palomino born in 1988, Fresco, a regal gray Portuguese with gorgeous long tresses, and six or seven other noble beasts. A performance showcasing the horses and their skills is staged in a central ring three times daily.

The remainder of the stables is given over to a comprehensive museum tracing the evolution of horseshoes, harnesses, saddles, and just about anything else you might associate with horses.

The château is closed Tuesday. Admission is 35FF to the château and 50FF to the stables and the Living Museum of the Horse.

ARRIVALS & DEPARTURES

Several trains leave the Gare du Nord daily for Chantilly and beyond. Fares are 76FF roundtrip and the trip is about 30 minutes each way. Or take the D line of the RER, which you can catch at Gare du Nord or Châtelet and which takes about 45 minutes. The bigger bus tour companies also offer half-day trips to Chantilly for about 300FF.

Cabs and local buses will take you from the station to the château, which is about a mile. Or, on a nice day, you can stroll to the château. Just walk straight out from the station into the woods a block away. After a brief walk down the open path you'll emerge at the famous Diane racecourse, pass by the awesome stables (you may at first mistake them for the château), and finally arrive at the moat surrounding the castle.

WHERE TO STAY & EAT

CHÂTEAU DE LA TOUR, *Chemin de la Chaussée, 60270 Gouvieux. Tel. 03.44.62.38.38, Fax 03.44.57.31.97. Rooms: 41. Double: 590-980FF. Restaurant.*

Located just west of Chantilly. A lovely almost Tudor-style residence from the turn of the century with an enormous park, its own small forest, a tennis court and pool, and good dining.

CHÂTEAU D'ERMENONVILLE, *60950 Ermenonville. Tel. 03.44.54.00.26, Fax 03.44.54.01.00. Rooms: 55. Double: 390-1,220FF. Restaurant.*

Located 22 kilometers (14 miles) southeast of Chantilly off the N330. A large, muscular castle where the philosopher Jean-Jacques Rousseau is said to have spent his last days. The castle with its soaring turrets is protected by a large moat and stands of trees.

LE PRIEURÉ, *60950 Ermenonville. Tel. 03.44.54.00.44, Fax 03.44.54.02.21. Rooms: 11. Double: 450-600FF. No restaurant.*

Located 22 kilometers (14 miles) southeast of Chantilly off the N330. Le Prieuré is a small but lovable inn in the village of Ermenonville. It is warm and comfortable, with antique furnishings and enchanting gardens.

MORE INFORMATION

Chateau de Chantilly, *B.P. 243, 60631 Chantilly Cedex. Tel. 03.44.62.62.62 or 03.44.57.40.40.*

DISNEYLAND PARIS

Disneyland Paris, Euro-Disney, Disney Village—they're all the same. The name seems to evolve in various ways for reasons that are never quite clear. In any case, now approaching the end of its first decade, the park has been the object of as much ink in the business sections of the regional newspaper and in the entertainment sections. Though there were naysayers who insisted the French would never attend a park dedicated to such an icon of American culture, it attracted 20 million visitors in its first two years and quickly became the most visited tourist stop in all of Europe. Still, things were bumpy financially the first few years, when the project lost hundreds of millions of dollars. That seems to have finally stabilized, and it appears that the park is here to stay.

We feel ambivalent about recommending Disneyland Paris. If you've come all this way, why not see France instead? Having said that, if you enjoy Disneyland and you don't mind spending a bit more than you would for the same rides back home, you'll no doubt have a blast, and that's the point of going on vacation.

Disneyland Paris is exactly what it sounds like — all the rides, shops, and parades you'd find at any Disney theme park. There are the familiar five sections to the park — **Main Street**, **Fantasyland**, **Frontierland**, **Adventureland** and **Discoveryland**. Attractions include the Pirates of the Caribbean, Sleeping Beauty's castle, the Mad Hatter's Teacups, the Dumbo flying carrousel — in short, all the fun stuff that made Disneyland such a hit in the first place.

The latest ride to open is quickly becoming one of the most popular — *Indiana Jones's Temple du Peril*, said to be the first Disney rollercoaster to pull full-throttle, upside-down, stomach-in-your-throat loop-the-loops.

Despite the pricey extra ticket for entrance, Buffalo Bill's Wild West show, with elaborately staged shoot-em-up cowboy and Indian skits, is ever popular — another tribute to the French's fascination with the myths of the American West.

You'll find lots of familiar food. Among the more notable establishments is **Annette's Diner**, with roller-skating waitresses zipping around with trays of burgers and fries. And the park's **Manhattan Jazz Club** pulls in some top performers.

Admission charges have been all over the map as Disney tries to shore up consumer interest and compete with French theme parks such as Asterix (it's the battle of the cartoon giants in a country that is obsessed with children's and adult comics). Recently, entrance fees that covered all rides was 220FF for adults, and 150FF for children. Prices also vary according to season.

ARRIVALS & DEPARTURES

A couple of years ago, the national railway opened a TGV station at Marne-la-Vallée to serve Disneyland Paris. Still, it's just as easy to catch the A4 line of the RER going 35 kilometers east to the Marne-la-Vallée/ Chessy stop (about a 30-minute trip for 70FF roundtrip). If you have a car, catch the A4 autoroute east toward Nancy and Metz and watch for signs.

WHERE TO STAY

Six hotels offer a range of prices and themes, from the fancy **Hôtel New York** to the almost too adorably southwestern **Hôtel Sante Fe**. *For information and prices, phone 01.49.41.49.10 or, in the States, call 800/ WDISNEY.*

If you'd like to stay outside the Disney complex, try:

LE MANOIR, *D402, 77610 Fontenay-Trésigny. Tel. 01.64.25.91.17, Fax 01.64.25.95.49. Rooms: 15. Double: 850-950FF. Restaurant.*

Located 22 kilometers (14 miles) east of Disneyland Paris off the N4. A stunning former hunting lodge surrounded by 40 acres of parkland, and featuring fine dining.

WHERE TO EAT

AUBERGE DE CONDÉ, *1 avenue de Montmirail, 77260 La Ferté-sous-Jouarre. Tel. 60.22.00.07, Fax 60.22.30.60.*

Located 22 kilometers (14 miles) east of Disneyland Paris off D407. Gourmet dining not far from the theme park, featuring lamb, lobster, magnificent desserts, and a lengthy list of Champagnes.

MORE INFORMATION

Disneyland Parisland Resort, *B.P. 100, 77777 Marne-la-Vallée, Cedex 4, France. Tel. 01.60.30.60.30 or 08.03.81.68.03.*

VAUX-LE-VICOMTE

Said by some to be the château that comes closest to perfection, **Vaux-le-Vicomte** is a symbol of symmetry, artistic success, and royal treachery. This is the home that Nicolas Fouquet built. He was appointed financial minister to France in 1653, served under Cardinal Mazarin and Louis XIV, and is said to have used all his genius in a mere eight years to successfully restore the royal treasury after its utter collapse.

Fouquet employed that same genius, an astute appreciation for the arts, and an acquaintance with the finest talents of the day to build this glorious château and its expansive gardens leading past several fountains to a lovely canal and sculpted grotto beyond. So proud was he of his home, he invited the young Louis XIV and his court to what was to be one of the most lavish balls of French history.

Legend has it that Louis XIV was insanely jealous of his host's grand home and had Fouquet arrested 19 days after the gala and imprisoned for the rest of his days. Indeed, Louis XIV absconded not only with many of Fouquet's art treasures, he also took charge of Fouquet's architect, garden designer, and decorator, ordering them to Versailles to build a château of unparalleled grandeur.

Political intrigue was as much the catalyst as jealousy, but whatever the true cause, Fouquet died years later in prison while Versailles arose to the west of Paris as a tribute to Louis XIV. Versailles may be more awe-inspiring in its regal excess, but the Vaux-le-Vicomte is the more refined and graceful of the two châteaux.

Several of the current small rooms at Vaux-le-Vicomte are now given over to some rather plain engravings, but there is plenty of greatness in the mansion. Note the marvelous tapestries depicting various months of the year in Fouquet's bedroom, the magnificent billiard table and ornamented rafters of **The Square Room**, the vibrant and sensuous painted ceiling of the **Salon des Muses**, and the *trompe l'oeil* in the **Hercules Salon**.

The latter part of the unguided tour walks you through several rooms on the main floor and the basement, recounting with the help of elaborately dressed mannequins and taped voices the unjust destruction of Fouquet's world at the hands of the young king.

In the gardens, be sure to walk to the end of the main terrace, where you will find a glorious view back toward the château, as well as a perfect vantage point overlooking the canal and, across the canal, the magnificent grotto. Up on the hillside above the grotto stands Hercules himself, surveying Fouquet's domain.

Admission to the château and gardens is 56FF. There is also a café with a modest menu but a pleasant outdoor terrace.

ARRIVALS & DEPARTURES

About the only unpleasant aspect of Vaux-le-Vicomte is that it's tough to get to, requiring you to rent a car or join a guided bus tour. About 60 kilometers (36 miles) southeast from the heart of Paris, Vaux-le-Vicomte is due east of the town of Melun. Take the N6 highway toward Melun, turning east just on the outskirts of Melun on N105 toward Meaux. The N105 is not adequately marked, but look for signs leading you to Meaux. Before long you'll see signs guiding you to the château.

WHERE TO STAY

LE MANOIR, located 25 kilometers north of Vaux-le-Vicomte. See "Disneyland Paris, Where to Stay," above.

MORE INFORMATION

Domaine de Vaux-le-Vicomte, 77950 Maincy. Tel. 01.60.66.97.09 or 01.64.14.41.90.

FONTAINEBLEAU

If you're looking for opulence on a massive scale and would willingly spend a bit more time on transportation if it meant you could avoid a tortuous crowd scene, **Fontainebleau** will suit your tastes better than Versailles.

Unlike Versailles, which was built largely under the rule of a single king, Louis XIV, Fontainebleau is a marvelous conglomeration of wings, courtyards, and gardens that were added and subtracted over the centuries according to the whims and decrees of several regal owners — François I (where you see an 'F' adorning an architectural element, the 'F' stands for François, not Fontainebleau), Henri IV, Louis XV, Napoleon and others.

The **gardens**, though designed by Le Notre, the same man who laid out the gardens at Vaux-le-Vicomte and Versailles, are not quite as magnificent as those at the other two châteaux. Still, they are well worth a stroll or a quick sandwich on a bench. Also, pass by the **Étang des Carpes pond**, where you will see some of the largest carps on the planet, having been well fed by the locals and tourists.

As with Versailles, the tour of the castle interior begins in chambers dedicated to portraits and landscapes that document the history of the château. Here, too, you will find a remarkable collection of painted plates, set into the walls and recounting the castle's past glories. Next, the **chapel**, as in Versailles, is an absolute gem of artistic excess, with sumptuous allegorical murals, and multi-colored marble and generous giltwork throughout.

A little further on, a stairwell sculpted in the 16th century for a favorite love of François I, resembles a boudoir, having been dedicated to the beauty of the human body, with frescos and sculptures of numerous voluptuous maidens being watched over by attentive cherubs.

The **Ballroom** is a triumph dating back to Henri II's time and rivaling even the Hall of Mirrors at Versailles for its splendor and elegance. It boasts one of the most impressive coffered ceilings we've ever seen. And the gilt-laden **Throne Room**, though a royal bedchamber until Napoleon had it transformed, exudes Raw Power.

There is more than enough here to keep you very busy for a very long time.

Closed Tuesday, and for lunch every day. Basic admission, 35FF. Guided tours of the gardens 25FF.

ARRIVALS & DEPARTURES

About 70 kilometers (42 miles) southeast of Paris, Fontainebleau can be reached by a combination of train (from the Gare de Lyon) and local bus from the Fontainebleau station. If you have a car (allowing you also to visit the remarkable forests that surround the village), take the N6 or N7 highways south and you will see signs leading you to this town of 16,000 people.

Another option is a tour bus. Various companies offer day and half-day trips to the château and the surrounding area.

WHERE TO STAY
In Barbizon (see below).

MORE INFORMATION
Château de Fontainebleau, *77300 Fontainebleau. Tel. 01.60.71.50.70.*

BEAUNE

If you have time for an overnight stay that is just a two-hour train ride to the southeast of Paris, this busy little town of 22,000, with its ancient central quarter surrounded by ramparts and a narrow park, is the prized jewel of the Côte d'Or and probably our favorite place in all of Burgundy. It is, in fact, the wine capital of Burgundy, so noted for several reasons, not the least of which is that many of Burgundy's best wines are produced in and around Beaune.

Amateur oenophiles (winelovers to you and me) while away untold hours sipping and philosophizing in Beaune's first-rate cellars and wine shops. You should be able to find no end of Côte de Beaune, Nuits-Saint-Georges, Meursault, Montrachet, Pommard, Volnay, and other vintage wines available for tasting.

But all is not hedonistic pleasure here. Serious business is conducted inside these city walls. In late November, a massive annual charity auction that hails back to the mid-1800s is hosted by the **Hospices de Beaune**, an organization that provides care for the elderly (see below for more detail).

The November **charity auction**, mentioned above, is a frenzied affair, live theater at its best (too bad it's a private affair). Wine produced in local fields, donated over the centuries to the Hospices, is up for sale. About 750 barrels, each containing the equivalent of 300 bottles of wine, are sold annually. The proceeds after expenses go to three nearby homes for the aged. The auction, though a charity, also sets the tone for the commerical pricing of each year's crop.

Whether or not you attend the auction and the public three-day bacchanalian bash preceeding it, the **Hôtel-Dieu** founded by the Hospices is well worth a visit. Built in 1443 as a hospital for the poor, the Hôtel-Dieu is just off the town's central Place Carnot. Its dreary exterior gives no hint of the expansive inner courtyard surrounded by hospital quarters topped with cheery multi-colored tile roofs.

Inside the infirmary, rows of canopied sick beds are lined up opposite a partial wall from the chapel – the proximity to the altar allowing even the dying to practice their faith. And the pharmacy still houses shelf after shelf of labeled jars containing the best known cures of long ago.

The Hôtel-Dieu, which ceased functioning as a hospital in 1971, also has a wonderful collection of tapestries and a dazzling polyptych painted by Roger van der Weyden in 1443 depicting the Last Judgment. The colors, guarded from the sun in a darkened room, are unbelievably radiant.

Other must-sees in town include the nearby golden-hued **Église de Notre-Dame** and the enormous **wine museum**, where you will gape at huge wooden presses, vats, and odd contraptions dating back to the 16th century. And shoppers hunting for crystal decanters, silver tasting cups, and original art will find plenty of enticing display windows throughout the town center.

While visitors often stop to sip wines at the Hospices headquarters, we much preferred the tour and tasting at the **Demeure Saint-Martin** on the edge of the central village. The former residence belonged to the first magistrate of Beaune, Jacques-Philibert, Marquis de Santenay. A captain in Louis XV's army, he was an avowed bachelor and unrepentant scoudrel.

"He had a terrible personality. Fought with everybody," said Gale Le Goff, our charming Canadian-born guide, who moved to Beaune years ago with her French husband. The three-story château just outside the ramparts had fallen into miserable disrepair until it was purchased in 1985 by Andre Boisseaux, a prominent local vintner who regularly buys a third of the wine sold at the Hospices auction.

He restored much of the château as a showplace of the Louis XV period and has stocked the sizable cellar with more than 100,000 bottles of regional wine, some dating back to the 1920s and many for sale to visitors (10-page catalogues are available). Madame Le Goff can tell you practically to the knoll where the grapes for each are grown.

Any visit to Beaune should also include a meal at the **Restaurant Bernard Morillon** adjacent to the Hôtel Le Cep (see *Where to Eat*, below). The restaurant, run by Bernard and his charming wife, Martine (who, with her artistic makeup and expansive gestures, resembles a diva), is set in two large rooms with muscular timbered ceilings set off by soft peach-colored fabrics on the walls and dining tables topped with pink roses.

WHERE TO STAY

LE CEP, *27 rue Maufoux, 21200 Beaune. Tel. 03.80.22.35.48, Fax 80.22.76.80. Rooms: 49. Doubles: 700-1,500FF.*

Next door to the exquisite Bernard Morillon restaurant. Stylish, and comfortable.

BLEU MARINE, *12 boulevard Foch, 21200 Beaune. Tel. 03.80.24.01.01. Fax 03.80.24.09.90. Rooms: 34. Doubles: 495-800FF.*

Next door to the very good Jacques Lainé restaurant. Contemporary, almost more like Italian decor. Good sized rooms. All the amenities right on the edge of the central part of the town.

WHERE TO EAT

BERNARD MORILLON, *31 rue Maufoux, 21200 Beaune; Tel. 03.80.24.12.06, Fax 03.80.22.66.22.*

One of the best meals we have ever eaten, with a superb wine list. Lots of game during mid-to-late fall. Dishes include starters of scallops and pigeon liver on a bed of watercress and a finely sliced wild duck breast and foie gras (the real thing) with truffles. Among the list of main courses were roast partridge and tender medallions of venison, both surrounded by a mix of cooked chesnuts, grapes, apples, and red current jelly. Try a sampling of regional cheeses and the dessert of grapefruit, caramel, and vanilla sorbets.

Gustav, Madame Morillon's tiny Yorkshire, will drop by the table periodically to check on your progress.

JARDIN DES REMPARTS, *10 rue Hotel-Dieu, Tel. 08.80.24.92.79.*

Michelin rates this charming spot the best in the village. During warmer weather, they open up the terrace, and the chef tends toward dressed up versions of such classics as foie gras de canard, beef tartare and poached pears.

PRACTICAL INFORMATION

• **Beaune Office de Tourisme,** *place de la Halle en face de l'Hôtel-Dieu, 21200 Beaune; Tel. 03.80.22.24.51.*

• **Comité Interprofessionnel de la Côte d'Or et de l'Yonne pour les Vins AOC Bourgogne,** *rue Henri Dunant, 21200 Beaune; Tel. 80.22.21.35.*

BARBIZON

Barbizon, a tiny hamlet of 1,400 residents a few kilometers northwest of Fontainebleau, is known as the village of painters. It served as a homebase in the mid-1800s for Rousseau, Corot, Diaz, Daubigny, Barye and other pre-Impressionists who were fond of wandering into the woods and setting up their easels in front of bucolic landscapes.

Several houses bear plaques claiming that so-and-so was once a resident in the house. Rousseau's and Jean-François Millet's former homes are now museums dedicated to the town and the artists.

Barbizon is still an art colony, though the quality of the pieces you'll see in the many small galleries will probably never grace the walls of the Musée d'Orsay. Still, the village is a pleasant stop and there are a couple of small cafés in garden courtyards that would be ideal for lunch. If you're in the mood for something grander, the **Bas-Breau** in the center of town has a Michelin one-star restaurant.

And if you're itching for a nature walk, Barbizon is set in the massive and, at times, spectacular **Fontainebleau forest**, which is home to several lovely glades, as well as dramatic outcroppings of rock and deep gorges.

ARRIVALS & DEPARTURES

Take the N7 highway out of the west end of Fontainebleau and turn northwest toward Paris. Before long you'll see signs to Barbizon. Some bus tours include Barbizon in their Fontainebleau itinerary.

WHERE TO STAY & EAT

HÔTELERIE DU BAS-BRÉAU, *22 rue Grande, 77630 Barbizon. Tel. 01.60.66.40.05, Fax 01.60.66.40.05. Rooms: 12. Double: 950-1,600FF. Restaurant.*

Right in the heart of town, this rustic former hunting lodge has been transformed into the lap of luxury with a magnificent garden and grand dining.

HOSTELLERIE LES PLÉIADES, *21 rue Grande, 77630 Barbizon. Tel. 01.60.66.40.25, Fax 01.60.66.41.68. Rooms: 23. Double: 320-550FF. Restaurant.*

Also in the center of town, this very comfortable hotel offers very good cuisine and a warm atmosphere.

HOSTELLERIE DE LA CLÉ D'OR, *73 rue Grande, 77630 Barbizon. Tel. 01.60.66.40.96, Fax 01.60.66.42.71. Rooms: 16. Double: 280-520FF. Restaurant.*

On the edge of the village, as well as of the forest beyond, this is a quaint one-time coach inn with antique-bedecked rooms and fine dining that won't cost you an arm and a leg.

MORE INFORMATION

Office de Tourisme, *Grande Rue, 77630 Barbizon. Tel. 01.60.66.41.87.*

LOIRE VALLEY

The **Loire** is France's longest river, covering more than 600 miles. It rises from the southeast not far from Lyon and arches gently this way and that until it reaches the Bay of Biscay just past Nantes at the base of the massive Brittany peninsula in the northwest.

This is **Chateau Country**, where, in the 15th and 16th centuries, royal families and the vulgar rich built hundreds of castles, each trying to outdo the other.

The result of this opulent game is quite remarkable. There is the epic castle of **Chambord**, with more than 200 rooms and a double-helix stone staircase rising up its center. There is **Cheverny**, still owned by the marquis de Vibraye, with its sophisticated architectural balance, prized tapestries, and pen of handsome hunting hounds. There is **Chenonceau**, with its meticulous gardens and massive stone wing spanning the Cher river in five graceful bounds.

The Loire also traverses two wine regions. Just to the west of Orléans, you enter the area where Vouvray and Chinon are produced. Much further west, near the coast, is Muscadet country, where the wine and the fresh seafood complement one another perfectly.

In short, the Loire is a vast and marvelous region. Too vast in our opinion for a frantic day-trip.

Our recommendation is to save the Loire for a separate trip, when you have a car for several days and can wander through the river valley at will, sightseeing at the château of your choice, exploring the countryside by tiny sideroads, or dallying at a vineyard for a tasting of the local wines. And there's nothing quite like bedding down in one of the elegant châteaux that have been converted into hotels — there are many.

ARRIVALS & DEPARTURES

Having said that, if you're determined to get a feel for the Château Country, our second recommendation is to take a day-tour by bus. Several of the major bus tour companies listed in Chapter 5, *Planning Your Trip*, offer one- and two-day guided and semi-guided tours (semi-guided meaning once you arrive at the château, you're on your own).

Prices run 800FF and up for a single day-tour, but that includes hassle-free transportation, admission charges, and lunch. Tours leave at about 7 a.m. and don't get back until just before dinner.

WHERE TO STAY

CHÂTEAU DE CHISSAY, *Route de Pierrefitte-sur-Sauldre, 41400 Chissay-en-Touraine. Tel. 02.54.32.32.01, Fax 02.54.32.43.80. Rooms: 24. Double: 490-1,000FF. Restaurant.*

Located 40 kilometers (25 miles) east of Tours off the D76.

With the look and feel of a real castle, the Château de Chissay has, in fact, hosted a couple of kings as well as de Gaulle himself. Rooms in the striking turrets are especially lovely, the dining is excellent, and the grounds offer a pool and tranquil walks through the gardens and adjacent woods.

HÔTEL DU BON LABOUREUR ET DU CHÂTEAU, *6 rue du Dr. Bretonneau, 37150 Chenonceaux. Tel. 02.47.23.90.02, Fax 02.47.23.82.01. Rooms: 28. Double: 400-700FF. Restaurant.*

Located 35 kilometers (22 miles) east of Tours off D40, very near the Chenonceau castle.

This isn't a manor house or castle, but it is a wonderful hotel with extremely good dining and is only a short stroll from the magnificent Chenonceau château. The hotel has three very cozy sitting rooms where you can daydream or enjoy a cocktail before dinner.

DOMAINE DE LA TORTINIÈRE, *Les Gués de Veigné, 37250 Montbazon. Tel. 02.47.34.35.00, Fax 02.47.65.95.70. Rooms: 15. Double: 680-1,150FF. Restaurant.*

Located 15 kilometers (9 miles) due south of Tours just off N10.

An absolutely superb Second Empire manor house on 30 acres overlooking the Indre River and various villages below. Incredible dining (lobster ravioli, for instance), a very good wine list, and a pool set in the grassy slopes beneath the white turreted château.

CHÂTEAU DES RÉAUX, *le Port-Boulet, 37140 Bourgueil. Tel. 02.47.95.14.40, Fax 02.47.95.18.34. Rooms: 17. Double: 450-950FF. Restaurant.*

Located just on the edge of Bourgueil north across the river from Chinon. This 15th-century historic monument is an absolute jewel, with its checkerboard-tiled turrets and the wonderfully warm reception. Dine with other guests at long tables (group dining like this is called *table d'hôte*, meaning table of the host), then sip after-dinner cordials with the very elegant and genial Madame Goupil de Bouillé.

CHARTRES

It's just like they've been saying for centuries: as you're hustling down the highway, looking out over the broad fields of this fertile plain south of Paris, suddenly in the distance you spot two spires. As you approach, the muscular **Notre-Dame de Chartres** cathedral, whose history reaches back more than 1,000 years, appears to rise out of the plains – practically floating on air. It's quite an impressive sight.

As is so often the case with such truly ancient landmarks, the early history of this cathedral is a bit murky. Early texts claim that a cathedral here was razed by the angry Duke of Aquitaine in the 740s. Another cathedral here was supposedly burned to the ground by a Viking conqueror 100 years later.

In 876, a third cathedral was consecrated here and presented with a strip of cloth said to have been worn by Mary when she gave birth to Christ. That relic, a modest swath of plain cloth still held in the cathedral treasury, is what first lured visitors to this hamlet by the thousands.

Though Chartres itself, a town of 40,000, is charming, the cathedral and its holdings are still what draw visitors here from all over the world. The cathedral you see now is yet another incarnation, having been dedicated in 1037 after the previous building was destroyed by fire.

There are many highlights, beginning with the three doorways of the **Royal Portal**, dating from the mid-12th century and adorned with sculpted portrayals of the kings and queens of Judah and other Old Testament patriarchs. Inside, standing beneath ceiling vaults that soar 120 feet high, you will find yourself gawking at the three massive circular stained-glass windows, or staring at the Jesse window (from about 1150) and wondering how the colors of the family tree that springs from a reclining Jesse's crotch can remain so brilliant.

Chartres is said, in fact, to have more than 150 stained-glass windows dating back to the 12th and 13th centuries, making it the preeminent showcase of this captivating medieval craft.

Inside, also note the remarkable stone choir screen. Wrapping around the choir, the 41 sculpted scenes that depict various moments in Mary's and Christ's lives, took two centuries to complete, beginning in the early 1500s. The high altar, executed in the 1770s, is also quite stunning, with its representation of Mary's ascent to heaven.

Behind the altar and up a stone staircase you will find a vault with a small, though dazzling, collection of embroidered ceremonial robes and golden chalices.

And be sure to walk around the outside of the cathedral to admire its buttresses and the steeples (the one on the right dates back to the 12th century, while the more elaborate Gothic version on the left was built in the 16th century). Also, stroll around to the very back of the church and enjoy the view of the town and the Eure River below.

ARRIVALS & DEPARTURES

Chartres can be reached by train from the Gare Montparnasse in Paris. Bus tours also offer half day trips. If you're driving, take the A11 or N10 highways southwest about 80 kilometers (48 miles).

WHERE TO STAY & EAT

ABBAYE DES VAUX DE CERNAY, *78720 Cernay-la-Ville. Tel. 01.34.85.23.00, Fax 01.34.85.11.60. Rooms: 55. Double: 410-1,900FF. Restaurant.*

Located about midway between Versailles and Chartres, just east of Rambouillet off the N306. Remarkable 12th-century abbey with the arched arcades bordering the central lawn, and 160 acres of parkland, fishing, a pool, tennis, and a fitness center. This stunning hotel was first renovated by the Baron de Rothschild, of fine wine fame.

CHÂTEAU D'ESCLIMONT, *Saint-Symphorien-le-Château, 28700 Auneau. Tel. 02.37.31.15.15, Fax 02.37.31.57.91. Rooms: 48. Double: 650-1,850FF. Restaurant.*

Located 22 kilometers (14 miles) west of Chartres off the N10 and A11. A visually imposing 16th-century castle complete with moat and manicured grounds. There is even a tiny pitch-and-putt golf course. First rate in every regard.

MORE INFORMATION

Office de Tourisme, *B.P. 289, Place de la Cathédrale, 28005 Chartres, Tel. 02.37.21.50.00.*

VERSAILLES

Versailles is a magnificent monument to opulence, excess, and ego.

Louis XIV, the Sun King, was supposedly so incensed by the elegance of the château at Vaux-Le-Vicomte owned by his finance minister Fouquet that he stole away Fouquet's architect, decorator, and master garden designer and ordered them to come up with something to top Vaux-Le-Vicomte. There was more to it than that, but jealousy was indeed a factor in the king's treachery.

Many still believe Fouquet's glorious home is the more perfect of the two, but none question the splendor that is Versailles. It's difficult even to select what is the most impressive because there is so much that dazzles.

There are the epic murals of the chapel ceiling, the many-hued masses of sculpted marble framing the windows of the **Hercules Salon**, and the *trompe l'oeil* porticos in the **Venus Salon** that are so real you feel as if you could step right into the walls they cover.

There are the brilliant golden cherubs guarding the corners of the **Mars Salon**, the sumptuous floral fabrics that decorate the **Queen's bedchamber** (and that Laura Ashley would die for), and the massive 40-foot canvases of the **Coronation Room** that glorify Napoleon's rise to power. And, of course, there is the **Hall of Mirrors**, a dizzying collection of chandeliers, mirrors, and murals looking out on the fountains below.

When you arrive at Versailles, stop at one of the small information booths and pick up a schedule that explains the various visiting options. Depending whether you are alone or in a group, and depending whether you want to see things for yourself or take a guided tour, you will be directed to specific entrances of the château. Remember, too, that once you are in and making the rounds, the press of human flesh will make it impossible to turn back.

While you look around with your mouth hanging open, remember that Versailles, made the seat of government by Louis XIV, was largely abandoned after the mobs came for Louis XVI and Marie-Antoinette and beheaded them in the name of the Revolution. The magnificence you see now is a credit to a hugely expensive restoration that began after World War II and was fueled by a great deal of American, as well as French, wealth.

And don't forget to leave time for the gardens. Some visitors even prefer the gardens to the château (and not just because they're free). Walk past the twin pools of the upper Water Terrace beside the château, down the green lawn to the Apollo Basin and the Grand Canal, where you can rent a rowboat or grab a bite to eat at the café.

If you want to get away from the crowds and were wise enough to bring a small bottle of water and a sack lunch, the **King's Garden** is a bucolic sanctuary. The gardens around the **Grand Trianon**, a small pink-marble mansion where the King dallied with sweet young ladies (not his wife) are also pretty and quiet.

You will no doubt notice that few if any fountains are on. The fountains are turned on most Sunday afternoons during the summer. The schedule is a bit wacky. For detailed information, with fountains ablaze with light and actors playing past royalty, write to **Office de Tourisme**, 7 *rue des Réservoirs, Versailles, or call 39.50.36.22. There are four "Grandes Fêtes de Nuit," with admission charges of 60 to 185FF.*

Mini-trains will ferry you around the Versailles gardens for 25FF for the day. You can get on and off whenever you like.

The château is closed Monday. Basic admission 45FF.

ARRIVALS & DEPARTURES

To reach Versailles, catch the C line of the RER at any of the stops in Paris, such as the Gare d'Austerlitz or Invalides, and go to Versailles-Rive Gauche (25FF roundtrip for about a 30-minute trip). The château is a short walk from the train station.

Beware: Do not catch the RER train going to Versailles-Chantiers, which is often marked Versailles-Ch.

WHERE TO STAY

LA FORESTIÈRE, *1 avenue Kennedy, 78100 Saint-Germain-en-Laye. Tel. 01.39.10.38.38, Fax 01.39.73.73.88. Rooms: 25. Double: 850-1,100FF. Restaurant.*

Located about 10 kilometers (6 miles) north of Versailles in the town of Saint-Germain-en-Laye, which is home to the château where Louis XIV was born. La Forestière is a lovely country-style estate with a generous garden, roaring fireplace, stylish rooms, and fine cuisine.

MORE INFORMATION

Château de Versailles, *123 avenue de Villiers, 75017 Paris. Tel. 01.30.84.74.00 or 01.30.83.77.88. For a recording, call 01.30.84.76.76.*

GIVERNY

In *The Masterpiece*, one of the best and certainly the most autobiographical of Émile Zola's remarkable Rougon-Macquart series of novels capturing French life in the 1800s, the main character is one of the founders of Impressionism who wanders off for several years to the French countryside, where he is inspired by all good things in nature.

Of course, that calls to mind **Claude Monet**, and intentionally so. Zola's Claude Lantier was a composite of Impressionists, and Monet was a prominent ingredient in the mix. Fortunately, Monet, who lived in **Giverny** from 1883 to his death in 1926, had a somewhat happier ending than did Zola's fictional character.

Giverny is a must if you're traveling mid-summer to early fall, when the magnificent gardens are ripe with colors and scents potent enough to inspire the artist in even the most curmudgeonly tourist.

You will see firsthand one of Monet's most common and captivating subjects: the lily pads floating on the ponds beneath the Japanese bridge. Breathtaking. And the experience will give you an even greater feel for the *Nympheas,* or *Water Lilies* works on view at the Orangerie in Paris (see Chapter 11, *Seeing the Sights*).

You can also visit the lovely green-shuttered house where Monet lived and which is now a museum, with reproductions of his paintings and photographs taken of him and his colleagues.

ARRIVALS & DEPARTURES

Giverny, about 50 kilometers (30 miles) northwest of Paris, can be reached by train from the Saint-Lazare station. Buy a ticket to Vernon, then catch a bus to Giverny, which is a couple miles from the station.

If you have a car, take the A13 and exit at Bonnières and look for signs to Giverny. Bus tour groups offer half-day trips.

WHERE TO STAY

CHÂTEAU DE LA CORNICHE, *5 route de la Corniche, 78270 Rolleboise. Tel. 01.30.93.20.00, Fax 01.30.42.27.44. Rooms: 38. Double: 400-700FF. Restaurant.*

Located 12 kilometers (8 miles) east of Giverney off the N13. This former home to Belgium's king Leopold II sits high above the Seine.

MORE INFORMATION

La Fondation Claude Monet, *27620 Giverny, France. Tel. 02.32.51.28.21.*

INDEX

THINGS CHANGE!

Phone numbers, prices, addresses, quality of food, etc, all change. If you come across any new information, we'd appreciate hearing from you. No item is too small! Drop us an e-mail note at: Jopenroad@aol.com, or write us at:

Paris Guide
Open Road Publishing, P.O. Box 284
Cold Spring Harbor, NY 11724

TRAVEL NOTES

TRAVEL NOTES

OPEN ROAD PUBLISHING

U.S.A.

America's Cheap Sleeps, $16.95
America's Grand Hotels, $14.95
America's Most Charming Towns &
    Villages, $17.95
Arizona Guide, $16.95
Boston Guide, $13.95
California Wine Country Guide, $12.95
Colorado Guide, $16.95
Disneyworld With Kids, $14.95
Florida Guide, $16.95
Hawaii Guide, $18.95
Las Vegas Guide, $14.95
National Parks With Kids, $14.95
New Mexico Guide, $16.95
San Francisco Guide, $16.95
Southern California Guide, $18.95
Spa Guide U.S.A., $14.95
Texas Guide, $16.95
Utah Guide, $16.95
Vermont Guide, $16.95
Washington Guide, $16.95

MIDDLE EAST/AFRICA

Egypt Guide, $17.95
Israel Guide, $17.95
Jerusalem Guide, $13.95
Kenya Guide, $18.95

UNIQUE TRAVEL

Celebrity Weddings & Honeymoon
    Getaways, $16.95
The World's Most Intimate Cruises, $16.95

SMART HANDBOOKS

The Smart Home Buyer's
    Handbook, $16.95
The Smart Runner's Handbook, $9.95

LATIN AMERICA & CARIBBEAN

Bahamas Guide, $13.95
Belize Guide, $16.95
Bermuda Guide, $14.95
Caribbean Guide, $21.95
Caribbean With Kids, $14.95
Chile Guide, $18.95
Costa Rica Guide, $17.95
Ecuador & Galapagos Islands Guide, $17.95
Guatemala Guide, $18.95
Honduras & Bay Islands Guide, $16.95

EUROPE

Austria Guide, $15.95
Czech & Slovak Republics Guide, $18.95
France Guide, $16.95
Greek Islands Guide, $16.95
Holland Guide, $16.95
Ireland Guide, $17.95
Italy Guide, $19.95
London Guide, $14.95
Moscow Guide, $16.95
Paris Guide, $13.95
Portugal Guide, $16.95
Prague Guide, $14.95
Rome & Southern Italy Guide, $14.95
Scotland Guide, $17.95
Spain Guide, $18.95
Turkey Guide, $18.95

ASIA

China Guide, $21.95
Japan Guide, $19.95
Philippines Guide, $18.95
Tahiti & French Polynesia Guide, $18.95
Tokyo Guide, $13.95
Thailand Guide, $18.95
Vietnam Guide, $14.95

To order any Open Road book, send us a check or money order for the price of the book(s) plus $3.00 shipping and handling for domestic orders, to: Open Road Publishing, PO Box 284, Cold Spring Harbor, NY 11724